Advance Praise
Credentials

"Credentials are fundamental to employment and opportunity, but also to personal identity. They are of interest to educators, employers, and policymakers. Yet despite their ubiquity and significance they are poorly understood; even more so every day as the number and type of credentials have exploded in the last two decades. Gaston and Van Noy provide an excellent framework to help navigate this proliferation. They plot an insightful way forward for college and university administrators, faculty members, academic advisors, and others as they design academic programs (and associated credentials) and help guide students to use credentials to achieve their goals."
—*Thomas Bailey*, *President, Teachers College, Columbia University*

"When trying to understand, let alone navigate, a landscape as chaotic and confusing as America's credential ecosystem, a guidebook from trusted experts is essential. This is that—the resource you'll want to read and reread to ensure you have a firm foundation for the journey."—*Scott Cheney*, *CEO, Credential Engine*

"A future-focused analysis of credentials and credentialism doesn't get any more timely than this. Over the past two decades, a Wild West of a credentials system has been developing throughout the United States and the rest of the world. The result is a complex and often chaotic environment that even PhDs can no longer navigate. Gaston and Van Noy draw on relevant history, pose challenges, identify opportunities, and, most importantly, suggest solutions for consideration by educators, advisers, and administrators. This is a must-read for higher education leaders today, but it may prove even more important for future leaders interested in a more equitable and sustainable future of work and learning."—*Parminder K. Jassal*, *CEO, Unmudl Skills-to-Jobs Marketplace; CEO, Practical Futures; and Adviser and Founder, Work + Learn Futures Lab, Institute for the Future*

"This is the first significant treatment of the history of credentials and its impact on higher education. The importance of this book is reflected in continuing calls for attention to quality and equity in education at all levels within postsecondary education. With government at both the state and national level, as well as other stakeholders seeking increased accountability through accreditation, this readable book could not be more timely."—*Leah Matthews*, *Executive Director, Distance Education Accrediting Commission*

"*Credentials* does a wonderful job of laying the framework of why credentials are important to an advanced society focusing on educating the workforce and building the economy. By looking back as a way to look forward, Paul Gaston and Michele Van Noy document the importance of well-defined credentials while suggesting what the competency-based credentials of the future will look like. What I like the most is how they advocate for quality and equity both within each credential and in the transitions made among credentials."—*Aaron Thompson*, *President, Kentucky Council on Postsecondary Education*

"Given the accelerating rate of change in the workplace, credentials have become an even more essential tool to ensure the relevance of skills. The authors' overview of the credentials landscape should help readers understand more fully the complex factors at work in how they are used by employers and educators."—*Van Ton-Quinlivan*, *CEO of Futuro Health; Former Executive Vice Chancellor of the California Community Colleges*

CREDENTIALS

CREDENTIALS

Understand the problems.
Identify the opportunities.
Create the solutions.

Paul L. Gaston and Michelle Van Noy

Foreword by Peter Ewell

STERLING, VIRGINIA

Published by Stylus Publishing, LLC.
22883 Quicksilver Drive
Sterling, Virginia 20166-2019

Library of Congress Cataloging-in-Publication-Data
Names: Gaston, Paul L., author. | Van Noy, Michelle, author. | Ewell, Peter, writer of foreword.
Title: Credentials : understand the problems. Identify the opportunities. Create the solutions / Paul L. Gaston and Michelle Van Noy ; foreword by Peter Ewell.
Description: First edition. | Sterling, Virginia : Stylus, 2022. | Includes bibliographical references and index. | Summary: "The credentials environment grows more complicated by the day, but this book answers key questions which help us understand why we must grapple with those complexities. The authors offer a broad view of the credentials environment, focus on categories of credentials, from the associate degree to doctoral degrees to non-degree credentials, and consider the implications for higher education leadership in volatile times"-- Provided by publisher.
Identifiers: LCCN 2021055760 (print) | LCCN 2021055761 (ebook) | ISBN 9781620369425 (cloth) | ISBN 9781620369432 (paperback) | ISBN 9781620369449 (library networkable e-edition) | ISBN 9781620369456 (consumer e-edition)
Subjects: LCSH: Degrees, Academic--United States. | Universities and colleges--Accreditation--United States. | Competency-based education--United States. | Vocational education--United States. | College graduates--Employment--United States. | Education, Higher--Aims and objectives--United States.
Classification: LCC LB2390 .G37 2022 (print) | LCC LB2390 (ebook) | DDC 378.20973--dc23/eng/20220110
LC record available at https://lccn.loc.gov/2021055760
LC ebook record available at https://lccn.loc.gov/2021055761

13-digit ISBN: 978-1-62036-942-5 (cloth)
13-digit ISBN: 978-1-62036-943-2 (paperback)
13-digit ISBN: 978-1-62036-944-9 (library networkable e-edition)
13-digit ISBN: 978-1-62036-945-6 (consumer e-edition)

Printed in the United States of America

All first editions printed on acid free paper
that meets the American National Standards Institute
Z39-48 Standard.

Bulk Purchases

Quantity discounts are available for use in workshops and for staff development.

Call 1-800-232-0223

First Edition, 2022

For our families, for our colleagues at Kent State University and Rutgers University,

and for

David Bills (1953–2021), University of Iowa, pathfinding scholar and esteemed friend.

CONTENTS

PART THREE: IMPLICATIONS FOR ACTION

It used to seem so simple. When I was growing up in the 1950s and someone referred to an individual's having "gone to college," it pretty much meant that the person had graduated with a bachelor's degree. This was before the founding of most community colleges. Graduate education was the province of only a few.

But even that was deceptive. A quick look at the most familiar of college credentials, the baccalaureate, reveals a surprising variety. Across the world, a "bachelor's degree" can involve study periods varying from three to seven years. Baccalaureate degrees can vary also in content (e.g., "Bachelors of Arts" and "Bachelors of Science"), can embrace particular fields of study (e.g., "Bachelor of Arts in History"), and can vary in implied quality (e.g., "honors" degrees or award designations like "cum laude").

This is nowhere near the proliferation of credentials at varying levels that students and policymakers face today. But it serves to illustrate that complexity in this arena has been with us for quite some time.

The purpose of this volume, ably discharged, is to make some sense of this proliferation. Paul Gaston and Michelle Van Noy tour the burgeoning credentials landscape from traditional degrees to emerging and unfamiliar new credentials and through nondegree credentials to apprenticeships, describing their characteristics and considering their applicability and quality. In doing so, they provide a very helpful introduction and analysis of an increasingly complex field.

A Taxonomic Point of Departure

To orient readers' thinking about this complexity at the outset, I would like to first propose a taxonomic point of departure under four headings. The first two headings address matters of classification: What is it exactly that a given credential represents? The next two headings address matters of veracity and trust: What is the nature and quality of evidence that the credential represents what it claims to represent?

Sufficiency/Level

The primary question is *how much* of *what* does the credential signify? This question arises from the fact that every credential first makes a claim that its holder possesses one or more identifiable (presumably valuable) attributes, qualities, or abilities that are either innate or are the products of instruction, the workplace, or the environment. The question then considers the place of this claim on an ascending or descending ordinal scale of some kind that will allow consumers to judge its sufficiency. These two properties—the claimed nature of the attribute and its identifiable level—provide an initial description of what the credential purports to signify.

Alignment

The primary question here is how does the credential *fit in with* existing definitions and established standards with respect to the specific claims that it makes? A significant consideration here is the extent to which it is consistent with or can be mapped to a known abilities or qualifications structure like the Liberal Education for America's Promise (LEAP) framework developed by the Association of American Colleges and Universities (AAC&U) or the Degree Qualifications Profile (DQP) underwritten by Lumina Foundation.

Another is the extent to which the credential explicitly references other credentials with verifiable descriptions of what they have in common. Evidence of alignment should allow viewers of a credential to determine the conceptual or empirical basis on which it is given.

Validity and Reliability

Validity and reliability are classic descriptors of any measure. Validity refers to the extent to which the measure in fact examines what it claims to examine. For a credential, this means the extent to which an individual who holds the credential in fact possesses the attributes, qualities, or abilities that the credential asserts. Reliability refers to the extent to which repeated attempts to apply the measure yield the same, or at least consistent, results. For a credential, this means the extent to which one can count on the credential to represent the claim it makes across a variety of circumstances. Although neither has anything to do with the actual content of the credential both are critical to establishing its veracity.

Error and Misrepresentation

While validity and reliability are general properties applicable to all credentials across circumstances, error is quite specific in application. Error occurs when the claim made for a credential is false, a situation that may or may not be deliberate or intentional. Misrepresentation occurs when the error is deliberate or intentional.

Two instances of the latter can occur. The first is where the misrepresentation is made by those issuing the credential: The claim made for the credential on the part of its provider is false or otherwise fraudulent. The second is where the misrepresentation is made by an individual who purports to hold the credential: Regardless of the underlying veracity of the credential's content, the claimant either does not possess it at all or the attributes or abilities supposedly addressed by the credential are not in fact present. Rectifying error or misrepresentation requires careful cross-checking and constant attention to detail. It also demands systematic follow-through, a thorough cross-checking process that must be performed for all relevant "downstream" applications of the credential. Regardless of circumstances, however, misrepresentation or fraud constitute the biggest overall threat to the credibility of any system of credentials.

Although many additional taxonomies affecting credentials are conceivable, these should provide readers with some initial guidance about how to think though the growing complexities of the credentialing landscape that are covered by this volume.

An Evolving Landscape

It may be also useful as an introduction to this topic to consider the future directions of credentialing—how might this landscape evolve in the decade or so to come? On this point, I would like to offer the following five suggestions.

The Prospect of Continuing Proliferation

The proliferation of credentials will continue unabated and will probably accelerate. Several factors suggest this conclusion. And new players in addition to traditional academic providers will expand in response to demand. We have already seen a good deal of this and, indeed, much of the current breadth and variety of the credentials landscape has been due to an increase in the number of nonacademic providers; Microsoft certification is a classic example of this. Moreover, there is a growing trend toward breaking up degrees into smaller certifiable pieces. For example, "stackable" certificates have become quite popular with certifications earned separately, sometimes from different providers, that may be assembled into broader credentials with greater value. This is attractive to providers because it increases their range of offerings significantly at little additional cost. Both these factors suggest that the current state of proliferation will both continue and increase.

Further Growth in Online Learning

Instruction leading to credentialing will increasingly move toward distance and online environments. There are several reasons to expect this development.

First, traditional postsecondary instructional provision was heavily impacted by COVID-19 with virtually all instruction moving online during the early months of 2020. While this proved to be a temporary condition, I believe that observers were correct in claiming that this shift would have long-standing impacts and that the post-COVID-19 postsecondary world would remain characterized by the prominence of distance and online provision.

Second, the limited breadth and content of most credentials, typically ranging from a semester to a year in nominal duration, make them especially suitable for distance delivery where such limitations are an advantage. Both these factors make it unlikely that future postsecondary instructional environments will return to the proportion of face-to-face provision that was true a year ago.

Competency-Based Credentials

Instruction leading to credentialing will increasingly move toward asynchronous mastery-based provision. I offer this prediction for reasons similar to those cited earlier. There has been a decline in the appeal of the traditional "college" experience involving on-campus attendance and face-to-face instruction. Partly this is because people do not have time for the traditional approach and partly because they are increasingly having to blend learning with work or other responsibilities. As a result, credentialing processes that mimic face-to-face instruction like synchronous online delivery will have a diminishing appeal when compared to those that can escape from these constraints. This trend also was exacerbated by the impact of COVID-19.

In fact, all postsecondary provision is moving in this direction including that leading to established degrees. The preeminent current example is Western Governors University (WGU), which is now 20 years old and has more than 120,000 graduates. WGU's degrees are all awarded on the basis of student performance on cumulative objective and performance assessments, and many of them can be modularized as "stackable" credentials as previously described. WGU's success means that it is becoming widely imitated, and this means that asynchronous mastery-based provision will likely become a "new normal" for all kinds of credentialing in the next couple of decades.

Increasing Demand for Information

There will be increasing demand for information about the full range of credentials, especially information addressing their credibility and quality. The accelerating proliferation of credentials will inevitably bring with it the need for various constituencies to evaluate their stature and worth. Possessors of a given credential will want assurance that it has value in the marketplace or otherwise in society. Employers and others who need to assess those individuals will demand a standard against which to determine their value. The emergence of information sources by means of which to make such determinations like Credential Engine is a natural and understandable result. But such information sources must have several important properties to be of real value. First, they must clearly identify the credential and distinguish it from others that may be competing or may resemble it. Second, as in the discussion of "alignment," they must provide a clear external standard or reference point that enables the value of the credential to be distinguished from possible pretenders or competitors. Third, they must provide a range of applicability within which the credential's claims are valid. Finally, they must provide concrete evidence of the credential's validity, reliability, and susceptibility to error. Several sources of such information are already becoming available, and I believe that more and more competing sources of this kind will emerge in the future. And because there is no single widely accepted standard of quality for such information, it will probably be up to the marketplace to sort them out.

A Challenge to Accreditation

All this will increasingly challenge the established role of accreditation as the principal arbiter of academic quality. While it governs many aspects of organizational condition and performance, institutional accreditation has historically centered on assuring the integrity and quality of the degree. This is even more the case for programmatic accreditation, which is focused on a specific academic or professional discipline. Insofar as this is the case, the explosion of credentials short of a degree, and the development of information sources that allow their credibility and quality to be assessed, pose a palpable challenge to accreditation. This is part of a broader set of trends. Most important among these is a growing decoupling of credentials from the institutions or programs that grant them; in this context, the credential itself is the prime unit of analysis with its quality assessed independent of its setting or provider. Another trend is the emergence of alternative sources of information to review or classify credentials. Examples include the Quality Assurance Commons (QAC) and the Rutgers Nondegree Credential Quality Framework. These alternatives should be welcomed because accreditation alone has never been wholly satisfactory in assuring academic quality or the integrity of a degree.

In Sum

I offer these suggested future directions for credentialing fully cognizant of the fact that forecasting is a risky business and is frequently wrongheaded. What is beyond dispute, though, is the fact that Paul Gaston and Michelle Van Noy have given us an important resource for navigating the increasingly complex world of credentials. Enjoy the read and learn from it!

—Peter Ewell, President Emeritus,
National Center for Higher Education Management Systems (NCHEMS)

Conceived initially as a book about *navigating an emerging environment*—one of proliferating credentials, providers, and modes of delivery—our study became a summons to *offer academic leadership for a volatile environment.* We are hopeful that the pandemic is now largely history, but it has had the effect of throwing the issues we are considering into high relief. Inequities have become more conspicuous, the proliferation of credentials has accelerated, the risks confronting students have become more onerous, and the challenges confronting administrators, faculty members, and academic advisors are now more urgent.

Although the closures and restrictions of 2020–2021 created logistical issues for us and for many other scholars and authors, the frustrations we experienced were offset by a sense that our work had become increasingly vital. The critical value of postsecondary credentials—for individuals, obviously, but also for the health of the economy and of society—had become increasingly clear.

The Credentials Environment

No book could address every facet of a credentials environment growing more complicated by the day. But there are questions any study of credentials must consider.

- Given the expansion in the variety of higher education credentials and in approaches to earning them, why are so many students disappointed with their postsecondary credentials?
- Despite the proliferation of credentials tailored to specific careers, why do so many employers complain that the preparation of their new hires is inadequate?
- Despite their investment in new programs meant to attract new enrollees, why are so many colleges and universities facing issues with student persistence, timely credential completion, and career success?

Fortunately, a book focused on credentials can for the most part avoid the abstract in favor of the tangible. Yes, college and university missions are complicated, but nothing they do is more important than offering credentials of value. Students should gain much from college beyond the pursuit of a credential, but they are unlikely to value their experience, however rich, unless they receive that credential and find it useful. Faculty members must meet a variety of expectations, but nearly all will identify as a priority the credentials they enable their students to earn. And administrators! Such jobs are complicated, but the most critical question is simple. Have the institution's administrators advanced its capacity to award credentials of value that will enable recipients to pursue education at a higher level or to enter their chosen careers? If the answer to that question is not persuasive, all other measures of institutional performance—on the athletic field, in the laboratory, in the community—may be of little account.

Our Primary Audiences

We seek to serve three primary audiences—college and university administrators, faculty members, and academic advisors. We hope that the book will prove useful also for many others, including public servants, agency principals, journalists, and foundation leaders and staff members, all of whom need to understand more clearly what is going on. Indeed, individuals who are not themselves educators have a vital role to play in promoting the understanding that both holds institutions to account and justifies their support by the public. And credentials lie at the heart of that understanding.

What This Book Seeks to Do—and What It Doesn't Do

We will suggest historical contexts where they may be relevant, but this is not a history of postsecondary education. We will describe many of the most important credentials on offer and address many of the issues that they raise, but this is not a reference book that lists all academic credentials. We will consider what credentials signify, how they may be evaluated, and how they function in the marketplace, but we have not written a theoretical study. Instead, as our title suggests, we seek to pose *questions* that leaders should ask, to clarify *choices* they may be facing or are likely to face, and to propose *initiatives* we believe they should consider. Well-informed, contemplative, and courageous leadership has never been more important to postsecondary education.

The plan of the book reflects this practical aim. In the first of three parts, building on Peter Ewell's foreword, we offer a broad view of the credentials environment—how credentials work, how the proliferation in credentials has created an unprecedented array of educational choices, and why this abundance has become a mixed blessing. In the second part, we focus on categories of credentials, from the associate degree to doctoral degrees to nondegree credentials. We conclude with two chapters that consider the implications of the information we have provided for leadership in volatile times. Throughout we focus on the importance at such a time of maintaining a priority on quality and equity. The first chapter introduces this binary concern. The final chapter offers 12 propositions for consideration and, we hope, for action.

In short, we offer this book to all leaders who must navigate a volatile environment. We seek to provide information they will find useful and to offer examples of creative and competitive initiatives well worth considering. We ask questions that deserve attention, even in—no, *especially in*—a period of operational and financial challenges. Finally, while we respect the risk of presumption in offering recommendations to experienced leaders—be they administrators, faculty members, or academic advisors—we accept that risk. Even in an environment as volatile as the current one, some priorities take precedence.

With the book's *usefulness* as our priority, each chapter begins with a prefatory paragraph that summarizes the emphases to follow and each ends with a list of initiatives (i.e., takeaways) that leaders (and those attentive to what leaders are doing) should consider.

ACKNOWLEDGMENTS

We want to thank our colleagues at Kent State University and at Rutgers University. We offer our particular gratitude to Tracy Cangiano, Victoria Coty, and Angelica Flores-Valencia who assisted in locating and verifying references.

We thank Peter Ewell, president emeritus of the National Center for Higher Education Management Services (NCHEMS), for the substantive foreword we will cite at several points. A colleague of long standing, he is the acknowledged U.S. authority on assessment, quality assurance, and institutional integrity.

We owe a debt as well to the colleagues with whom we have discussed the issues we are addressing, to those who have offered valuable guidance, and to those with whom we have collaborated on issues concerning credentials. In particular, we have learned much through our work with Scott Cheney, CEO of Credential Engine, and his staff, and with the leadership and members of the Non-Degree Credentials Research Network (NCRN) based at the George Washington University Institute of Public Policy. We have benefited also from the encouragement of Lumina Foundation, which supports the NCRN and many other initiatives related to quality credentials and to equity. Our participation in the foundation's Quality Credentials Task Force in 2018–2019 led to our collaboration on this book.

For their expertise, experience, and willingness to review parts of an early draft, we are grateful to Roy Swift and his colleagues at WorkCred, to Steven Crawford and his colleagues at George Washington University, and to the late David Bills of the University of Iowa. Finally, we owe much to our editor, David Brightman of Stylus Publishing, who has shepherded this project from its inception.

From the myriad studies, whitepapers, web postings, and recommendations concerning credentials, many of which appear in the References, we want to acknowledge three in particular.

First, the annual reports on the total number of the different U.S. credentials published by Credential Engine (CE) using analyses provided by the Center for Regional Economic Competitiveness (Arlington, VA) represent a point of departure for any consideration of credentials. Each CE report has improved on the previous ones in method, accuracy, and inclusiveness. We do not attempt to replicate the level of detail provided by these reports but recommend that you consult the most recent one as a useful context for our narrative.

Second, *The Credential Society*, by Randall Collins (1979), offered an early warning for a concern we will take up in some detail, that the expansion of the credentials environment would exacerbate rather than ameliorate stratification in higher education. A paperback with a new preface appeared in 2019.

Finally, we thank our NCRN colleague Sean R. Gallagher (2016) for his thoughtful and helpful study, *The Future of University Credentials*. Our focus is broader than that of Professor Gallagher, but his thorough study of "the intersection of higher education and hiring" offers a point of departure for anyone studying postsecondary credentials—those offered by colleges and universities and the many these days that are not.

While it is customary at this point to thank helpful libraries—and we do express our appreciation to helpful librarians at Kent State and Rutgers— we must also acknowledge the extent to which we have had to rely on information online. During the period in which libraries were closed, we were particularly grateful for the quality reporting of *Inside Higher Education* and *The Chronicle of Higher Education,* as well as that of compilation sites such as *The EvoLLLution, University Business,* and Lumina Foundation's daily digest of postsecondary education stories. Of course, prudent scholars must be cautious when relying on a virtual library. To that end, we have attempted wherever possible to locate multiple sources, to consider the possibility of conflicting interests, and, above all, to ensure that the links we provide are "live" at the time of publication. We apologize for any that are no longer current by the time you are reading this book.

Finally, we want to thank one another—and, for their support and toleration—our respective families. Collaboration on the writing of a book, though never easy, becomes much more difficult when communications must be limited to the exchange of drafts and electronic communications. We think that through a combination of patience, persistence, and shared values, we have made it work. But you must be the judge of that.

ACRONYMS

Not a comprehensive list but a guide to many of the acronyms used in this book.

AA	Associate of Arts degree
AAA	Associate of Applied Arts degree
AAB	Associate of Applied Business degree
AACC	American Association of Community Colleges
AAC&U	Association of American Colleges & Universities
AAMC	Association of American Medical Colleges
AASCU	American Association of State Colleges and Universities
AACSB	Association to Advance Collegiate Schools of Business
AACN	American Association of Colleges of Nursing
AAS	Associate of Applied Science degree
AAU	Association of American Universities
ABA	American Bar Association
ACBSP	Accreditation Council for Business Schools and Programs
ACE	American Council on Education
ACEJMC	Accrediting Council on Education in Journalism and Mass Communications
AHA	American Historical Association
ANA	American Nurses Association
ANAB	Accreditation National Board (of ANSI)
ANSI	American National Standards Institute
ANSI-ASQ	American National Standards Institute National Accreditation Board
APLU	Association of Public and Land Grant Universities (formerly NASULGC)
AS	Associate of Science degree
ASPA	Association of Specialized and Professional Accreditors
ASU	Arizona State University
AuD	Doctor of Audiology degree
BA	Bachelor of Arts degree
BS	Bachelor of Science degree
CAA	College Art Association
CBE	Competency-based education

C-BEN	Competency-Based Education Network
CCC	City Colleges of Chicago (IL)
CE	Credential Engine
CEU	Continuing Education Unit
CEW	Center on Education and the Workforce (Georgetown University)
CFP	Certified Financial Planner
CGS	Council of Graduate Schools
CHE	*Chronicle of Higher Education, The*
CHEA	Council on Higher Education Accreditation
CIC	Council of Independent Colleges
CLEP	College Level Examination Program (College Board)
COA	Certified ophthalmic assistant
CR	Credential Registry (Credential Engine)
CSA	Society of Certified Senior Advisors
CTDL	Credential Transparency Description Language (Credential Engine)
DBA	Doctor of Business Administration
DEAC	Distance Education Accrediting Commission
DM	Doctor of Management degree
DNP	Doctor of Nursing Practice degree
DO	Doctor of Osteopathic Medicine degree
DPT	Doctor of Physical Therapy degree
DQP	Degree Qualifications Profile
EAB	*Name of an education technology research company—not an acronym*
EACEA	Education and Culture Education Agency
EC	European Commission
ECS	Education Commission of the States
EdD	Doctor of Education degree
ELO	Essential Learning Outcomes
GED	General Educational Development Test
GPA	Grade point average
GT	Georgia Tech
GWU	George Washington University
IACBE	International Accreditation Council for Business Education
IHE	*Inside Higher Ed*
IPEDS	Integrated Postsecondary Educational Data System
IRAP	Industry-Recognized Apprenticeship Program
IT	Information technology
ITCC	Ivy Tech Community College (IN)

JCU	John Carroll University (OH)
JMU	James Madison University (VA)
LER	Learning and Experience Record
LPN	Licensed Practical Nurse
MA	Master of Arts degree
MBA	Master of Business Administration degree
MD	Doctor of Medicine degree
MFA	Master of Fine Arts degree
MOOC	Massive Open Online Course
MIT	Massachusetts Institute of Technology
MS	Master of Science degree
NA	New America
NACE	National Association of Colleges and Employers
NAICU	National Association of Independent Colleges and Universities
NASULGC	National Association of State Universities and Land Grant Colleges (Now APLU)
NCCA	National Commission for Certifying Agencies
NCES	National Center for Education Statistics
NCHEMS	National Center for Higher Education Management Systems
NCRN	Non-Degree Credentials Research Network
NCTQ	National Council on Teacher Quality
NDC	Non-Degree Credential
NEU	Northeastern University (MA)
NGA	National Governors Association
NILOA	National Institute for Learning Outcomes Assessment
NSCRC	National Student Clearinghouse Research Center
NYU	New York University
PAYA	Partnership to Advance Youth Apprenticeship
PCCC	Pennsylvania Commission for Community Colleges
PharmD	Doctor of Pharmacy degree
PhD	Doctor of Philosophy degree
QA Commons	Quality Assurance Commons
RA	Registered Apprenticeships
RCAM	Regional Center for Advanced Manufacturing
RN	Registered Nurse
ROTC	Reserve Officer Training Corps
SLCC	St. Louis Community College (MO), Salt Lake Community College (UT), South Louisiana Community College
SNHU	Southern New Hampshire University

SRE	Standards Recognition Entities
SUNY	State University of New York
UCF	University of Central Florida
UIUC	University of Illinois Urbana-Champaign
USDE	U.S. Department of Education
USDL	U.S. Department of Labor
WGU	Western Governors University
WICHE	Western Interstate Consortium for Higher Education

The State University of New York (SUNY) has defined the micro-credentials it offers through Taxonomy of Terms that may be accessed at https://system. suny.edu/academic-affairs/microcredentials/definitions/. Those that appear in this book differ somewhat from the SUNY taxonomy but are not inconsistent with it.

PART ONE

The Promise and the Problem

The need for this book has become increasingly urgent. Accounts of individuals squandering thousands of dollars on programs leading to worthless credentials have shaken public faith in postsecondary education. Frequent institutional closures have led to devastating results for students, faculty members, and communities. Employers have expressed dissatisfaction with the academic preparation of their new hires. Enrolled students with access to academic advising have found it difficult to choose among competing opportunities, while students unaffiliated with any institution have had little or no access to trustworthy advice. Concerns that tuition has become too expensive, that institutions are investing in the wrong priorities, and that oversight of institutional performance fails to assure quality are shared by many policymakers and opinion leaders.

And for "tens of millions" seeking additional education during a period of unemployment and financial stress, making wise choices has become more difficult. They have found themselves confronted with "an increasingly confusing, and sometimes predatory, market of education and training experiences" (Cheney & Sponsler, 2020). Every concern emerging a decade ago has become more urgent.

But first things first. If we are to consider how to address what has been called "credential pollution," we need to answer a fundamental question: What is a "credential"?

Credentials and Credibility

Sometimes used as an adjective ("a credentialed teacher") but more often as a noun, *credential* signifies a formal award from a credible body that corroborates the recipient's knowledge, skill, and competence for employment or further study. By extension, a credential is a physical or digital document that attests to what has been accomplished. Not all learning results in credentials, but all credentials signify learning—or should.

Derived from the Latin *credere* (to believe) and *credent-* (believing-), the word "credential" denotes veracity. Related words include *creed* and *credo* (a profession of truths believed), *credence* (truthfulness), and *credibility* (a reputation for truthfulness). Hence, a fraudulent credential should be a contradiction in terms.

But as Peter Ewell observes in his foreword, credentials in the 21st century can in fact prove untrustworthy. For a fee, a person can obtain an impressive but deceptive document purporting to be a college degree or certificate. With just a bit more effort, an individual can register for instruction at a diploma mill, perhaps write a brief paper, and receive what may have the appearance of a legitimate credential. More often, honest individuals will invest considerable time and money in earning credentials of ostensible value—only to find them of little worth in the marketplace. With innumerable providers and credentials from which to choose and little reliable guidance on how to discern value, confusion can lead to unfortunate choices.

Simple—But Not So Simple, After All

From one perspective, the credentials environment is not that complicated. Peter Ewell categorizes credentials according to their substance (what they signify in terms of knowledge and ability) and their integrity (the extent to which they may be considered trustworthy)—points of reference worth keeping in mind. Another eminently practical approach appears in questions raised by Sjur Bergan of the Council of Europe at a Lumina Foundation invitational conference in 2009. How much time is required to earn the credential? Does it meet the expectations of employers or qualify recipients for admission to advanced programs? How much effort is required? What form does instruction take? And what are the learning outcomes? When a person is awarded a particular credential, what should that person know and be able to do?

These questions as well as Ewell's two broad categories offer useful points of departure, but they also lead to the more complex questions that arise in practice. For instance, the length of a program in terms of weeks and months hardly begins to describe the extent of commitment required of the student. Some programs may require only a few hours each week, while others become practically full-time jobs. Quality? It all depends. One employer may welcome associate degrees from the local community college. Another in the same industry may regard graduates from that college as unqualified—not always on rational grounds! Inequities can reveal prejudices and misunderstandings concerning institutions, programs of study, and ethnic groups. All credentials are transactional. Their value lies in how they are perceived.

Ewell's categories and Bergan's questions are important stepping-stones leading to more complicated issues. We will follow these issues beginning with the next chapter.

A Changed Environment

As noted previously, problems that have developed over time have been exacerbated by the volatility of the past few years. But the search under duress for urgent solutions may in some instances have revealed potential improvements.

A Confusing Environment Has Become More Opaque

This book was prompted by a paradox. A proliferation of credentials has created "too much choice," a situation in which misjudgments become more likely and risks may outpace benefits. Some providers in this new environment offer genuine innovation and strong quality control focused on student accomplishment. Others invest more in advertising and recruiting than in curricular development or delivery. Rolling out untested approaches, providing little in the way of student support, and offering shortcuts to credentials, they are likely to disappoint those most in need of the advantages credentials can provide.

Both the complexity of the credentials environment and its risks have increased. Many prosperous, capably led institutions enable their students to make progress down clear pathways to success, while students at challenged colleges and universities are likely to face their own challenges that can easily become impediments. And any circumstances opportune for quality distance education can create an opening for inexperienced, inept, and disreputable providers.

Many Institutions Vulnerable Prior to the Pandemic Have Become More So

Students deserve assurance that their satisfactory pursuit of a credential will lead to an award. That assurance has become less reliable. A yearlong task force on quality credentials convened by Lumina Foundation in fall 2018 offered five recommendations, one of which was especially blunt: "Plan for institutional closures and mergers." Among the practical proposals was one calling for a comprehensive student records system capable of recording an individual's cumulative learning up to and beyond the award of a credential. Advantageous in any event, easily accessible records could prove a godsend in the aftermath of an abrupt institutional closure. In addition, the proposal called for states to take an expanded role in reassuring employers "that an institution's closure need not mean that its credentials lack value" (Lumina Foundation, 2019).

Student Advising Has Become More Critical

In order to choose among different opportunities and to navigate the complexities of a curriculum, students need well-informed, focused, and creative advice. Course scheduling, the most conspicuous function of such advising, is far from the most important one. Effective advisors seek to understand the preparation, the capacities, and the aspirations of their advisees so that they may tailor their advice student by student in terms of the opportunities from which they may choose. Obviously, as choices proliferate, guiding students to choose wisely among curricular options and modes of delivery has become even more critical.

But few students rely on a single institution, and fewer still do so now than was the case a decade ago. Academic advisors must therefore be willing to look beyond the walls of their institutions to advise on the full breadth of educational choices. Ideally, there should be a professional role comparable to that of the certified financial advisor whose practitioners would offer independent and objective advice. Short of that, in situations where the interests of the student may differ from those of the institution, academic advisors must be both willing and prepared to place their advisees first. The need for academic altruism has become a priority.

Challenges Require Solutions

At a time when making wise choices among educational alternatives has never been more important, the risk of making unwise ones has never been greater. Higher education faces many challenges, but these challenges have one thing in common: *They all directly or indirectly concern credentials.*

Hence our title: this is a book finally about leadership, the kind of leadership that finds expression in clear *understanding of the problems*, in resourceful *identification of the opportunities* becoming available, and in an active *commitment to create solutions*.

I

THE PURPOSES OF CREDENTIALS

How They Work

While credentials command respect because of what they signify and because of the reputation of the provider, their value to the recipient lies almost entirely in what they enable, that is, in how they function. Theories of human capital and economic transaction can provide useful insights. Savvy administrators, faculty members, and academic advisors should bear in mind these insights as they seek to strengthen their programs, serve their students, and shore up their institutions. But it is also important to be aware of the many other ways in which credentials function but may not function well.

For 25 years, Elizabeth Caitlin assisted Mennonite women in upstate New York as they were giving birth. She held a relevant credential, that of a certified professional midwife, from the North American Registry of Midwives. Nevertheless, she was arrested in early 2019 by the state police. Her credential was the *wrong one*. To be licensed to practice in New York, a midwife must "pass an exam by the American Midwifery Certification Board, have a master's degree and meet other qualifications" (Pager, 2019). Caitlin's case has become complicated beyond the scope of this book, but we mention it because it illustrates vividly the single most important principle so far as credentials are concerned—that a credential has value only to the extent that it is *judged* to have value.

What Credentials Do

Credentials introduce a recipient to others. Although they cannot signify all of the qualities of an individual, they have clear advantages over less formal descriptors. They provide information meant to be most clearly relevant to a possible hire, affiliation, or enrollment, and they usually do so in ways that allow comparative evaluation. If an organization learns through experience that the credentials awarded by a particular program or institution are reliable in identifying well-qualified candidates, it is likely to assign greater credence to them. And if three candidates with associate degrees from Hypothetical Tech perform well on the job, the next candidate who presents an HT degree may be more likely to receive favorable consideration.

That simple overview cannot convey the deeper appreciation that administrators, faculty members, and academic advisors should share if they are to serve students well. But it does express the important insight that while credentials take the form of documents (perhaps digital ones), they assume value only as they point both backward and forward. They record the completion of a program of study or training to testify to the candidate's preparation and aptitude for further study, training, or employment. They may not be sufficient apart from complementary forms of documentation, but they do establish a threshold for communication and provide a framework for consideration. Credentials are thus not static but dynamic. To misquote Archibald MacLeish, unlike a poem a credential should not "be" but "mean."

Why credentials can do what they do rests on two simple assumptions— that they are descriptive and that they are truthful. Although some credentials are neither, as Peter Ewell observes in the foreword, credentials are *intended* to enable recipients to make a *credible* appeal for evaluation. In turn, credentials enable those evaluating a recipient to assess with some assurance of reliability the applicant's aptitudes, experience, and capacity for growth.

The Realm of Theory

To understand the value of a credential—and to appreciate why there has been such a proliferation of credentials and providers in the 21st century—it is important to consider the variety of ways in which a credential may function and the different purposes it may serve. What does a credential *embody*? What assumptions, positive or negative, can a credential prompt? What may a credential *accomplish*? Under what circumstances?

Access to tangible gains—employment, a promotion, admission to graduate study—may represent the most important value of a credential for an individual. But tangible rewards are often not the only ones. Whether the credential is a Bachelor of Arts from a liberal arts college or a certificate in welding from a registered apprenticeship program, what a credential accomplishes for an individual may be intangible as well. At any graduation ceremony, the joy graduates share expresses more than their ambitions for the future. Like family photos and certificates of appreciation, diplomas and academic certificates imply character and identity as they point to future opportunity.

Other limitations to be found in pertinent theories will appear in the examples to follow—but so will the usefulness of these theories. Those on which we focus appear to hold particular value during an era when the transactions enabled by credentials have become less predictable.

The Usefulness of Theory

Credentials are above all transactional. Graduations that only "hang on the wall" (to quote Billy Joel's "Allentown") fail to fulfill their intended purpose. Particularly when employment is the objective, transactions and the protocols they reveal can be highly complicated. If administrators, faculty members, and academic advisors are to prepare their students to navigate the process, they need to understand the most critical factors.

Paradoxically, however, an administrator, faculty member, or academic advisor may find an awareness of theoretical perspectives useful precisely because transactions involving credentials cannot be reduced to a standard set of governing assumptions. Awareness of theory can offer guidance through the complex variability of such transactions.

Differing Perspectives on the Roles of Credentials

By reviewing some of the major perspectives on what credentials signify and how they operate in the marketplace we can more readily understand what must be done to prepare recipients for the complexity of that environment. Then we can look more closely at how credentials function in different kinds of transactions.

Credentials as Vouchers for Skills: Human Capital Theory

Human capital theory views education as a conveyer of skills and abilities needed by workers in society. By this perspective, workers with higher levels of educational attainment typically offer proportionately greater skills and abilities and thus qualify for greater economic rewards (Becker, 1993).

Colleges and universities regularly allude to human capital theory in advertising the advantages they offer. As an experiment, search Google for the phrase "Success Starts Here." In February 2019 Massasoit Community College (MA), Johnson Community College (KS), Georgia State University, South Central College (MN), Atlanta Technical College, Simpson College (IA), Wisconsin-Eau Claire, the Newberry School of Beauty (CA), and

Northeast Community College (NE) were among the many institutions advertising the same promise: "Success Starts Here."

Their confidence in making this promise finds support in analyses documenting the higher wages more educated and skilled workers typically receive. Such analyses may make a reasonable leap of faith in suggesting that credentialed workers are more highly paid because their credentials have given employers confidence in their potential for greater productivity. But that leap rests on two assumptions, that employers act rationally by hiring workers who are demonstrably more highly skilled and that they reward them for their superior skills with higher wages. But neither assumption is always reliable. The education documented by a credential does not always ensure productivity because education does not always create the knowledge and skills that translate to effectiveness on the job. And higher wages may reward academic achievement that in practice may prove unrelated to an organization's priorities.

On the other hand, credentials can testify to qualifications that transcend academic achievement, thereby justifying the premium earnings of credential recipients in a particular field compared with the earnings of individuals who present comparable educational experience but lack the credential (Flores-Lagunes & Light, 2007). Even though the on-the-job abilities of those without a credential may be comparable, the credential recipient typically enjoys an advantage in that the credential may testify to such valuable intangibles as persistence, focus, and follow-through. Second, credentials typically document completion of a "program," a coherent presentation of learning organized according to clear goals rather than a hotchpotch of disaggregated courses and experiences. It should not be surprising that many employers attach value to the assurance credentials represent.

Suggesting Intangibles: Theories of Signaling and Screening

Such intangible values are the focus of what are known as "signaling theories." As has just been suggested, an individual who completes education or training that results in the award of a credential may have developed qualities an employer finds desirable (Bills, 2003). Similarly, "screening theories" argue that credentials enable an evaluator to assume that a candidate has previously been favorably evaluated by others for admission to a program and for graduation. In other words, such graduates arrive "prescreened" (Bills, 2003).

But these intriguing explanations for employer preferences take us only part way to understanding how employers value credentials in hiring prospective employees. For one thing, these explanations rest more on wages earned by employees than on direct data concerning employer decision-making.

For another, they do not take into consideration important factors such as local labor markets or the social contexts of organizations. Nor do such explanations account for the prestige that may attach to credentials from highly respected providers. And they do not acknowledge that two individuals presenting identical credentials may have experienced differing levels of academic success.

For an example of how both "signaling" and "screening" can enhance confidence in the evaluation of candidates, consider a premise of Reserve Officer Training Corps (ROTC) programs, namely that college students who pursue an interest in officer training programs and who qualify for advancement are likely to offer an appropriate pool of potential talent for military leadership. By having met admissions standards, demonstrated their ability to learn, and shown a sustained interest in military education, such students have in a sense "prequalified." During the course of their undergraduate careers, the Armed Services (their potential employers) will track how well they are realizing their potential. When students invited to further military study in their junior and senior years complete both their academic and military educations, their employers can assume that the cadets they commission are well-prepared for the further training and the assignments they will undertake.

ROTC programs are not unique in this regard. The implicit covenant they illustrate, whereby certain credentials inspire confidence, appears as well in such notable credentials as the Harvard MBA, the Stanford baccalaureate, the Miami-Dade associate degrees in allied health sciences, the University of Michigan MD, or the University of Virginia PhD in English. Any credential both declares objectively (courses taken, programs completed) and suggests subjectively (virtues demonstrated, aptitudes confirmed)—but some do this more persuasively than others. Beyond the information available in a traditional transcript, savvy hiring officers are likely to infer in some credentials both the knowledge and skills required for success on the job and the "soft skills" organizations seek in potential leaders. An ability to work well with others, to navigate a complex environment, and to demonstrate loyalty to an organization are frequently associated, and not without reason, with a college degree (Brown, 1995).

Conflict Theory: Credentials as Sources of Status and Power

Because credentials differentiate those who have earned them from those who have not, they typically offer recipients competitive advantages in the marketplace. Providers advertise such advantages when recruiting students. For instance, Walden University (2019) promises those who earn their "accelerated" master's degrees "an edge over job candidates who didn't continue their education past the bachelor's level." In a 30-second advertisement aired during the 2009 Super Bowl, Luis Proenza, then president of the University of Akron (2009), touted "the Akron Advantage"—a promotion that still lives on YouTube. More recently, advertising its graduate degrees, Northeastern University (2017) asks, "Want to set yourself apart from the rest of the workforce?"

Of course, prestigious institutions may not need to make such promises. Whether justly or not, the competitiveness of their credentials is often assumed. That is in part because privileged, well-prepared students tend to choose institutions that enroll other privileged, well-prepared students, while underprivileged and underprepared students are more likely to attend institutions that answer to the modesty of their aspirations. But there are many institutions not considered prestigious that may offer greater value added by enabling both well-qualified and challenged students to overcome impediments and find success.

That observation echoes "conflict theory," which focuses less on what credentials signify in terms of experience and knowledge and more on how they confer status and power, that is, how they enable recipients to claim preferential access to the limited resources within an economy (Bills, 2004; Collins, 2019). There are different strands within such theory, but they all agree that education, often touted as a sure impetus to social mobility, can just as easily be invoked to reinforce social immobility and exacerbate inequality.

One of the principal results of this phenomenon may be found in an individual's seeking advanced credentials in order to maintain an edge in the labor market—for example, the (name your institution) "advantage." Colleges and universities thus promote their credentials by appealing to student and parent concerns about economic competitiveness. Some wealthy families, as recent admissions scandals have shown, will go to great lengths, even illegal ones, to make sure that the credentials their children earn are prestigious. For others, creating an advantage may be a matter of investing in the cost of additional credentials. But even students who are not wealthy may be persuaded that earning a graduate degree, notwithstanding the additional cost (and additional debt), may be necessary to their success.

The Consequences of Unexamined Assumptions

Another way that credentials perpetuate status and power may appear in the assumptions of the colleges that award them, assumptions about student preparedness and potential that may betray the unexamined conjectures of White middle- and upper-class culture (Bourdieu, 1984). Administrators, faculty members, and academic advisors may assume, for example, that all of their students arrive with the "college knowledge" needed to navigate complex program options, available resources, and expectations (often unstated) as to what is required to be successful in college. By failing to provide essential guidance to students who need it, institutions may place such students at a disadvantage and thus inadvertently protect a hierarchical status quo favoring the "college knowledgeable." Conversely, institutions may assume that students who fare less well on standardized entrance examinations have less potential for college success and may be diverted to low-yield "developmental" sections.

Such errors of judgment may have implications for the long term, in that the skills and knowledge gained through earning credentials are often associated with status and power for a lifetime. Privileged students who have gained savvy denied to others may be more likely to choose institutions offering programs that foster independent thinking, teamwork, and initiative as well as greater knowledge of art and culture. By so doing, they prepare themselves for occupations such as those in finance, management, and technology that may place greater value on such competencies. By contrast, students who lack a strong secondary school education and who face financial insecurity may be inclined to focus more on narrowly defined technical skills than on the broader skills associated with leadership. Some institutions and programs enable students to learn to be leaders. Others may be more likely to prepare students to serve as compliant workers who follow instructions and do not question authority (Bowles & Gintis, 2002).

Community Colleges and the Opportunities They Offer
What of the claim that community colleges make to the contrary (i.e., that they effectively address and ameliorate such inequities through programs that allow their students to overcome impediments and compete effectively with those holding supposedly more prestigious credentials)? Certainly, many thousands of community college alumni can testify to career success and professional growth their credentials have made possible. The commitment of St. Louis Community College (SLCC, 2020) to "launch students into new and better careers, four-year degrees and richer lives" so as to "strengthen St. Louis one student at a time" is typical. But there remains a concern that such "launches" occur too infrequently. Some critics have questioned whether community colleges may divert students from the goal of a bachelor's degree by encouraging them to enroll in workforce training programs (Brint & Karabel, 1989).

Because only 20% of students who begin their education at a community college eventually transfer to a four-year institution, there clearly is more work to be done. The National Student Clearinghouse Research Center (NSCRC) suggests that there is "space for the institutional evolution of student transfer practices in order to promote higher educational attainment for postsecondary students." That is putting it diplomatically, in that such "space" includes "curricular and cultural gaps" between community and four-year colleges, "environmental differences" between the two, a shortfall in articulation agreements, and "disparities in student academic preparedness" (NSCRC, 2019).

Maintaining Justifiably High Standards—or Creating Artificial Barriers?
The broader implications of what may appear as the discriminatory structure of postsecondary education, one track for the privileged, another for the less so, appear in an increasing concern with "credentialism," the disproportionate influence assigned to having a postgraduate credential (as opposed to not having one) and to some credentials rather than others. (See chapters 2 and 10 for a more thorough discussion of this concern.) The result of such disproportionate influence? Disproportionate benefits for those with the most highly regarded credentials—and disproportionate restrictions on access by others to the pursuit of such credentials.

Presumably in an effort to ensure quality, nearly all occupations and professions maintain some form of "entrance standards." For many, they have grown higher over time—often, but not always, for good reason.

One example may be found in the evolution of legal education. Throughout much of the 19th century, a customary path to practicing law in the United States was through a practical legal apprenticeship. By "reading law" with an attorney, one would gain knowledge and experience gradually until prepared to take a bar exam.

But with the appointment of its section on Legal Education and Admission to the Bar in 1893, the American Bar Association (ABA) began to move in the direction of a mandate that a formal law school education rather than an apprenticeship should be the preferred means of access to the profession. The ABA's publication of Standards for Legal Accreditation in 1921 and its initial listing of law schools in compliance established a protocol that continues to this day. While theoretically voluntary, accreditation remains essential for most schools of law because in all but about five states, graduation from an ABA-accredited law school is required for admission to the bar exam (Staver & Staver, 2003). Schools that cannot qualify their graduates to sit for the bar exam "naturally have difficulty attracting enough students to be financially viable" (Lao, 2001, pp. 1035–1036). Therefore, "the ABA's clout is considerable" (Gaston, 2014, p. 161).

One could argue that the restriction of access and the enforcement of more stringent standards has been prompted by a desire to justify greater public confidence in those practicing law and in the practice of law itself. And, commendably, having acknowledged the underrepresentation of women and people of color in the profession, the ABA is pursuing the issue through a resolution (ABA 113) and related initiatives.

The intent is not to criticize the ABA or any other professional gate-keeper, but to urge careful scrutiny of "screens" that may limit access to an occupation or profession. Many may be well justified. Some may not be. What is clear is that some standards have led to exclusion from occupations and professions ranging from some trades (restricting access to particular apprenticeships) to some professions (limiting access to those accepted by a restricted cohort of approved programs). It should not be surprising that elite groups may protect their privileged access to certain credentials that offer them advantages (Brown, 1995; Collins, 2019). But it should be objectionable.

Guiding Students to Their "Appropriate" Stratum?
A less visible—because more widely accepted—phenomenon may be found in a practice we will examine in several different contexts, one of directing students to "appropriate" programs of study. The process may be benign. Effective advising should lead students to programs that align well with their abilities, interests, and aptitudes. But assessment should be objective, not conjectural, based on data, not on assumptions. The concern is that postsecondary education may select students according to perceptions of class and status, whereupon some will be prepared for managerial and professional cultures through education in the appropriate attitudes and dispositions—and others will not (Brown, 1995, 2001; Collins, 2019).

Whether or not administrators, faculty members, and academic advisors can confirm this concern through their own experience, they should find it a useful prompt to remain vigilant against all forms of prejudice and exclusion. Far from a mere posture, such vigilance should include practical strategies such as (a) reviewing the principles of professional societies and accrediting commissions to determine their position on inclusiveness and diversity, (b) securing funds for scholarships that enable the formerly excluded to pursue highly selective professional education, and (c) auditing the institution's academic programs to measure the depth of their commitment to recruit the underprivileged and underrepresented.

Theory focused on priorities such as these is not rarified and hypothetical but offers a compelling perspective on social and ethical issues as well as educational and economic ones. By providing us with language to discuss such issues and to make judgments about them, theory can enable us to act. Ameliorating inequity in postsecondary education is not only a moral imperative, it also can be an important means toward improved institutional health, indeed, to survivability.

Institutional Theory: Credentials as Creators of Social Roles

A somewhat less often considered perspective—but one related to the phenomenon we have just described—highlights how credentials help to determine roles in society and how they can influence the individuals who occupy these roles (Meyer, 1977). A presumed alignment between education in specific arenas of knowledge and experience, on the one hand, and related positions in the social network, on the other, can create expectations concerning individuals.

Hence some credentials may inspire authority and respect out of proportion to the explicit knowledge and experience they document. For instance, individuals who receive a medical degree often report a conspicuous increase in the authority they are able to exercise and the respect they are given, even though their epistemic authority (their superior knowledge of medical matters) need not and should not entitle them to "order" a patient's behavior (Applbaum, 2017). But that sense of authority and respect can influence behavior. Consider how a 35-year-old MD might in all likelihood introduce themself to a new patient who happens to be a distinguished professor with a PhD: "Hello, Sam, I'm Dr. Baker." Credentials can both create and legitimize roles within society.

That process of creation and legitimization can also reflect and support social and economic growth. The introduction of a new credential in response to an emerging need dramatizes how a discipline, the credential it awards, and the perceived value and authority of that credential in society can evolve together. A case in point would be computer technology. Fifty years ago, departments of mathematics began offering a few courses in computer science that enabled students to develop expertise in a growing subdiscipline. Eventually the baccalaureate or master's degree in mathematics would seem inappropriate for a discipline grown increasingly independent of its parent. Hence the growth of computer science led to new departments and programs that would award new credentials—bachelor's and master's degrees in computer science—entitling recipients to new social roles and economic opportunities.

We spoke earlier of some of the intangible values of a credential that graduation ceremonies celebrate. No wonder that many degree recipients in the spring of 2020 found online ceremonies a pale imitation of the real thing. Daniel Holohan, a graduating senior at Arizona State, complained, "We don't get to walk across the stage, we don't get to have that closure." He added, "It feels like your education . . . is a letdown" (Myskow & Hansen, 2020). He received the credential—but not the desired public acknowledgment of the social role for which he had qualified.

Credentials and the Providers That Award Them

A presumed correlation between what a credential purports to document and the value a credentialed candidate represents for a potential employer may be found, at least in part, in the credibility of the institution that has granted the credential. In the most basic sense, the authority educational providers receive from states, the federal government, and accreditors gives their credentials legitimacy. But all credentials are not created equal. Because universities may draw on centuries of custom and practice as a source of their legitimacy (Meyer et al., 2007), a degree documenting mediocre performance at an Ivy League college may exert greater sway in some marketplaces than a *cum laude* degree earned at a public regional university.

For some credentials, however, the satisfaction of third-party standards may take precedence over (or at lease complement) institutional repute. With nursing or teaching or aircraft maintenance, for example, a credential from a wide spectrum of institutions may serve as a legal prerequisite for licensure. The spectrum may reflect recommendations prescribed by the appropriate professional group. In other cases, states may reach their own determinations on what programs may pass muster and on the requirements that applicants must meet.

In less formally regulated occupations and professions, the conventions of the discipline may serve as an indicator. For instance, the award of a Master of Musical Arts degree typically signifies that the recipient aspires to a career as a professional performer. But the recipient of a Master of Music degree will be more likely to seek advanced study toward a career as an educator. This distinction is likely to hold regardless of the institution.

That example, by the way, offers a further reminder that the *understanding* of the link between credentials and occupational roles may be more important than the actual link (Meyer et al., 2007). As we have conceded, an employer may use credentials to assign people to occupational roles based on *assumptions* regarding the credential without assessing directly the knowledge and experience of recipients. "The individual knows he or she is a student, acquiring credentials and therefore possessing certified knowledge and capacity. Others know it, too. Under these conditions, it is less relevant whether the knowledge actually exists or is possessed by the student" (Meyer et al., 2007, p. 208). The important issue is the *perception* of a linkage between the credential and the occupational role.

That can change once the successful applicant begins work. Then success is likely to depend more on the employee's contributions to the organization in applying the competencies indicated by the credential. That is the limitation of a perspective that relates credentials and occupations without defining the competencies that the credential holder should have. Hence—a drum roll for the obvious conclusion—individuals presenting the same credential may not achieve the same level of success!

Similar Credentials With Different Results

That drum roll introduces the question that arises when graduates of different institutions present the same credential in the same discipline: What determines their comparative value in the marketplace? Obviously, differences in emphasis from one program to another may make one credential preferable to another for an employer with clearly defined priorities. But without detailed information concerning such differences or any other metric for ranking institutional and program quality, the value assigned a credential is likely to depend in part on subjective factors.

A credential awarded by a well-known institution may inspire greater confidence than one from an obscure institution—even if the lesser known institution is otherwise comparable or perhaps even to be preferred for the strength of its program. With this in mind, administrators, faculty members, and academic advisors may be able to enhance the competitiveness of their graduates by awarding detailed transcripts attesting to experiences and competencies or by requiring them to develop online learning portfolios to supplement their transcripts.

But "pipeline preference" is likely to remain a factor, as some employers will give precedence to graduates (a) who have already established a link with the hiring organization or (b) who have graduated from institutions with a positive track record within their organizations. (Consider that 80% of those who complete an apprenticeship accept employment with the sponsor of their apprenticeship program.)

Finally, there may be a less easily defined (and perhaps less easily justified) issue of "institutional category allegiance." It would not be surprising if employers with Big 10 degrees were to favor graduates from Big 10 universities, or if an employer who had begun their postsecondary education at a community college were more likely to favor applicants who had made the same choice. Such subjective matters complicate the effort to understand how credentials function in the marketplace, but they cannot be ignored.

Graduates seeking employment should be aware of such subjective influences in order to choose strategies for taking advantage of them when possible and for compensating for them when not. Those whose credentials have been awarded by an institution that may be unfamiliar to a recruiter may want to add a brief but informative institutional profile. Graduates from a university in the Atlantic Coast Conference should learn which corporations hire most aggressively in ACC institutions. And those who will present an associate degree or a four-year degree built on an AA may want to document the success of others who have earned the same credentials by the same path. Because strategic approaches often will increase the likelihood of success, institutions should prepare their graduates to develop and follow them.

Credentials in Social Contexts

We have considered "credentials as creators of social roles," noting, for instance, how credentials contribute to the definition of social roles and how preparation for credentials can acclimate candidates to assume those roles. (The hypothetical young MD entering an examining room provided our example.) We did not examine, however, how credentials function within social structures that include labor markets, organizations, and occupations.

Different Labor Markets, Different Prospects

Most workers and employers work within local regions, and the labor markets and the social structures characteristic of these regions can influence how credentials bear on hiring. Unions in one region may be powerful, in another, weak. One region may show a predominance of strong nuclear households, while in another families may be less conventional and perhaps less stable. Cultural norms in one region may prescribe a strong work ethic. In another, such values may be less evident. Any of these factors can influence the way credentials function.

There are also significant differences among organizational social contexts—not only from one industry to another, but also within particular industries where historical differences have led to different institutional and organizational dynamics. For instance, although the contrasts between Silicon Valley and Boston's Route 128 are no longer as pronounced as they once were, there remain clear differences in their cultures. That of Route 128 has long been characterized by large corporate employers that expect loyalty and provide long-term careers, while that of Silicon Valley has been known for a continual movement of employees from one firm to another in search of new ventures and opportunities (Saxenian, 1994).

Similarly, wages within the same industry may differ from one geographical area to another. Although it is not always possible to account for such variances definitively, some obvious factors include regional differences in demand for workers, in the qualifications of the local labor force, in the desirability of the area for potential employees, and in the cost of living.

Different Organizations, Different Prospects

Although employees are hired not by "labor markets" but by particular employers, we can acknowledge some fairly obvious principles. First, large firms tend to spend more resources on hiring and to take a longer time to hire workers than smaller ones. Those that employ personnel trained in human resources, compensation, and quality improvement are more likely to employ standardized processes with explicit criteria. Such an approach can offer increased efficiency and consistency as well as greater impartiality.

Second, firms that draw principally on their own workforce in recruiting for leadership positions tend to screen entry-level credentials more thoroughly. Instead of asking whether a candidate is qualified for an entry-level position, they ask whether the candidate is likely to earn promotion. Thus those with "internal labor markets" (groups of related jobs) especially tend to recruit employees with the expectation that they will advance through building on their skills and knowledge (Althauser, 1989; Rosenfeld, 1992). Because the stakes are higher in a hiring process meant to identify likely candidates for eventual promotion, credentials are likely to receive greater scrutiny (Bills, 1988b).

On the other hand, firms operating according to union contracts may use more bureaucratic, less personal methods in the evaluation of credentials. Indeed, especially for union shops, the contract may in some respects *define* the hiring process. And while public sector organizations may also respond to labor regulations, they must respond also to public administrative procedures, to bureaucratic preferences for methodological formality, and to regulatory oversight. The result? Reviewing candidates and credentials often takes considerable time.

Anyone entering the employment market with a newly earned credential should be aware of these differences—as should administrators, faculty members, and academic advisors. One need not be a human resources expert to recognize that some students are more likely to find success in a small business than in the corporate world. But other students should be encouraged to embrace the more competitive challenge. The more aware we are of how credentials function in the marketplace, the more effective we can be in enabling credential recipients to navigate it.

Credentials—and the Occupations They Enable

The value assigned to credentials reflects also the status of the occupations for which they are a qualification. Hence, recalling our hypothetical Dr. Baker, a medical degree offers its recipient a measure of prestige less directly associated with their knowledge of anatomy and physiology than with the esteem the medical profession enjoys. By contrast, while a bachelor's degree in psychology may signify deep knowledge, it is likely to offer only limited opportunity for employment. Typically only an advanced degree will enable practice as a psychologist.

In sum, credentials offer access not only to occupations, but also to the social roles and environments identified with them. Even credentials that do not lead to earmarks for particular professions—bachelor's degrees in broad liberal arts fields, for example—may suggest a spectrum of respected capacities and capabilities. Of course, assumptions that bachelor's degree recipients present social skills, critical thinking skills, and other aptitudes for successful employment superior to those presented by recipients of the associate degree may not prove to be justified. In the most obvious instance, an associate degree program well aligned with the requirements of a particular industry may indicate far more appropriate preparation than a bachelor's degree in an unrelated field. But many employers may give precedence to candidates with four-year or advanced degrees whether such degrees represent an essential qualification or not.

Credentials at Work: Theory and Practice

This is not a book principally about the theory of credentials. However, as we have already seen, some awareness of theoretical perspectives can enable us to acquire a more fully informed acquaintance with the different kinds of significance credentials carry for their recipients and for those responsible for evaluating them. When we observe, for instance, the significant distinction in the state of New York between different midwifery credentials, when we attempt to appraise innovative programs awarding unfamiliar credentials, or when we attempt to assess the earning potential of those who hold such credentials, our acquaintance with perspectives encompassing human capital theory, conflict and control theory, and institutional theory will offer useful signposts. Similarly, our brief review of certain issues in labor market sociology, industrial sociology, and the sociology of work and occupations should prove useful as we approach complex questions.

The Usefulness of Theory in the Real World

Beset with concerns about the perceived inadequacies of their graduates, the costs of their programs, and the ways in which some students may be misled by unscrupulous providers, administrators, faculty members, and academic advisors may be tempted to ignore theoretical perspectives so as to focus on the energy and promise of a challenging era. But to overlook perspectives on how credentials function would be a disservice to students.

For instance, students should be made aware that their newly minted credential will signify in many ways—as an attestation to knowledge and ability, as a pointer to networks and social strata, as a surety for perseverance, as a talisman of regional identity. Graduates will deserve a moment's self-satisfaction when the credential is in their hands, but they should know that its value for them will depend in part on how they present it—and themselves—and in part on whether they are prepared to negotiate and perhaps disarm marketplace misconceptions.

"Academic" Versus "Vocational"

A rigid and ill-informed distinction between "academic" and "vocational" credentials, perhaps the most pervasive of the misconceptions, is problematical in two respects. "Academic" learning, including "liberal" learning, should enable preparation for a vocation. And "vocational" learning should offer preparation not only for employment but also for continued learning, for participation in civic life, and for satisfying lives.

An essay by Mark Rose in *The American Scholar* makes the point well. Quoting a speech President Obama delivered at a community college in Troy, New York, in 2009, Rose concurs that "the power of these institutions [is] to prepare students for 21st-century jobs." But having studied the motivations of students attending a community college in a depressed sector of Los Angeles, Rose defines that power more broadly. Yes, the students he describes share an interest in obtaining remunerative employment. They want to learn to weld and to become employed as welders. But such students "want more out of college than the prospect of a job," Rose says. "They want to do something good for themselves and their families. They want to be better able to help their kids with school. They want to have another go at education and change what it means to them. They want to learn new things and to gain a sense—and the certification—of competence. They want to redefine who they are" (Rose, 2011, para. 7).

Rose's point is not that these students must study subjects in addition to welding—though they may in fact wish to do so. The point is that learning to weld is about far more than mastering a rudimentary skill. Students learn about "metallurgy and electricity." They "develop a level of literacy and numeracy." They learn "problem solving, troubleshooting, decision making—thinking in a careful and systematic way about what they're doing and why" (Rose, 2011, para. 14).

Why, then, is there a tendency to relegate so-called "vocational" learning to a separate tier of postsecondary education, a default for those who choose not to attend college? Rose suggests that one reason lies in our fixation on the economic benefits of education at all levels to the exclusion of all other benefits such as intellectual, moral, cultural, and civic development. We should both expect and acknowledge such benefits in vocational education.

The Risks of Unexamined Assumptions
There are risks for students in assumptions such as that between academic and vocational credentials. Those who have earned so-called "second-tier" credentials may find themselves unable to compete even when they may be ideally qualified for the job on offer. But there are risks for employers as well. Unexamined assumptions of several kinds may lead them to overlook potential employees who would offer their organizations value.

For instance? Some employers may instinctively relegate holders of associate degrees to one category of openings and holders of baccalaureate degrees to another—when either might be suitable. Or they may have an unexamined preference for graduates from particular kinds of institutions (e.g., liberal arts colleges or Big 10 universities). Or the recipient of an MD may hold an edge over the recipient of a DO. Or vice versa—even though there are few meaningful distinctions between the two any longer.

Such misconceptions may lead to a lack of alignment between the competencies signaled by credentials and those required in the jobs being filled. But the risks of misalignment become even more likely when employers do *not* respect credentials as reliable indicators of preparation and likely performance. A complicated, unpredictable, and often stressful process at best, hiring motivated by unexamined assumptions may not work to the benefit of either the candidate or the hiring organization.

A perhaps more benign instance occurs when credentials function less as indicators of knowledge and ability and more as indicators that recipients (a) have already passed multiple screenings and (b) have demonstrated the kind of persistence identified with productivity. (We introduced "screening" theory earlier in this chapter.) Credentials used primarily for "screening" may offer more reliable guidance than intuition alone, but there is likely to be a greater risk that hiring decisions will be less objective and less responsive to the actual needs of the organization.

There are steps that administrators, faculty members, and academic advisors can take so that the credentials awarded by their institutions serve their graduates (and the potential employers of their graduates) well. First, they can enrich student transcripts so that they provide useful information beyond courses, grades, and credits. For instance, online portfolios of student work can attest to leadership experience, point to particularly demanding coursework, and document potential for further intellectual and experiential development. Second, educators can join forces with employers so as to understand how to create documentation that will enable enhanced evaluation of the credentials they award. Finally, they can make certain that their students are well prepared to identify opportunities, to appreciate the value of timely and thorough applications, and to avoid unwitting discourtesies than can blight otherwise competitive candidacies.

In Sum

As we examine what credentials are available, what they mean, and how they work effectively—or not—this chapter may appear in retrospect as an orderly portico leading into a raucous and confusing arena. But the perspectives introduced here will serve us well. They will enable us to avoid focusing on a particular credential to the extent that we lose sight of the wider and ever evolving landscape of credentials. They will warn us against taking familiar assumptions for granted. Above all they will remind us continually that the questions are often more important than the answers—and that there are many questions remaining to be answered.

Takeaways

By understanding how credentials work in the marketplace (as well as ways in which they may not work well) administrators, faculty members, and academic advisors can take steps to improve the efficacy of the credentials they award and to enable their students to gain maximum advantage from the credentials they earn. Working collaboratively, they should consider the following:

- Clarifying alignments between the credentials their institution awards and any requirements for licensure that recipients may have to address.
- Offering diploma "supplements" that clarify the significance of course and credit information provided in the transcript or requiring students to maintain an online learning portfolio that documents both curricular and cocurricular experience. Or both!
- Consulting with principal employers to determine what information about graduates they would find most useful and in what form they would prefer to receive it. An obvious opportunity for discussion: a template for student's learning portfolios.

- Enabling students to understand, to appreciate, and to communicate effectively both the tangible and intangible elements of their college experience.
- Enabling students seeking employment to understand how different organizations approach the hiring process in different ways so that they may ask appropriate questions and respond to employer expectations *and* enabling students seeking acceptance by other academic institutions to meet the requirements of differing application processes.

2

THE PROMISE OF
ABUNDANCE

An Opportune Environment

Having considered how credentials work, we should consider how the credentials environment has expanded. The result is unprecedented opportunity for students, who now have many more choices, and for institutions, that can make many more choices available to their students. By disaggregating the elements of this environment, we will be better able to appreciate why offering reliable guidance to students has never been more critical, why faculty members need to look further than ever beyond the status quo, and why administrators should regard the current competitive era as an opportunity to weigh the value of what might be done against that of what is being done at present.

An already inscrutable credentials environment became more so during 2020–2021 as a pandemic forced postsecondary education to modify its assumptions and operations—at least temporarily—while opening up new opportunities to innovative providers. There is a positive legacy of this period, in that some expedients (expanded distance education, increased student interest in short-term credentials, a focus on effective asynchronous pedagogy, etc.) have survived to the benefit of postsecondary education. But guiding students to appropriate educational choices now means enabling them to navigate within a credentials environment that has become more complicated by the day.

The Many Dimensions of a Complicated Environment

To acquaint students with worthwhile opportunities that respond to their interests, their abilities, and any challenges they may have while enabling them to avoid the risks that have emerged we have to look beyond a formidable increase in the sheer number of credentials so as to recognize that

- there are *many more kinds of credentials,*
- there are *many more credential sequences,*
- there are *many more providers* and *kinds* of providers, and
- there are *many more approaches to delivering programs.*

Competitive institutions will respond strategically to these layers of complexity. Administrators will work with faculty members to make sure that the credentials on offer are described in terms of the expectations the institution will have of the student and the expectations the student should have for the credential. Faculty members dedicated to student success will make a point of understanding the range of options their students may consider. And academic advisors, recognizing that their increasingly diverse advisees deserve increasingly sensitive and creative guidance in making wise choices, will look beyond familiar curricular structures.

There Are Many More Kinds of Credentials

Despite claims to the contrary, there are few, if any, new *categories* of credentials. In addition to degrees, there are nondegree credentials such as certificates, certifications, and badges that tend to offer a more highly focused approach to a specific career—often (but not always) for less time and money. But while the categories have remained fairly stable, new credentials within these categories now offer students many more choices. And while this wider range of choices may be most conspicuous in terms of short-term, nondegree programs, even the familiar bachelor's degree now appears

SIDEBAR
The "Academic" and "Vocational" Divide
Some credentials are *directly* focused on preparation for employment while others are *less so.* But the distinction between "academic" and "vocational" programs must be made with care. Credits earned toward an applied associate degree may count toward a baccalaureate degree. A baccalaureate degree program may include a certification in a powerful job-ready credential. The safest approach is to avoid assuming that any credential, however "applied" or "academic" it may appear to be, may be safely relegated to one category or the other.

in "many more kinds." The traditional bachelor's program in which a student encounters both breadth (general education) and depth (a major) still offers many students a competitive advantage, but that advantage can now be enhanced by innovations we will describe—embedded certificate or certification programs, for instance. In addition, there are now *applied baccalaureate* programs that promise highly specific expertise in narrowly defined fields.

There Are New Majors, New Minors
This is not the place for a comprehensive inventory of new credentials. To list recently introduced programs in cybersecurity alone would require several pages. But the *range* of new offerings and the kinds of questions they can prompt may be suggested by five new credentials announced in just a two-month period in early 2020.

- **Rocky Mountain College** announced a new **Doctor of Medical Sciences** degree. This program is meant for physician assistants who possess the master's degree.
- A Bachelor of Science degree in **outdoor products** planned by **Oregon State University-Cascades** (2020) teaches both the "design, development, manufacturing, testing, [and] sustainability" of outdoor products and the values of "corporate responsibility and stewardship of natural lands."
- Two "studies" programs, one leading to the associate degree, the other, to a master's, are to be offered, respectively, by **Holyoke Community College** (n.d.) **in Latinx studies** (https://www.hcc.edu/latinx-studies) and by the **Franciscan University** (n.d.) **of Steubenville** in **Catholic studies**.
- Following the legalization of recreational cannabis in Illinois, Western Illinois University (2020) announced a new minor in **cannabis production**.

There Are New Programs in Unfamiliar Disciplines
There are also new credentials that introduce unfamiliar disciplines. For instance, **Delgado Community College (New Orleans)** offers an opportunity to become a "**health coach**." Despite the name, the credential is only tangentially related to providing health care. Rather, students learn "techniques to help patients take an active role in identifying and adopting healthy lifestyle choices to improve their health outcomes." Success in the program enables students "to be tested for board certification through the National Board of Medical Examiners" (Delgado Community College, 2019).

Georgia Tech has embraced the new field of cybersecurity through a multifaceted offering. Available both on campus and online, the GT (2020) master's program offers three tracks, so that students may "study cybersecurity in the context of information security, policy, and energy systems." These contexts are offered, respectively, by the College of Computing, the College of Liberal Arts, and the College of Engineering. While it makes sense that a complex field would be offered through different facets of the university, a student will likely require some guidance in choosing the most appropriate.

There Are New Combinations
Finally, in some instances, the issue is not one of new credential "elements" but of new "compounds." Recognizing the value of the liberal arts disciplines while acknowledging concerns as to their marketability, the **University of Illinois Urbana-Champaign** (2019) offers "**recombinant degrees**" that combine study in an arts and sciences discipline with computer science. New programs enable students in philosophy or linguistics or anthropology "who plan to pursue technical or professional careers in arts and sciences areas requiring a sound grounding in computer science" to gain "novel perspectives in interdisciplinary work."

Approaches to Managing the Confusion
Such offerings testify to the creativity and entrepreneurship of postsecondary education and to the potential for further innovation, but they also point to the likelihood of increased confusion.

The most obvious response is the one we continue to emphasize. Each institution must clarify the costs and benefits of the credentials it offers, make its students aware of expanding curricular opportunities, and acquaint them with criteria they should consider in evaluating those opportunities whether found "in house" or elsewhere.

The next is more ambitious. We must continue to develop a national credentials taxonomy, a public standard for nomenclature that would enable students to compare credentials readily within recognizable categories. Beyond state taxonomies used to track allocations and a federal taxonomy used for focused comparisons, the most promising initiative in this direction is CE's Credential Transparency Description Language (CTDL). Its objective is to enable individuals "to make 'apples to apples' comparisons between and among credentials" (CE, 2021, p. 4). More than half of the states are using or considering the taxonomy, which records information about credentials, providers, competencies, outcomes, pathways, and other information. With encouragement from federal agencies and foundations, other states appear likely to get on board.

There Are Many More Credential Sequences

"They're doing college backwards." That's how Dave DesRochers, an authority on higher education pathways, describes an increasingly frequent phenomenon, that of students seeking an associate degree or nondegree credential *after* receiving a bachelor's degree. At community colleges, according to the American Association of Community Colleges, more that 8% of their students fit that description (Marcus, 2020).

That trend runs counter to the familiar sequence: Qualified high school graduates enter a community college or four-year college and earn associate or bachelor's degrees. Graduates who require advanced study may then earn a master's degree. Or even a doctorate. One stage offers preparation for the next. Those who cannot qualify for this sequence or have no wish to do so may seek career-focused credentials such as certificates or certifications instead.

While such a continuum remains familiar, the breadth of variations continues to increase. In addition to new and creative sequences, there are new combinations. For instance, while a bachelor's degree is a prerequisite to qualify as a certified financial planner, one may pursue the degree and the certification simultaneously. Or a bachelor's degree recipient may initiate such study through a graduate program. The Certified Financial Planning Board of Standards (CFP Board, 2020) website describes several such options and lists institutions that support them. There is even a new verbal coinage used to describe degree programs that include earning a nondegree credential: "credigrees."

SIDEBAR
Bachelor's Degrees With a Difference
The final report in December 2020 on a project focused on "integrating high-quality, industry certifications into bachelor's degree programs" makes a strong case. Recommendations developed through separate convenings of representatives from specific sectors (health care, cybersecurity, liberal arts, manufacturing) call for accessible pathways enabling students ("especially those historically underserved") to acquire *an industry certification while pursuing a bachelor's degree.* Acknowledging the need for affordability, for "rapid prototyping, model building, and information sharing" as means to implementation on a broad scale, and for engagement with employers, the report envisions "robust and ultimately sustainable pathways" (Workcred, 2020). Administrators, faculty members, and academic advisors searching the landscape for singular opportunities should not overlook this one.

Many certificates (important differences between certificates and certifications are described in chapter 8) can be wild cards "playable" at almost any point. Earning a certificate in nursing, for instance, can offer a first step along a career path leading to an LPN or RN program. But certificate programs can serve also as capstone or transitional credentials. The proliferation of nondegree credentials has created more such opportunities for learners but at the cost of greater complexity that must be navigated if credentials are to work together in meaningful ways.

The attractive idea of "stackability," that short-term credentials may be aggregated to create a platform for the pursuit of a degree, remains appealing for many and can be one criterion for the evaluation of a nondegree program. But there are now many patterns. Those with master's degrees may undertake a career change by earning an associate degree. A PhD in English may seek a Microsoft digital badge. A graduate in political science may earn a certificate and become a firefighter. Perhaps an image more helpful than that of a "stack" is that of a LEGO construction. Pieces are made to fit together in a variety of directions for a variety of purposes.

At least, they *should*. The challenge implicit in the image of the LEGO construction may be clarified by using an entirely different metaphor, that of islands separated by broad straits. Programs (both degree and nondegree) too often appear isolated on a credential "island" that students inhabit until they receive the credential. A student on the point of completing one credential may gaze across the strait to other islands, but the few available ferries are difficult to locate and inconvenient to schedule. Moreover, there are unsettling rumors that gaining access to the next island may be more complicated and more expensive. What are the costs and benefits of attempting the crossing? In terms of this metaphor, what is needed is a commitment to create convenient and inviting links enabling students to travel from one island to the other when it is to their advantage.

Under present circumstances "many sequences" offer many opportunities to fall "out of sequence," thereby increasing the likelihood of unproductive and time-consuming effort required to earn a credential. One effective remedy may lie in so called "career pathways," a specific approach to "well-articulated sequences of quality education and training offerings . . . that enable educationally underprepared youth and adults to advance over time to successively higher levels of education and employment in a given industry sector or occupation" (Mortrude, 2014). Incorporated in the Perkins Career and Technical Education Act, the Workforce Innovation and Opportunity Act, and the Higher Education Act, the approach has engaged many states and local educational institutions. Through this approach, postsecondary institutions coordinate their efforts with those of other institutions to ensure that their students can earn credentials that connect meaningfully and efficiently.

There Are Many More Credential Providers

Prior to the current century, providers of academic credentials were mostly the familiar ones: accredited community colleges and four-year colleges. That structure remains dominant but is no longer exclusive.

The Familiar Hierarchies of Carnegie and U.S. News

Since 1970, the Carnegie Classification of Institutions of Higher Education (2017) has offered both "a way to represent and control for institutional differences" and a means whereby research studies may "ensure adequate representation of sampled institutions, students, or faculty" (para. 3). Currently there are 37 different "Carnegie Classifications," such as "Doctoral Universities: Very High Research Activity," "Baccalaureate Colleges: Arts & Sciences Focus," and "Associate's Colleges: High Career and Technical-High Traditional." This configuration of institutions often translates into assumptions regarding the kinds of credentials they offer.

More popular approaches to rankings within this hierarchy appear annually in competing commercial publications, the most prominent of which is *U.S. News and World Report.* Although the rankings of "best colleges" draws the most attention, the magazine and its website provide "nearly 50 different types of numerical ratings and lists to help students narrow their college search" (*U.S. News*, 2020). The rankings of "national universities" and "liberal arts colleges" draw the most attention, but there also are lists for regional universities and colleges, for historically Black colleges and universities, for "Top Universities for International Students," even for "A+ Schools for B Students." The weights assigned to different values such as admissions selectivity and alumni engagement are regularly reconsidered, but few surprises appear from year to year. Reputation—measured in part through surveys of academic leaders—continues to matter. A lot. Well-known and well-respected institutions tend to earn the higher rankings that reinforce their prestige—and that of the credentials they award.

The Mix of Providers Is Wide and Deep

The breadth of the postsecondary spectrum is a challenge. In addition to the familiar institutional categories, there are institutions with highly specific vocational emphases, colleges emphasizing a priority on the spiritual growth of their students, "institutions" that open to meet pop-up training needs, and marginal niche operations that emerge only to disappear.

SIDEBAR
CE's New "Finder"
Following the completion of our initial draft, Credential Engine announced in its web-based monthly bulletin for September 2021 a "new version" of its Credential Finder, an application "that allows users to search, find, and compare credential information." The purpose of the redesigned application according to CE is "to make it easy for people—learners, workers, educators, providers, employers, etc.—to find and act upon the various credential opportunities available to them."

Under "Colleges," The Real Yellow Pages (2019) for Atlanta shows 444 entries. A quick glance will suggest that an accurate count of discrete institutions would be difficult. But it is obvious that a student in Atlanta attempting to use this reference would have to consider more than 150 entries, from those for well-known universities such as Emory, Georgia Tech, and Oglethorpe, to those for less well-known institutions such as the Dogwood Institute for Medical Training, the Luther Rice University & Seminary, and Malk College. And the list does not include the myriad of providers available to students online! Even those who have already made a clear career choice will face a challenge. Interested in a truck driving school? In Atlanta, there appear to be no fewer than 10.

There Are Many More Approaches to Offering Credentials

Prior to 2020, despite an increasing frequency of innovative approaches, the most traditional model of postsecondary education remained the dominant one. Students register for classes, show up on time at their appointed classrooms, record notes, and take exams. Their "seat time" translates into credit: 45 hours = 3 semester hours—with occasional adjustments for the quarter system or other alternate calendars. Labs and one-on-one instruction (e.g., in music or in art) translate into credit according to different but comparable formulas. And credits, accumulated to meet qualitative and quantitative requirements, translate into credentials.

The most conspicuous exception to this model has been distributed (or distance) education, from the venerable "correspondence course" to online learning. Another has been the College Level Examination Program. Introduced in 1967 by the College Board and still widely in use, CLEP offers what now appears as a precursor to "direct assessment," the evaluation of competences irrespective of how they have been acquired. And competency-based education (CBE) has had enthusiastic supporters in both familiar institutions and unfamiliar new providers.

But the pandemic created a sea change—at least temporarily. Virtually overnight, in-person learning became the exception. Education at a distance became the rule. One end of the delivery spectrum, that emphasizing close interaction between individual teachers and students, was largely suspended. The other end of the spectrum, instructional methods that do not offer such interaction in person, became the dominant approach.

While a more typical balance between in-person and online learning has emerged since then, the shift in favor of distance education appears likely to continue at some level. In the meantime, savvy administrators, faculty members, and academic advisors will make themselves conversant with a broad range of instructional options and with the advantages and disadvantages of each. They will thereby be in a better position to choose the instructional methods that align most closely with their respective missions, the spectrum of their students, their pedagogical resources, and the credentials they award. They will recognize that learning can occur in many ways. While credentials typically reflect formal learning that is instructor led and classroom based, they are more and more likely to document learning that occurs informally in other settings and is more learner directed (Van Noy et al., 2016).

A few reminders about broad methodological categories may be useful.

Direct Instruction in Multiple Guises
Tutorials, classroom instruction, supervised application, thesis direction, and the like create their own spectrum, from in-depth, highly personal interaction between teachers and students in studio classes to the anonymity of mass lectures. Although the values of such in-person learning have been and continue to be widely acknowledged, they have now become increasingly subject to scrutiny. Effective instructors and motivated students never forget that instruction, however delivered, should offer a coherent, purposeful educational experience leading to the award of appropriate, respected credentials aligned both with student interests and with the needs of the marketplace. But for this to happen, administrators, faculty members, and academic advisors must make certain that the curriculum embodies clear intentions that are transparent to students and realized in practice.

In other words, articulating the distinct advantages of direct instruction has become obligatory. No longer the assumed default, direct instruction must justify itself as a choice in terms of results—in terms of credentials. Lawsuits filed by students during the pandemic claimed that distance education, at least in the forms made available to them, had failed to meet their needs in ways that justified their tuition. But their dissatisfaction should not have reassured educators hanging on to the status quo. The challenge in the future will be to demonstrate that direct instruction can be *at least as effective* as the most effective online learning.

Learning at a Distance

Online learning had emerged as a principal ground of innovation in post-secondary education long before there was a compelling need for sudden and unprecedented expansion. In September 2019 *The Chronicle of Higher Education* identified three highly dissimilar institutions as "super innovators" in this regard (CHE Innovators, 2019).

Arizona State (ASU) is one of the nation's largest public universities. Southern New Hampshire University (SNHU) is a private university with just over 3,000 students on its 338-acre campus. Western Governors University (WGU), a private not-for-profit institution created in 1997 by 19 state governors, does not even have a campus. But the three have in common a highly entrepreneurial approach to online education focused on credentials. ASU aggressively markets its online programs to the public, works with corporate partners to expand online access for employees, and sponsors research to enrich and expand online education. In addition to its modest on-campus enrollment, SNUH enrolls more than 100,000 online students. WGU, operating solely online, also enrolls more than 100,000.

SIDEBAR
New Converts to Online Learning
Restrictions on online learning have long been the rule in disciplines that qualify credential recipients for licensure in fields such as law and medicine. But change is appearing even there. Medical students learn techniques of effective telemedicine and may supplement their in-person instruction with online tutorials. The American Bar Association has recently approved eight "hybrid" programs that combine instruction at a distance with periodic campus residencies. And in August 2021, St. Mary's University School of Law (San Antonio, TX) announced that it had received ABA approval for an online-only program.

Such innovative institutions fulfill—and then some!—an observation made by Peter Brooks (2011) nearly 10 years ago: "No university that I know of is oblivious to the revolutions of network and Web" (p. 11). But not remaining oblivious is a far cry from taking an entrepreneurial approach to identifying and responding to emerging opportunities. What's required? Academic advisors must become more knowledgeable about the use of online learning to supplement course work on campus. Faculty members who may have doubted that "online courses can achieve student learning outcomes at least equivalent to in-person courses at any institution" (Lederman, 2019) may need to learn new pedagogies, rethink course content, and focus closely on ends (i.e., learning outcomes, student success, and credentials) as well as on the pedagogical means.

But as 2020–2021 offered a golden opportunity for proponents of online learning, it also revealed the limitations of such learning and made inequities in access and quality conspicuous. Here, too, this chapter's catchphrase, "expanding opportunity, increasing confusion," applies. To a far greater extent than with direct instruction, the terms *online learning* and *distance education* suggested a broad spectrum of effectiveness that included untried pedagogical approaches, inequitably distributed resources and opportunities, and halting approaches to documenting quality. Some online courses provided intense one-on-one exchanges with instructors and other students, while others offered little or no personal contact. Some incorporated sophisticated pedagogical advances specifically geared to online learning. Others offered taped lectures. Some enabled students to work toward competitive credentials of documented value. Other courses led nowhere.

SIDEBAR
Virtual Ivy
An announcement by the University of Pennsylvania that it would offer a 100% online Ivy League bachelor's degree suggested that a reputation for exclusivity can offer an advantage in the competition for the world's connected students. Marketing its expensive degree to "working adults and other non-traditional students who want to pursue an Ivy League education . . . built with career enhancement in mind," Penn Online (2021) points to its reputation in a direct appeal: "Whether you already have an associate's [*sic*] degree, some college, a high school diploma, or GED, Penn LPS Online makes the Ivy League experience accessible to you." Of course, we may assume, without the ivy.

Imperatives for administrators, faculty members, and academic advisors are increasingly clear. The most strategic will maintain robust "online readiness" henceforth. One useful resource in this regard may be found in an assessment tool created by the Distance Education Accrediting Commission (DEAC). Incorporating standards that DEAC (2020) has developed, the (SEA)RESULTS tool enables providers to "assess their distance education effectiveness across academic, organizational, operational, and technical dimensions, to better understand their strengths and weaknesses" (para. 2) and create a strategy for strengthening their capacity for effective distance education, and to measure their performance over time.

SIDEBAR
Learning Through Duress
Lessons learned through having "to re-engineer courses to active learning" in 2020 remain applicable to in-person instruction. Colleges can continue to "flip" the classroom: provide online instruction prior to the class meeting, confirm student understanding of the material, build on that understanding through "group problem solving and project-based learning," and assess the results (Craig, 2020, para. 13).

Whether through use of this tool or through some other means, assessment of distance education capacity and effectiveness are critical. But equally critical may be a continued effort to secure an enduring shift in the culture forged on the anvil of credentials: from "my courses" to "our students." As opposed to assuming that the curriculum will enable students to earn credentials of value, the student-centered institution begins with credentials by considering the learning outcomes (both implicit and explicit) each credential should guarantee. Curricula that will enable students to accomplish these outcomes can then be developed. Whether the approach be through in-person instruction, distance education, or one of the "hybrid" approaches that combine the two, effective educational providers put first things first.

Competency-Based Education

A direct line between learning and credentials can be drawn. Students earn credit not by accumulating seat time but, as the term suggests, by demonstrating mastery of competencies. In order to gain such competencies, students may attend classes, but they may instead pursue programmed instruction, self-directed learning, massive open online courses, and so on. As with qualifying for a driver's license, the issue is not how you have acquired the necessary competences, but how well you can demonstrate them.

For the credentials earned through this approach to be credible, however, there are two requisites.

First, competencies must be clearly defined in terms of the knowledge and skills that students can demonstrate. For degrees, examples of demonstrable competencies may be found in the *Degree Qualifications Profile.* Other kinds of credentials require different approaches. Many apprenticeship programs offer models of well-defined competencies. Certifications may have experiential or academic prerequisites, but they can be earned only through the demonstration of competencies on examinations. Similarly, certificates may be awarded on the basis of assessed competencies.

Second, the examinations and assessments used to measure competences must do so reliably through protocols that will ensure the comparability of credentials earned through CBE with those awarded conventionally.

CBE, still in the early stages of what appears likely to be wide acceptance, has a strong advocate in the Competency-Based Education Network (C-BEN, 2020), whose members are pursuing three priorities: (a) enabling students, employers, and others to appreciate the advantages of CBE so as to increase demand; (b) enabling "leaders from a wide range of disciplines and perspectives" to assert their influence in building capacity; and (c) eliminating regulatory barriers to CBE. While there is much work remaining, it would be prudent for administrators, faculty members, and academic advisors to become conversant with the principles of CBE and to inform themselves about its early adopters. One useful reference is *A Leader's Guide to Competency-Based Education* by Deborah J. Bushway, Laurie Dodge, and Charla S. Long (2018).

Work-Based Learning
By gaining practical experience through apprenticeships, clinical education, internships, and informal learning that can occur through job shadowing and career academies, students may earn credit toward the award of a credential. The category is a broad one, encompassing both formal and informal learning, but programs emphasizing work-based learning characteristically focus both on (a) the acquisition of technical skills required for performance and (b) acculturation (i.e., the development of essential soft skills such as collaboration, adaptability, and an appropriate work ethic; Alfeld et al., 2013; Raelin, 2008).

Criteria for Navigating the Many Dimensions

Given the number and the range of providers and credentials, academic administrators, faculty members, and academic advisors face a formidable challenge in guiding their students to make responsible choices. Fortunately, there are some objective standards that can inform that guidance, but they must be well understood and thoughtfully communicated.

The Power of Accreditation

Among the standards to be considered in assessing quality, accreditation may be the most important. It also may be the least well understood. At a minimum, anyone with a stake in postsecondary education should understand first that an institution's accreditation by a U.S. Department of Education (USDE) recognized accreditor (a) provides assurance that the institution is regularly evaluated, (b) indicates that the credits awarded by the institution should be considered for acceptance by other institutions, and (c) confirms that enrolled students will be eligible to apply for federal financial aid. In addition, because institutional accreditation does not focus on the quality of any particular program, it is important that students be made aware of the possible value of programmatic accreditation.

With this understanding as context, institutions would be well advised to clarify both their institutional accreditation and the specialized accreditation earned by any of their programs. Students in turn should be aware that some institutions are "accredited" by organizations not recognized by the USDE and that others may not be accredited at all. While there can be value in credentials offered by unaccredited providers, faculty members and advisors should remind students that they may not qualify for federal aid at such institutions, that the credits they earn there may not be accepted by other institutions, and that the credentials they receive may not be widely accepted.

So far as programmatic accreditation is concerned, an institution should be transparent as to which of its programs that are eligible maintain accreditation—and why. Every one of the 67 accrediting organizations listed by the Council on Higher Education Accreditation (CHEA, 2021) is distinctive. Not all programmatic accreditations are essential to every institution, and those that may be essential may be so for different reasons. For instance, credentials that lead to licensure must typically be earned through accredited programs. Without a degree from an accredited program in law or nursing, for instance, you cannot sit for the licensure exam. In other fields, such as journalism and mass communication, accreditation may be discretionary, a question of value for money. Administrators, faculty members, and academic advisors should be able to offer informed guidance. For instance, an aspiring journalist concerned about a program not accredited by the Accrediting Council on Education in Journalism and Mass Communications (ACEJMC) may find reassurance in learning about prestigious programs that have chosen not to seek accreditation. At the same time, programs that are accredited by ACEJMC may want to clarify the benefits that such recognition can provide. Of course, for some disciplines, especially those in the liberal arts and social sciences, there are no accrediting commissions.

SIDEBAR
Major or Alma Mater: Which Matters More?
Jeffrey Selingo describes as a "myth" the premise that choosing a major matters more than choosing an institution—at least so far as potential earnings are concerned. "Students who graduate from more selective schools tend to make more money. . . . The better the college, the better the professional network opportunities, through alumni, parents of classmates and eventually classmates themselves" (Selingo, 2017). Of course, the choice of a major, whatever the institution, can have a significant impact on earnings.

Just to make things more complicated, there is one further wrinkle. A few disciplines may have a choice among *competing* programmatic accreditors. In business, especially, it is important that institutions specify whether their programs are accredited by the Association to Advance Collegiate Schools of Business (AACSB International), the Accreditation Council for Collegiate Business Schools and Programs (ACBSP), or the International Assembly for Collegiate Business Education (IACBE). Because the three differ in their emphases, some employers or graduate business schools may prefer one over the others.

For-Profit and Not-for-Profit

Another important difference to consider is that between for-profit and not-for-profit providers. Administrators, faculty members, and academic advisors at both kinds of institutions should be prepared to explain the differences as significant but not necessarily invidious. There are for-profit institutions that achieve regional accreditation, document impressive student satisfaction and success, and recruit potential students according to high ethical standards. Moreover, a for-profit institution's frank disclosure of its status offers an opportunity to disarm preconceptions and to distance itself from problematical providers that may have received negative attention.

But students should also be reminded that the for-profit sector has had more than its share of problematical providers. While the not-for-profit sector also includes substandard providers with abysmally low six-year graduation rates, inferior facilities, or mismanaged priorities, that sector overall is fairly stable compared to the for-profit one, an industry still "seeking to reorganize and rebrand itself after years of aggressive government oversight, financial problems, and scathing press coverage" (Bauman & Blumenstyk, 2018).

A summary of movements within the for-profit sector as of March 2018 revealed no fewer than seven recent realignments, including the acquisition of a for-profit (Kaplan University) by a not-for-profit state university (Purdue), a merger between formerly competing for-profit providers (Capella and Strayer), an institution's bid to move from for-profit to not-for-profit status (Grand Canyon University), and the closure of 21 of 24 campuses by the Zenith Education Group (Bauman & Blumenstyk, 2018). A recent acquisition occurred in August 2020 with the University of Arizona's "purchase" (for $1) of Ashford University, an online, for-profit provider with 35,000 students and a problematical history. Even more recent? The disclosure in September 2021 that Brandman University, a private, nonprofit, principally online institution, would take on a new affiliation and a new identity as UMass Global. The "Global Administration" offices of UMass Global, which will offer online, hybrid, in-person, and self-guided courses and programs, are located 3,000 miles from Amherst, MA, in Irvine, CA.

None of these actions need prompt an advisor to discourage students from considering a particular institution or program. Indeed, the new opportunities they are developing may be ideally suited for some students. But the volatility of the for-profit environment—its closures, mergers, acquisitions, affiliations—should prompt due diligence regarding the likely sustainability of the programs and institutions being considered.

Responding to the New Environment

How should leaders—administrators, faculty members, academic advisors—respond to the complexity of the credentials marketplace and the confusion that the complexity creates? We have a few suggestions.

Begin With Credentials

For most institutions, a strategic approach will begin with *credentials*—those they are offering, those that are being offered by their competitors, those that are emerging in new disciplines, and those of long standing now responding to increasing demand. A needs assessment will consider surveys of (a) current, former, and prospective students; (b) employers that regularly hire the institution's graduates or might if additional programs were to be offered; and (c) faculty members, academic advisors, and student affairs professionals. Discontinuation or reorganization of underperforming programs following an analytic inventory and consultation with stakeholders may create a reinvestment opportunity.

Having reflected on their challenging experience in 2020–2021, savvy institutions will maintain curricular and pedagogical modifications that now appear to represent genuine improvements. These might include greater reliance on distance education, the creation of "hybrid" courses and programs combining in-person and distance learning, a greater focus on high-impact pedagogy, and, above all, the offering of more clearly defined learning outcomes for degrees, programs, and courses. Options already familiar for some institutions—weekend colleges, evening programs, and flexible summer programs—may offer opportunities others will find worth considering.

Institutions should also consider the *structure* of their degree programs. There could be no better time to integrate appropriate nondegree credentials into two-year and four-year degrees, to align synergistic disciplines as attractive double majors, and to offer attractive alternatives for popular but highly competitive majors such as pre-medicine and architecture.

In addressing such priorities, leaders that know their institutions and their students, that develop their strengths and avoid imprudent experiments, and that measure themselves regularly in terms of the demands they address and the competition they face are far more likely to remain effective and successful.

But the credentials environment will continue to evolve. Without attempting to predict the long term, we recognize several likelihoods. First, growth in demand for nondegree credentials is likely to continue. Second, while new credential providers will continue to emerge, others will continue to disappear through closure or consolidation. Third, at least within the near term, what was already an inscrutable credentials environment will probably become even more indecipherable.

Credentials and "Credentialism"

"In 1972, people without college degrees were nearly as happy as those with college degrees. Now those without a degree are far more unhappy about their lives" (D. Brooks, 2020). That finding, reported by columnist David Brooks, provides one perspective on "credentialism," a source of the disproportionate advantages said to be enjoyed by those with academic credentials at the expense of those who lack such credentials. Brooks's reference is an article by J.M. Twenge and A.B. Cooper (2020), "The Expanding Class Divide in Happiness in the United States, 1972–2016."

In the previous chapter, we acknowledged that credentials function as sources of status and power. So long as there is equitable access to credentials and due respect for ability and achievement not ordinarily credentialed, there may be nothing wrong with that. But because access is rarely equitably distributed, status and power tend to be inequitably distributed as well. Those who "valorize" degrees "both as an avenue for advancement and as the basis for social esteem" may not appreciate both "the hubris a meritocracy can generate" and "the harsh judgment it imposes on those who have not gone to college" (Sandel, 2020, p. 26). Evidence for the resentment credentialism can create is not difficult to find.

It should therefore not be surprising that as views of higher education have become increasingly partisan, public support for what has long been prized as a public good has declined. "Once widely seen as an engine of opportunity, the university has become, at least for some, a symbol of credentialist privilege and meritocratic hubris" (Sandel, 2020, p. 104).

Two premises lie behind "credentialism." The first is that academic skills are somehow of greater value than skills enabling vocational competence and craftsmanship. The second is that the possession of a higher education credential offers entitlement to social privilege, generous remuneration, and a lofty sense of self-satisfaction that other credentials—or the lack of a credential—do not provide. While both premises reflect reality to an extent, both are misguided and harmful.

Even as we affirm the importance of academic credentials and the advantages they can offer, we should affirm also the recognition that knowledge and ability associated with the trades and crafts are no less worthy of respect and may often be of greater moment. "Applied" programs and apprenticeships emphasizing direct preparation for a career provide positive alternatives to baccalaureate programs and may offer as secure a path to economic security and leadership. And while there is a traditional sequence for academic degrees based on assumptions of increasing specialization, challenge, and autonomy, there should be no hierarchy of value. When you need a licensed electrician, you will not attempt to locate someone with a Harvard MBA.

While we recognize "the tyranny of merit" as a reality, we believe that those who enjoy the advantages society offers the academically accomplished must recognize that they "are not self-made and self-sufficient" (Sandel, 2020, p. 227). Their good fortune does not confer entitlement. To the contrary, as Michael Sandel (2020) concludes, the recognition of that good fortune should lead to a personal commitment to greater humility grounded in "a lively sense of the contingency of our lot" (p. 227).

In Sum

The solutions for the issues we have considered in this chapter are ones that administrators, faculty members, and academic advisors are uniquely positioned to offer. The resources of the academy can be directed to the education of the academic community with regard to the complexities of the credentials environment. And its ceremonies, its structures, and its values can encourage the reevaluation of "credentialism" that is required. In chapter 10, our "Takeaways" will include specific steps colleges can take. Paradoxically, by questioning "credentialism," college leaders can clarify and strengthen the rightful value of credentials for those who receive them and for a society that needs what they have to offer.

Takeaways

Institutions have a clear responsibility to guide students in making wise educational choices among an unprecedented spectrum of opportunities. The issues and approaches covered in this chapter should offer a starting point, but the common thread is that responsible educators make the interests of their students their priority. "Responding to the Changed Environment" offers many of the most important "takeaways." So far as curricular planning for the future is concerned, the balance may continue to shift in favor of those that can be completed in less time and at less expense. That trend is one with important implications.

- Because of inadequate state and national data on noncredit credentials, leaders must familiarize themselves with trends within their disciplines by consulting with employers, disciplinary associations, economic development bodies, and—most importantly—with their students.
- Savvy administrators and faculty members should acknowledge but not rely too heavily on the "brand advantage" that degree programs share. The most traditional degree program can become a platform for innovation (e.g., consider restructuring the credential to include nondegree credentials aligned with clear employment opportunities).
- In addition to advising students as to the growing spectrum of credentials, academic advisors can offer effective counsel to their colleagues, administrators, and faculty members. Advisors are the "distant early warning" system for postsecondary education.
- Providers that seek to expand online programming should consider several elements of good practice:
  - Monitor current online market share, avoid sectors that are becoming oversaturated, and pursue opportunities consistent with institutional strengths, mission, and image.
  - Choose audiences carefully. That the University of Washington seeks students worldwide for its online Continuum College does not mean that a small liberal arts college in the Midwest would be wise to do so. But a community college serving a region with a single large industry may want to consider developing additional online programs specifically tailored to the needs of that industry.

o Maintain credential quality. An *IHE* survey confirms that "neither faculty members nor digital learning administrators believe online learning is less expensive to offer than its on-ground alternative" (Lederman, 2019). Institutions that cut corners are likely to relinquish any potential advantage that distance education otherwise might offer them.

o Confirm through rigorous assessment that courses offered online are *at least equivalent* to on-campus courses in rigor, effectiveness, and, most importantly, student success. Ideally, they should offer an example of clear intent and continuous improvement.

o Acknowledge both the limitations of online instruction and the salutary example it can offer for the improvement of in-person instruction.

3

THE PROBLEMS OF PROLIFERATION

A Risky Environment

Having examined the opportunities offered by growth in the number and variety of credentials, we now give particular attention to the problems that can occur. An environment that offers an extraordinary range of educational options invites extraordinary mistakes. Without access to guidance concerning the design, meaning, and outcomes of credentials—and about the effectiveness and reliability of the providers that offer them—today's students and employers face significant challenges. Institutional administrators, faculty members, and academic advisors—as well as policymakers—must understand this challenge in order to address it.

As we observed in chapter 2, the higher education "store" has expanded dramatically in ways both unpredictable and volatile. "Every day the options within this highly complex landscape of credentials change as new credentials are created, some are removed, occupational requirements shift with employer needs, and the economy continues its perpetual evolution" (Credential Engine [CE], 2018, p. 3). As a result, the credentials environment has become "vast, complex, expensive, and inefficient" (CE, 2021, p. 5).

The Growth of the Credentials Environment

Nearly one million. That is a recent (February 2021) count of credentials in the United States by CE. Of these, nearly 920,000 are postsecondary credentials. Note that these numbers reflect "unique" credentials, not the total number of credentials awarded! There are three postsecondary provider

TABLE 3.1
Providers and the Credentials They Offer

Providers	Number	Types
Postsecondary institutions	359,713	Degrees, certificates
Massive open online course (MOOC) providers	9,390	Course completion certificates, etc.
Nonacademic providers	549,712	Badges, course completion certificates, licenses, certifications, apprenticeships

categories. Table 3.1 shows what kind of credentials each kind of provider offers—and approximately how many.

Although the CE report has become more detailed and more informative with every iteration, the recognition in the 2019 report that "we still know very little about the full range of credentials offered across the country" continues to ring true. That is in part because the count depends on estimates of some categories such as occupational licenses and bootcamp certificates. But the knowledge gap reflects also the fact that many of the new providers fall outside of familiar institutional categories. They may promise a fast track to employment by focusing on skills within a limited range of fields, such as business, health care, and computer technology. Some can point to robust quality assurance in the form of third-party oversight. Some cannot. Some are "accredited" by "nonacademic" evaluators. Some are not.

The issues created by the expansion of the credentials environment cannot be attributed solely to new providers, however. Even if we were to limit our consideration to familiar providers, we would still find considerable potential for confusion. The result of this proliferation has been to make what were once fairly straightforward choices into at best a complicated process of categorization and discernment—at worst a risky stab in the dark.

From a "Small Town" to a "Metropolis"

In 1950, of the 15% of high school graduates who chose to attend college, nine out of 10 chose four-year colleges in order to study for a bachelor's degree (Snyder, 1993). They may have been aware of a few other credentials, such as the master's and doctoral degrees earned by their faculty members and the professional degrees displayed by their doctors and dentists, but you could count the categories of credentials on both hands.

We might picture that uncomplicated environment as a small college town offering easy navigation among familiar landmarks. Of course, a halcyon environment for some students at that time proved unwelcoming for others. Students of color, students beyond traditional college age, students bound to full-time jobs, and students with family obligations often had few alternatives: "evening colleges," correspondence courses, vocational schools, and the like. But traditional students found the environment trustworthy, their choices, straightforward. There was little risk of making truly calamitous decisions.

By contrast, the current credentials environment evokes a metropolis with opportunities on every corner. If you can make it there, you can make it anywhere. But the transit system is confusing and irregular. Traffic jams occur frequently. A gaggle of clamorous advertisers competes for business. And good advice is hard to find. For the savvy, there are many good prospects in such an environment. For many others there's an abundance of risk.

Navigating an Environment of Unprecedented Complexity

What do students make of this "highly complex landscape"? In theory, those with highly focused interests and needs should be able to locate programs within a reasonable distance that correspond closely to what they are seeking. Wide choice should offer greater opportunity. And when the system works, that is what happens.

Say you're a licensed practical nurse (LPN) seeking to become a registered nurse. But your full-time job leaves you little time to attend classes on a college campus. There's an accredited online program for that at Indiana State University. "Equivalency exams allow students to earn credit for knowledge gained while working as LPNs and accelerate their completion of the degree, graduating in as few as three years" (Indiana State University, 2019).

Or you're a recent high school graduate with an interest in automotive technology. You want to earn a two-year degree and find a good job right away, but you want to maintain your options for further education. There's a program for that at Montana State University Northern. The Automotive Technology Fast Track program will enable you to earn an accredited associate of applied science (AAS) degree in three semesters. If later you want to become a corporate technical representative, service manager, specialized diagnostician, or midmanager, much of the work you have done to earn the AAS will count toward the bachelor's degree in automotive technology (Montana State University-Northern, 2019).

A Dilemma Becomes More Difficult

What are the challenges? One of them is simply "too much choice." Facing so many options can prove overwhelming. In fact, studies of decision-making have found that individuals faced with an overabundance of choices may run up against limitations in human cognitive processes. There is only so much information individuals can collect, process, and absorb in making decisions (Kahneman, 2011).

Such a dilemma becomes even more likely when one must somehow make sense of conflicting projections. For students considering fall 2021 programs, there were often more unknowns than knowns. Would their programs be offered in person or online? Would a volatile variant of the virus upset projections of economic recovery—or would international rates of infection impede international exchange? Would the short-term credentials that had enjoyed greater popularity continue to appeal to increasing numbers of students? Or not? With little of the information required for wise decision-making, many thousands of students then—as now—played their hunches.

For others, such an environment can lead to "analysis paralysis," an inclination to put off decision-making until only a few options—often not the most appropriate ones—remain. Or the student may instead make an impulsive decision so as to get beyond the decision-making process. Either response is likely to prove risky—and this is especially the case when those making the decisions lack knowledgeable family members and friends who can refer to experience and offer advice (Bruch & Feinberg, 2017). Inequities in society can translate directly into catastrophic educational choices.

Administrators, faculty members, and academic advisors have a particular responsibility at such a time to guide students in choosing wisely among the options available to them (Bailey et al. 2015; Scott-Clayton, 2011). Faculty members in particular must become more aware of the choices facing their students and better prepared to offer assistance. And academic advisors have an especially critical role in clarifying alternate paths from which students might choose wisely. (Pathways can help. See sidebar on p. 54.) But as difficult as it may be to secure such support within institutions, students who have not yet formed an institutional affiliation will find themselves at an even greater disadvantage.

An Unprecedented Challenge

The spring 2020 pivot from in-person to remote education distanced millions of students from readily available student services. Just as options were becoming increasingly opaque, guidance for weighing them became less accessible. While some students already had gained experience with distance education, many more felt isolated by a lack of experience and resources.

In the fall of 2021, with a gradual return to in-person and hybrid offerings, faculty members and academic advisors were in a better position to identify students most in need of guidance and to intervene as appropriate in offering such guidance. But we know now from enrollment figures that many of those who would have benefited most from such guidance were not present to receive it. As the economy grows, institutional operations return to normal, and enrollments return, especially to the community colleges that saw the sharpest declines, effective advising should again offer many students—at least those who have returned—the guidance they need.

But there is much ground to make up, especially among those from disadvantaged backgrounds. They are likely to have discovered that the proliferation of choices "has brought risk rather than opportunity, confusion rather than access, frustration rather than accomplishment" (Lumina Foundation, 2019). As the CE (2018) report observes, decisions made impulsively often carry "considerable consequences for making wrong choices" (p. 3). Students admitted to reputable programs may find the cumulative costs insupportable. Or they may complete their programs only to discover a lack of demand for the credentials they have earned. Or they may experience the unexpected closure of their institution or the cancellation of their program before they receive a credential. Since 2015, such closures "have displaced more than 100,000 students" (Vasquez, 2019).

SIDEBAR
The Data Is Limited
The federal Integrated Postsecondary Educational Data System (IPEDS) and U.S. Department of Labor (USDL) reporting offer a reliable count of (a) degrees from institutions authorized to offer federal student aid (Title IV institutions), (b) for-credit certificates and online degree programs offered by such institutions, and (c) *registered* apprenticeships. But counts of occupational licenses, certifications, unregistered apprenticeships, badges, and bootcamp certificates necessarily reflect "rough estimates." In some respects, the CE (2019) had to start from scratch: "The country has never had a good estimate of the number of credential programs, much less a strong accounting of their various characteristics and potential returns" (p. 6).

Searching for an Answer

Where lies the answer? Students must make their own educational choices, but the principal responsibility for enabling them to make *wise* ones still is that of educational institutions. Not only should colleges make available clear information about their own programs—their length, estimates of all costs (not just tuition), the average rate of completion within specified time frames, and verifiable information about placement and success—but they must be willing and able to guide students in interpreting that information and in making informed comparisons among different opportunities, including those offered by competing institutions.

A fully adequate approach cannot be found solely within institutions, however, because many students who need guidance have no affiliation with any institution. To address this challenge as a part of their commitment to education as a public good, administrators, faculty members, and academic advisors should consider creating collaborative, multi-institutional sources of academic and career advising to serve students who have not yet chosen an institution or who are considering making a transition from one institution to another. The marketplace may eventually address this need through the creation of independent, entrepreneurial advising services. Elsewhere we call for the emergence of professionals certified to offer such advice. But until that call is answered, institutions have the opportunity and the responsibility to respond. By doing so, they would serve their students *and other students* while building a competitive advantage in the changing marketplace.

The Changing Marketplace

Having considered the expansion of the postsecondary "store" now offering more credentials in far greater variety, we should acknowledge that the "customers" have changed as well. Broad societal trends evident in the first two decades of the century had created a more highly diverse spectrum of students. But such students found themselves increasingly challenged by volatile swings in the economy as some employment sectors (tourism, retail, heavy manufacturing) experienced temporary but dramatic contraction while others (health care, light manufacturing, engineering) continued to expand. To an already volatile environment for postsecondary institutions, add an unprecedented public health crisis, the global pandemic. Students who at one time could choose with confidence from a wide range of reliable educational providers had to make themselves aware of institutional vulnerabilities. In November of 2020, according to Moody's Investor Service, 30% of American public universities (public and private) were running deficits (Kamin, 2020). Some colleges closed, while many of those that survived cut programs, faculty, and academic departments.

The reasons for some of the sharpest cuts—at the University of Alaska, the University of Akron (OH), the University of Evansville (IN), Elmira College (NY), the University of Vermont, Ithaca College (NY), Marquette

University (WI), and Hiram College (OH), to name just a few—could be found in pandemic-caused enrollment declines, discouraging demographic trends, the cost of increased student aid, inadequate public health responses, reductions in state support, lost housing revenue, and the need for immediate unplanned investments in distance learning. In such an environment, a single questionable decision (e.g., to build a new football stadium or to invest in a new degree program) without a thorough needs assessment could prove calamitous. Caveat emptor had never been more relevant. That remains the case.

A credentials marketplace already forbiddingly opaque has thus become even more unpredictable, with the result that institutions seeking to attract students and to serve them well must work harder to understand the student population in all its complexity and to respond strategically and responsibly to its needs. In such a climate, the responsibilities and opportunities that lie at the heart of this book become more compelling than ever for administrators, faculty members, and academic advisors.

An Expanding Student Population

Notwithstanding some enrollment declines at the beginning of the decade, many more students are now seeking postsecondary credentials. With the exception of 2020–2021, that increase has been building steadily. While in 1980, 40% of high school seniors reported that they would pursue a bachelor's or graduate degree, the National Center for Education Statistics (NCES) reported that by 2016 that number had climbed to 60% (2019b). As of 2012, close to two thirds of the parents of high school juniors were reporting they expected their child to attain a bachelor's or graduate degree (NCES, 2019b).

The percentage of credential holders in the population has risen accordingly. In 1980, fewer than one fifth (17%) of adults over 25 years of age held a bachelor's degree or higher (NCES, 2019c). In 2019, one third (35%) held at least a bachelor's degree (NCES, 2019c). The growing enthusiasm for credential attainment has been met by (and to an extent encouraged by) the expansion in the credential marketplace.

Even more encouraging than the increasing numbers of credential recipients has been their increasing diversity. In the broadening mix of students, the majority are now "nontraditional," a category that includes students who are older than traditional college-aged students, that attend part-time and may work full-time while attending, that have dependents, that are single parents, or that have a GED rather than a traditional high school diploma.

From just under two thirds in 1986, the percentage of these students had grown to three quarters in 2012 (Horn, 1996).

Over time, this trend has dramatically changed the profile of the typical college student, thereby requiring an increased priority on accommodating students whose preparation is likely to include a wide range of life experiences, whose approach to learning is likely to be far more pragmatic and employment oriented, and whose obligations beyond academic ones must often take precedence. There have always been "students who work," but more and more campuses, classrooms, and distance learning platforms are dominated now by "workers who study."

Within this cohort, colleges are now enrolling substantially greater numbers of low-income students and students of color. In 1980, about one third (32.5%) of recent high school completers enrolled in college were considered low-income. This percent increased to close to two thirds (65.4%) in 2016 (NCES, 2019d). In 1980 fewer than one fifth (19%) of students enrolled in postsecondary institutions were students of color. This figure increased to 47% in 2017 (NCES, 2019d).

For many such students, particularly those who have been underrepresented in postsecondary education, earning a credential with documented market value holds particular promise. Beyond offering the likelihood of a financial advantage, the recognition a credential provides can be particularly important for students with limited access to the social networks that can facilitate hiring. These heartening increases reflect social factors such as improved high school graduation rates, a decrease in the availability of secure jobs requiring only a high school degree, and the greatly increased accessibility of postsecondary education in the form of community colleges.

But there are important external influences as well. Major changes in the labor market (that we consider later in this chapter) have prompted students to reconsider their needs and goals and have encouraged their interest in the emergence of new kinds of credentials. Administrators must understand these changes so they can understand the extent to which their credentials respond the needs and goals of students for whom employability is the first priority.

A brief review of recent trends will suggest ways in which postsecondary education must respond, both to needs that have developed over time and to those that have recently emerged.

The Promise of Earnings From Credentials

A significant factor contributing to enrollments is the recognition of potential economic benefits associated with postsecondary credentials. Students, parents, employers, and state agencies responsible for funding postsecondary education expect that meaningful credentials will entitle recipients to better paying jobs. In fact, the college premium (the estimated lifetime earnings of a postsecondary credential recipient in comparison with those of a high school graduate) has increased in recent years (Pew Research Center, 2014), further fueling the popular assumption that college graduates on average earn more than others (Angrist & Chen, 2011; Oreopoulos & Petronijevic, 2013).

Two factors bear on this assumption.

The first is that, in general, the higher the level of the credential, the higher the gain in earnings. According to the National Association of Colleges and Employers (NACE), "Earning an advanced degree [such as a master's] has been especially beneficial for those in non-career-related fields, such as humanities." But findings from a 2019 survey show that "holding a master's degree can also reap benefits for those in career-related fields" (NACE, 2019, para. 3). Two disciplines illustrate the point. In business administration, a 2019 graduate earning a bachelor's degree was "projected to earn a starting salary of $57,133" while an MBA recipient "can expect to earn $84,580" (para. 2). In computer science, a bachelor's degree recipient was "projected to earn a starting salary of $68,103" (para. 4), but a master's degree recipient could hope to earn $82,275.

There is a dark underside to this bright coin that we will describe in chapter 6, which focuses specifically on the master's degree. That is the offering of presumably prestigious and certainly very expensive master's degrees to students whose chosen fields will offer only very modest remuneration. Such degrees can suggest the principle that the level of the degree and the prestige of its provider may matter less than the field in which it is earned.

A positive perspective appears in a report from Georgetown University's Center on Education and the Workforce, "The Overlooked Value of Certificates and Associate Degrees." While agreeing that a bachelor's degree can still offer reliable access to remunerative employment, "program of study and major matter even more to potential earnings than education level" (Carnevale et al., 2020, p. 2)—a finding of particular importance to those unable or unwilling to pursue a degree. In an environment where workers with a high school diploma face decreased opportunity, the right kind of "middle-skills" pathway combining short-term nondegree credentials is becoming more and more attractive. Succinctly put, "less education [in the most competitive fields] can often be worth more" (p. 2) than more education in less competitive ones. The report shows that "some certificate holders can earn more than those with an associate's or bachelor's degree, and some associate degree holders can earn more than those with a bachelor's degree" (p. 2).

With the field of study as a critical differential, the range of median earnings for those with "less education" is very broad, from a low of $20,000–$30,000 for those earning associate degrees in education or the fine arts to over $50,000 for those with such degrees in engineering or architecture. The range is even more pronounced so far as certificate holders are concerned, from low median annual earnings of less than $20,000 in cosmetology to as high as $150,000 in engineering technologies or drafting (Carnevale et al., 2020).

In sum, while the bachelor's degree continues to offer on the whole a reliable advantage so far as employment opportunities and earnings are concerned, less costly and less demanding programs in some high-demand disciplines may offer a comparable or even greater competitive advantage.

Broader Social Forces at Work

Although an analysis of all the factors bearing on the alignment between credentials and earnings lies beyond the scope of this book, educators who recognize the presence (and possible influence) of broader social forces are likely to respond more effectively to the needs of their students.

As we have observed, one of these social forces is that well-paying unionized manufacturing jobs once available to high school graduates have decreased sharply, thanks in part to globalization and to the decline of union membership. According to the Pew Research Center, "the share of American workers who belong to labor unions has fallen by about half" (DeSilver, 2019, para. 2). Moreover, unskilled workers are now less likely to find employers willing to train them. To an increasing extent, employers expect that employees will have developed the necessary work readiness skills while in school (Cappelli, 2012).

One further social force may be found in increased job mobility—or, from another perspective, in the volatility of employment. As we noted in the preceding chapter, lifetime jobs leading to a secure retirement are becoming fewer by the year as examples of sustained loyalty to one organization are increasingly the exception. Jobs are increasingly short-term and project-based as consultants replace salaried employees with benefits. This dynamic environment has placed the undereducated, many of whom lack the skills required for navigation of a mutable environment, at a particular disadvantage. By the same measure, such mutability has heightened interest in programs that develop adaptability and an aptitude for independent learning, skills that can offer a degree of protection during labor market shifts.

SIDEBAR
Pathways Promote Progress
The guided pathways reform model, widely adopted by community colleges as an alternative to the "cafeteria model" students might otherwise experience there, promises a more coherent and student-centered way of organizing college programs and services (Bailey et al., 2015). There are a few key ideas: mapping out program pathways so that students know what is needed to attain a particular credential; assisting students in making choices about programs and careers so that they choose a credential aligned with their goals; helping students to stay engaged so that they attain the credential they seek; and ensuring that the credential encompasses a "coherent set of learning outcomes" (Bailey, 2017). Institutions with a priority on student success—not just community colleges—should offer all students, traditional and nontraditional, a choice of facilitated and supervised pathways leading efficiently and effectively to the timely award of credentials.

Administrators, faculty members, and academic advisors should acknowledge in these factors both obligations and opportunities. Institutions that approach all education, including liberal education, as "real-world" preparation are more likely to attract and retain committed students. That means clarifying and delivering on explicit learning outcomes, course by course, program by program. And it means making sure that such outcomes include those aligned with proficiencies employers say they want: critical thinking, an enthusiasm for diversity, experience in working within teams, a penchant for independent learning.

Can the Cost of Postsecondary Education Be Justified?

Students deserve the assurance that their commitment, their investment of time and money in the pursuit of a credential, will create both tangible and intangible advantages leading to anticipated benefits. To put the point bluntly, the more postsecondary education costs, the more it must deliver in terms of tangible (employment) and intangible value. Reductions in public funding of postsecondary education, the resulting rise in tuition costs, and steady increases in student debt easily justify the growing insistence among students, their families, and the public that credentials lead to well-paying careers (Fry, 2014; Lee, 2013).

An institution unaware of or insensitive to an apparent disconnect between program costs for students and the tangible benefits associated

SIDEBAR
New Degrees, Sobering Results for Providers
A November 2020 report from Burning Glass Technologies on new under-graduate and graduate (but not doctoral) degree programs, *Bad Bets: The High Cost of Failing Programs in Higher Education*, observes that "roughly half of the programs that first graduated students in the 2012–2013 or 2013–2014 academic years reported five or fewer conferrals in 2018." Even more sobering? "A staggering two-thirds of new programs produced 10 or fewer graduates in 2018" (para. 3). The Burning Glass findings should encourage exceptional due diligence on the part of institutions prior to the launch of any new program.

with the credentials it awards is either not clarifying those benefits in terms that their students will appreciate or failing to consider a possible imbalance of costs and benefits. To be sure, colleges must also look out for their own interests. Those that close because of revenue shortfalls will serve no one. Since the decline in public funding for public higher education began in the 1970s, public institutions have found themselves increasingly pressed to generate increased tuition income (Desrochers & Hurlburt, 2014). Private institutions have faced corresponding pressures in the increased costs of doing business. Finding ways to offset revenue declines has become a critical survival skill.

The sweet spot in curricular planning lies in programs that educate students effectively and efficiently while creating adequate income for the institution. That is why in our discussion of the different categories of credentials (chapters 4 through 10), we will emphasize the importance of conducting inventories that distinguish successful programs from underperforming ones. Institutions focused on preserving the status quo rarely position themselves for the future. To prepare the next generation of entrepreneurs, colleges and universities must themselves become more entrepreneurial, committed to the success of their students while keeping an eye on the bottom line. The pursuit of new opportunities will doubtless lead to difficult decisions concerning undersubscribed heritage programs, but strong administrators, faculty members, and academic advisors know that leadership may require reallocation from legacy programs to innovative ones that will address emerging needs.

Of course, traditional programs can themselves be more clearly attuned to such needs. Some offer precisely the proficiencies most needed in a volatile, project-based employment market. But traditional approaches to such programs may not serve well either institutions or students. By demonstrating a close alignment between the specific learning outcomes they offer and the documented needs of employers, institutions can argue effectively that liberal learning is real-world preparation for careers.

SIDEBAR
The Vocabularies of Postsecondary Education
"Competitive branding"—the search for an advantage through innovative credential titles—has further complicated what was already an opaque environment. As an example, the familiar Master's in Business Administration (MBA) has produced such varied offspring as the Executive MBA (EMBA), the somewhat different MBAE at Purdue (distinct from the MBAE that signifies the master's degree in biological and agricultural engineering at North Carolina State University and from the MBA in human resource management at Loyola Marymount), the international IMBA at the University of Chicago, and the part-time MBA (PMBA) at Kent State (OH). Master's degrees can be similarly recondite, and there is an even greater welter of new descriptors for baccalaureate degrees. A recruiter for IBM may find herself comparing candidates for the Bachelor of Business Administration (BBA) at the University of Georgia with those who will earn a Bachelor of Arts (BA) or Bachelor of Science (BS) in business at Arizona State and with those working toward the Bachelor of Science in business administration (BSBA) at Drake (IA). Looking for even greater complexity? Arizona State offers 47 differentiated bachelor's degrees in business, from the BS in nonprofit leadership and management to the BA in Digital Culture.
—Gaston (2014, pp. 8–9)

The Significance of Employers

As we have insisted throughout, employers represent a cornerstone in the credentials environment, a powerful influence on the ways in which that environment continues to evolve, and a bellwether for change. They deserve more consideration than they often receive. The concerns they express about the graduates they hire represents critical intelligence for academic institutions.

For instance, surveys have revealed employers' disappointment in the computational and problem-solving skills of new hires and in their reading and writing skills as well (Cappelli, 1997). Work attitudes and aptitudes (e.g., motivation, good work habits, social skills) represent another concern.

The ability to engage in nonrules-based communication that involves building trust and rapport is another. Such skills are particularly important in an economy no longer reliant principally on routine manufacturing and administrative support (Levy & Murnane, 2004).

Employers express also an important distinction between entry-level skills and those essential to advancement. An important 2021 report by Ashley Finley for AAC&U shows, for instance, that while only 60% of employers believe "that college graduates possess the knowledge and skills needed to succeed in entry-level positions," only 55% "believe they possess the knowledge and skills required for advancement and promotion" (Finley, 2021, p. 15). As we observed in chapter 1, employers who hire with an awareness of a candidate's potential for eventual promotion are likely to do so more deliberately.

A particular source of employer dissatisfaction lies in a disconnect between assumptions particular to certain credentials—what the recipient of a BSBA should know and be able to do, for instance—and the competencies of those presenting the credential. When considering a potential hire, they are likely to ask whether both objective (e.g., the candidate's grade point average) and subjective (e.g., the reputation of the candidate's alma mater) factors inspire confidence. But they are likely to question also the reliability of the credentials themselves—how well they document the readiness of the candidate to undertake the requirements of the job.

We acknowledged in chapter 1 the contributions of the late David Bills toward our understanding of how employers use credentials. His study of hiring transactions in six Chicago area firms offers a valuable perspective on just how complex such questions are (Bills, 1988a, 1988b). His interviews show how widely employers vary in how they evaluate an applicant's knowledge and aptitude (as documented by a credential) in the context of their own estimate of the quality of the applicant's experience. That prompts an obvious follow-up. Why are specific credentials associated with higher earnings if employers do not establish in advance that such credentials serve as surrogates for the needed skills?

Part of the answer may lie in the "credentialism" we consider in chapters 1 and 11, but a more persuasive answer may lie in a recognition that credentials are rarely the sole (and may not be the principal) determinants in hiring decisions. Although the evaluation of candidates for employment will almost always *begin* with their credentials, evaluation usually proceeds to other factors such as the candidate's personality, enthusiasm, knowledge of the hiring organization, and sociability—factors demonstrably related to success. Unfortunately, factors likely to be irrelevant (age, gender) and ones certain to be so (race, sexual orientation) may also come into play. In fact, particularly with regard to racial discrimination, there appears to have been only modest improvement over time (Quillian et al., 2017).

Economic circumstances are likely to bear on employment as well. A tight labor market may encourage a more generous evaluation of applicants, while one offering an abundance of job seekers may enable a more discriminating approach. In either case the hiring officer may reasonably consider both the urgency of the organization's need for the hire and how readily the applicant would be able to adapt to its culture.

But the weight of the credential itself remains conspicuous, most notably in its capacity to influence how employers *perceive* the requirements of an open position and how they *perceive* the alignment between candidates' credentials and those requirements. The logic of decision-making includes at least three complex variables. First there are the qualifications a potential candidate has to offer—irrespective of the requirements of a particular position. Then there is the question of the relationship between those qualifications and the job requirements. A candidate who presents impressive qualifications may not be well qualified for a particular job. Finally, there is the question as to how faithfully the *perception* of the requirements of a job reflects the *actual* requirements of that job (Van Noy, 2011). Employees whose credentials indicate a clear alignment with the requirements for a position *as advertised* may nevertheless stumble into a catastrophic misfit because the advertisement does not reflect what the position actually requires. And it is equally possible that candidates profoundly well suited to fill a particular opening may be eliminated from a search because of criteria unrelated to the needs of the job.

Other factors can make an already complex and often stressful process more so. For instance, some employers may emulate the hiring practices or standards of their competitors because such practices or standards appear to have become normative. Those that limit their hiring to candidates with college degrees may assume that that such credentials confer a particular legitimacy or aptitude without ever having examined that premise. Conversely, organizations that consider bachelor's degree recipients overqualified for some openings may overlook the benefits such candidates can offer despite their qualifications.

Candidates are likely to experience stress as well. Some may feel insecure because they lack confidence in the reputation of their credentials provider. Others may feel entitled to preferential consideration because their degree is prestigious. As students, they may have become familiar with the roles for which their education has prepared them. As candidates, they may present themselves according to such roles. And they may miscalculate.

The complexity of this dynamic underscores how important it is that credentials speak for themselves as thoroughly and persuasively as possible. The European "diploma supplement," which documents what a credential means in terms of learning outcomes and educational experience, might be an ambitious undertaking for the United States, but credentials accompanied by succinct, well-organized portfolios, whether online or in hard copy, could go a long way toward supporting and expanding the role of credentials in employment decisions. And candidates prepared to speak to the capabilities their credentials document and committed to address any deficiencies they may reveal are likely to be more successful than those that choose to stand or fall on the basis of the credential alone.

Here, again, the importance of well-informed advising cannot be overestimated. The more fully the complexity of the hiring process is shared with graduates by knowledgeable advisors, the better candidates for employment will be able to navigate it. Faculty members and academic advisors can have a profound influence on the success of their students by preparing them to anticipate and to address these variables.

But employers themselves have an important role to play. Colleges of business and other disciplines with a clear vocational focus routinely invite employers to advisory boards. But all disciplines would benefit from regular, in-depth, genuine consultation with the employer community. By "genuine" we mean a two-way conversation leading to greater awareness among both employers and academic leaders. Employers have much to gain from articulating more clearly what their *actual* job requirements are and how these requirements inform the priorities assigned to hiring officers. There are many organizations that manage their employment practices through a sophisticated perspective on the issues we have considered, but there remain many others that largely fly by the seat of their pants.

When employers do accept opportunities to clarify their expectations, faculty members and advisors have much to gain from paying attention. The other side of the conversation should express a resolve to create a closer alignment between what a credential promises and what its recipients will be able to demonstrate in terms of measurable proficiencies. And faculty members should conduct curricular audits to make sure that their students can achieve those proficiencies.

Every party to the complex courtship of a hiring process can play its role more effectively. Employers by defining their expectations in terms of actual job requirements. Faculty members by creating curricular paths based on such requirements. Advisors by becoming more appreciative of the courtship's complexities so as to prepare potential graduates for them. Administrators by clarifying an institutional priority on student success relative to well-defined learning outcomes and well-aligned opportunities.

SIDEBAR
A Credential Transparency Roadmap for States

Seeking greater clarity regarding what credentials mean relative to employment, CE has developed a 10-step process to enable state leaders to "prioritize and create better credential transparency." As of September 2020, CE reported "work already underway in 19 states and regions." The steps include the following:

1. *Learn and articulate the benefits of credential transparency.*
2. *Use examples to show the benefits of greater transparency for constituencies.*
3. *Agree to use a common language defining essential data about credentials and competencies.*
4. *Focus on quality and equity.*
5. *Conduct an inventory of credentials available in the area under consideration.*
6. *Using the common language, publish credentials (and their competencies) to the Credential Registry and the open Web.*
7. *Align credential data with contextual information.*
8. *Encourage the development of applications that increase the accessibility and usefulness of CE data.*
9. *Seek policies that will mandate the continuous improvement of credential transparency.*
10. *Create any additional infrastructure that may be needed.*

—Rafel et al. (2020)

Achieving a closer alignment between academic credentials and employer expectations will be a continuing challenge—but one well worth the effort on both sides.

In Sum

The postsecondary educational morass of providers, disciplines, delivery methods, quality assurance agencies, funding sources, and the like cannot easily be deciphered even by seasoned observers. The environment is too volatile, too unregulated, too alluring to those seeking an immediate windfall. But by focusing closely on credentials—how they are to be understood, what is required to earn them, what competencies they document, and how they function in the hiring process—it is possible to make sense out of what is most important. The shared priority is that students obtain access through their credentials to satisfying careers, perhaps to further education, and, ultimately, to satisfying lives as learners and productive citizens.

Takeaways

While some of the opportunities listed have particular relevance to a specified professional sector, most will require an institutional commitment to collaboration, both within the institution and externally.

Administrators should consider

- collaborating with other institutions (peer institutions, regional neighbors, system partners) to limit unnecessary duplication of credentials, to ensure broad public awareness of credentials currently available, to identify and respond to (perhaps cooperatively) gaps in regional offerings, and to offer guidance to students presently without an institutional affiliation;
- clarifying in all university materials and communications the content, costs, and trustworthiness of its credential programs;
- confirming that the essential institutional learning outcomes are expressed concretely, that they appear conspicuously in institutional information, and that academic programs assure the accomplishment of those outcomes by credential recipients; and
- clarifying their expectations that all disciplines will consult regularly and meaningfully with their respective employer stakeholders and with institutions that enable their students to pursue further study.

Faculty members should consider

- becoming better informed regarding new credentials and providers within their respective disciplines so as to acquaint their students with an expanded range of alternatives and to provide guidance on making wise choices;
- aligning credentials more closely with demonstrated labor market need; and
- framing educational pathways enabling students to navigate the credentials environment more effectively and efficiently.

Academic advisors should consider

- mastering the complex credentials environment (even programs that may lie beyond the purview of their institutions) so as to enable their advisees to make fully informed choices;
- guiding students to available curricular pathways while remaining sufficiently flexible to entertain proposals for idiosyncratic but thoughtfully conceived pathways;

- matching student needs and aptitudes more closely with different pedagogies;
- introducing advisees to the broad range of credentials, avoiding hierarchies that privilege some degrees over others—or that privilege degrees over nondegree credentials;
- enabling potential graduates to understand and to navigate successfully the complex environment of the hiring process; and
- making time to offer guidance to unaffiliated students.

Administrators, faculty members, and academic advisors should work together

- to make certain that all credentials offered by the institution are clearly described in terms of the educational outcomes students are meant to achieve and that all credentials are clearly described according to widely understood nomenclature;
- to remain aware not only of "new credentials" but also of credentials that are being introduced in response to "new disciplines"; and
- to continue refining the delivery and assessment of online learning.

PART TWO

Degrees of Difference

Of all academic credentials, the *degree* is the most widely recognized. Unlike most other credentials, degrees are *relative* rather than *absolute*. As with thermometers (30 *degrees* Celsius) or criminal justice (a third-*degree* misdemeanor), an academic *degree* points to a step on a scale. Marketing slogans that advertise "degrees of difference" playfully echo that recognition.

But there are important "degrees of difference" among nondegree credentials (NDCs) as well. Increasingly, these two categories can complement one another. Some degree programs are being designed to include NDCs. And some NDCs lead their recipients to degree programs. That is a good thing. In Part Two, we will examine both the familiar degrees, one by one, and the most prominent NDCs.

Degrees Past to Present

The origins of our degrees are important because they shed light on distinctions separating the most familiar and most often awarded ones. For instance, it is worth knowing that the European universities from which we have inherited degrees had themselves adopted an Islamic template offering "now familiar institutions like lectures, professors, [and] *qualifications called degrees*" (MacCullough, 2009, p. 399). In such origins we find a familiar degree ladder that would have been recognizable as early as the 13th century. Notwithstanding local variations, there was typically an initial credential (a "scholar's" degree), the more comprehensive "bachelor's" degree (which signified progress toward "mastership"), and an advanced degree ("master" or "doctor") qualifying the recipient to lecture at a university.

Over time variations developed. Differences between the credentials available in one nation or another became more pronounced. Nomenclature became confusing. By the latter half of the 20th century the resulting hotchpotch was limiting the mobility of students and faculty, complicating the transfer of credits, and compromising European competitiveness in both academic and economic terms. The solution? A multifaceted approach known as the Bologna Process that in some respects has turned back the clock. Since 1999, the now 38 "Bologna" nations have pursued a broad range of reforms called "action lines," but their signal accomplishment has been the regularization of degrees: a "short-term" degree similar to the U.S. associate degree, a three-year bachelor's degree, a two-year master's, and a four-year doctorate. There are a few exceptions to this standard, but for the most part the structure is again one that would have been recognizable in Bologna 700 years ago!

In a sense, U.S. credentials have provided an incentive for the structure restored through the Bologna Process. During the 19th century our bachelor's degree became an increasingly desirable entry-level credential for employment. Those who wanted to teach in college would proceed to earn a master's degree. A new credential called the "associate degree" appeared at the same time to enable students to begin their education at a local "junior" institution before completing their academic work at a "senior" institution. And the doctorate for the most part maintained its status as a capstone degree, an educational pinnacle.

Degrees of Difference

This *structure* continues to serve even as the *function* of degrees grows more variable. For instance, even though some associate degrees may lead to higher earnings than some master's degrees, no one would claim on structural grounds that an associate degree is equivalent to a master's degree or that a bachelor's degree awarded by an Ivy League college trumps a doctorate earned at a regional state university. There remains an understanding that the degree ladder, from associate to doctoral degrees, should attest to incremental growth in an individual's knowledge and competencies. That assumption appears in accreditation standards and in the criteria states employ to authorize programs.

One endeavor to define the differences between associate, bachelor's, and master's degrees, regardless of discipline, focuses on gains in proficiencies recipients of each should be able to demonstrate. We have already mentioned how the *Degree Qualifications Profile* (published by Lumina Foundation, 2011 and 2014) organizes learning proficiencies in five broad categories and describes the incremental growth expected from one degree level to the next. Avoiding familiar but vague goals such as "ability," "awareness," and "appreciation," the DQP favors active verbs (e.g., "evaluates," "differentiates," "identifies") that describe how students should be asked to demonstrate their attainment of proficiencies.

More than 800 U.S. institutions of higher education have made use of the DQP as a framework for clarifying both the educational objectives of their degrees and the differences between them. Notably, the framework can be just as useful in evaluating prior learning that may not be course based. "The student, not the institution, is its primary reference point" (Schneider et al., 2015).

SIDEBAR
A Difference in Name Only
One apparent "degree of difference" is less significant than it might seem. Although there are degrees in the "arts" (BA, MA) and those in the "sciences" (BS, MS), the distinction is mostly a matter of institutional preference. Degrees in the liberal arts most often appear as BAs and MAs—but not always. And those in the sciences and social sciences are usually listed as BS and MS degrees—but not always. If a university wishes to award a BA in chemistry, it can do so, just as the University of Colorado does.

Degrees of Change

Since the turn of the century, the U.S. educational topography that emerged in the late 19th century and that provided a relatively stable firmament in the 20th has been showing signs of tectonic stress. The ground has been shifting in four ways.

- Increasing skepticism about the priority that degrees have enjoyed traditionally—or, to make the same point more positively, increasing enthusiasm for highly focused NDCs.
- Growing concerns about the viability of *particular* degrees, particularly those that may not offer a clear path leading to employment.

- Emerging innovative and entrepreneurial approaches to redefining familiar degrees and introducing unfamiliar ones. Ditto for NDCs.
- Mounting readiness to question the authority credentials exert in the workforce and in society. Should academic credentials, whether degrees or NDCs, retain their privileged influence on status and income?

The needle on the academic seismograph is swinging widely.

Credentials Defined by What They Are Not

As we will observe, there should be a more positive designator for short-term, highly focused credentials that offer both alternatives and complements to degrees. Why do we refer to NDCs in terms of what they are *not*? Such credentials, often developed and implemented fairly quickly in response to emerging marketplace demands, are typically more affordable, more readily attainable over a short time span, and more directly focused on specific skills and knowledge. After chapters 4, 5, 6, and 7 describe how degrees are evolving, chapters 8, 9, and 10 will document the increasing popularity and value of credentials such as certificates, certifications, and apprenticeships—as well as the less familiar "badges," bootcamp completion certificates, and credentials available through corporate programs.

As such credentials continue to gain currency, degrees may become one option among several. We are not yet at that point. Over the past eight years NCES figures show only modest growth in the relative number of certificates awarded. In 2017–2018 954,738 certificates were awarded by all providers. By contrast, there were 1,980,644 bachelor's degrees, 1,011,487 associate degrees, 820,102 master's degrees, and 184,074 doctorates awarded—for a total of 3,996,307 degrees. The "market share" of certificates has indeed increased since 2011–2012, from 21% to approximately 23%, but on average there are still four degrees awarded for every certificate. The trend becomes more complicated, of course, when the consequences of the pandemic, including an apparent spike in NDC registrations, are taken into consideration and more complicated still when *all* NDCs, both those that can be documented and those that cannot, enter the conversation.

The Credential Engine count, which focuses not on the number of credentials awarded but on the number of discrete credentials, shows (for 2020) 122,000 "Title IV" certificates, 40,000 certificates offered by non-Title IV providers, 8,500 course completion certificates from MOOC platforms, and 120,000 online course completion certificates—with significant growth in almost all categories from one year earlier. On the other hand, the number of unique degrees offered by Title IV providers showed a modest decline of 213,000 in 2019 to 196,000 in 2020 (CE, 2021). (Reductions in duplication of data may account for some part of the decline.)

The fact is that both degrees and NDCs are essential to a postsecondary education system capable of serving students with diverse abilities, needs, challenges, and priorities. Even as the recognition that "not everyone needs a college degree" should be heard as an endorsement of alternate credentials, the college degree itself has become a platform for further testing innovative modes of delivery, implementing creative curricular structures, and addressing new areas of knowledge. The recognition that credentials other than degrees can expand awareness, confer valuable knowledge and skills, and offer secure pathways to success does not belie the conclusion that a college degree remains the most widely respected, most coveted, and most marketable credential on offer.

4

THE ASSOCIATE DEGREE

A 19th-century U.S. contribution to postsecondary education, the associate degree emerged with a new kind of institution that would award it, the junior (later "community") college. Framed at first as an award for the first two years of study toward a bachelor's degree, the degree has become also a credential enabling immediate access to a career. An innovation in itself, the associate degree has since become a platform for further innovation.

As early as the 13th century a "scholar's" degree designated academic preparation qualifying its recipient to begin the pursuit of the bachelor's degree, itself one step on the path to "mastery." Other "short-cycle" degrees are now appearing internationally. But both the American version of the "scholar's" degree and the community colleges that specialize in offering it are largely home grown.

A Degree Defined in Word and Action

The title of the credential, "associate," is defined as suggesting the status of someone "who belongs to an association or institution *in a subordinate degree of membership*" (Oxford English Dictionary, 1989). Those who chose the term might have been more assertive. Limited understanding of what the degree signifies can be problematic as well. Although the percentage of associate degree recipients relative to the general population has increased within the past 30 years, currently only about 10% of U.S. individuals hold an associate degree, as compared with nearly 33% who hold a bachelor's degree (Ryan & Bauman, 2016).

But a greater obstacle to understanding and appreciating the credential may lie in its multifaceted nature. The associate degree may serve either as an end in itself, as a means to an end, or as both an end and a means. At their inception, associate degrees documented the first two years of a four-year college degree program. That they would offer credit "for transfer" was more or less a given. However, as community colleges expanded and diversified their missions to include more emphasis on workforce preparation, the associate degree more highly focused on preparing learners for immediate access to employment began to appear.

A clear distinction appears in the title of a 2002/2003 article in the *Occupational Outlook Quarterly* by Olivia Crosby:

"Two years to a career or a jump start to a bachelor's degree." But "or" is problematical. Even by that time, the once clear distinction between "transfer" and "vocational" programs had begun to erode. "Or" was becoming "and." Students may now complete a career preparation program only to apply their degree as one step toward a baccalaureate. Other students may discover that their "transfer" degrees offer sufficient preparation in themselves for employment—at least for the time being.

While the erosion of what was once a clear (if never absolute) distinction can complicate understanding of the credential, the additional flexibility can be a positive for students in two respects. First, it enables those who receive the degree to consider how best to deploy it to their greatest advantage. Second, it allows associate degree programs to accommodate a range of educational priorities. One student may choose an associate degree program in automotive technology as a sufficient qualification toward a life-long career. Another may eventually come to regard success in the pursuit of an associate degree in automotive technology as a platform for further study toward a bachelor's degree. There are associate degree options for both. Community college administrators, faculty members, and academic advisors share an obligation to educate their students as to these options—and to interpret that flexibility for employers and senior institutions.

The "Transfer" Associate

Transfer degree programs encourage the expectation that recipients will apply the credits they earn toward a bachelor's degree in a four-year institution. Such programs typically offer general education courses (similar to those offered by baccalaureate institutions) as well as some preparatory instruction in a specific field. The Associate of Arts (AA) and Associate of Science (AS) are the most familiar. Most community colleges facilitate the transfer of their students through articulation agreements with the four-year institutions that their students most often choose.

By design the AA and the AS are intended for transfer. But as we have suggested, recipients of "applied" associate degrees such as the Associate of Applied Science (AAS) also may decide to continue their education and thus may seek to transfer many of the credits they have earned. We argue throughout this book that no degree should be seen as "terminal," as an "island" isolated in the midst of the strand. For those who wish to travel, there must be convenient ferry service from one island (the associate degree) to another (a bachelor's degree program).

The Alamo Colleges District (TX) has launched a fleet of such ferries. Elements of its program include clear links from its two-year colleges to 26 partner baccalaureate institutions, highly personalized "inescapable" student advising, and continuous program assessment. The backbone of the program lies in more than a thousand different "Transfer Advising Guides" that define, program by program, what courses are required for seamless transfer to a baccalaureate program.

Ideally, the program will become simpler over time. Are a thousand different paths necessary? And is there sufficient accommodation for students who, having identified one transfer university, finally choose another? But it is difficult to argue with the outcomes. Because transfer students who follow the advising guides "are guaranteed to only lose a maximum of three credits, or one course, upon transfer, compared to a national average of 13 credits," their programs tend to be much more efficient than the national average (65 hours versus 80). Moreover, the Alamo district's transfer students are both more likely to graduate with bachelor's degrees than the national average would predict and more likely to do so *in less time than the baccalaureate institution's four-year students* (Lavinson, 2021, para. 5).

SIDEBAR
A "Cross-Border" Opportunity
A transfer agreement concluded in January 2020 between the Pennsylvania Commission for Community Colleges (PCCC) and the private, nonprofit Southern New Hampshire University (SNHU) signaled a "coup for SNHU" (Blumenstyk, 2020, para. 3). Under the terms of the agreement, according to the PCCC (2020), "students from all 14 Pennsylvania community colleges will be able to transfer up to 90 credits to SNHU and complete their bachelor's degree online with a 10 percent tuition reduction" (para. 2). The agreement offers a path to transfer far smoother than the paths available through many institution-to-institution articulation agreements.

The range of state transfer policies is broad. Some states mandate that their four-year institutions accept the AA awarded by in-state community colleges as satisfying their general education requirements in full. Others mandate the acceptance of credit from the transfer programs but allow four-year institutions to impose additional course requirements. And there can be an additional challenge in assessing college credits earned in high school

SIDEBAR
One Problem, Three Potential Solutions
The Problem: Although 80% of community college (CC) students intend to earn a bachelor's degree, only 25% transfer to a four-year institution, and only 13% actually earn a bachelor's degree within six years.
Solution A: *Encourage and enable transfers from community colleges to private liberal arts colleges.*
Ithaka S+R recommends that community colleges and independent four-year colleges collaborate on transfer pathways inviting for students and efficient for institutions (Wilson et al., 2020). Transfer students may find a nearby independent college more convenient than a distant public university, and when increases in public institution tuitions are taken into account, an independent college offering financial aid may prove less expensive overall. Many independent colleges might develop a more welcoming enrollment front porch. Ithaka S+R sees potential gains for equity as well. "The lifelong benefits of a liberal arts baccalaureate must be extended to those who have been historically excluded, namely the large numbers of students of color, first-generation learners and students from socioeconomically disadvantaged backgrounds for whom community colleges are the gateway to higher education" (Wilson et al., 2020).
Solution B: *Create a community college within a university.*
Drake University (IA) has created its own two-year college to offer associate degrees. With an annual tuition of $18,500, John Dee Bright College is more affordable than the parent university, which has a sticker price of nearly $60,000 annually. Drake's president, Marty Martin, describes the college as "a new pathway into Drake University that will be uniquely tailored to meet the educational needs of a diverse array of students who have often not seen Drake as their potential collegiate home" (Drake University, 2020, para. 2). Because the John Dee Bright credentials will serve both as "career" and "transfer" degrees, the new dean of the college envisions that "graduates will be prepared to launch their careers or pursue a four-year degree at Drake or another institution. . . . They will graduate with new skills and refined approaches for thinking critically, problem solving, collaboration and communication" (para. 4).

Solution C: *Create a "university center" within the community college.*

With 11 four-year colleges and universities as its partners, Macomb (MI) Community College is one of the many two-year colleges that provide an on-campus center enabling students to learn about opportunities for transfer to four-year institutions. Macomb also enables its students to apply for transfer admission through its center and even to take classes offered at the center by a transfer institution. "Yes, you can earn bachelor's, master's and doctoral degrees in Macomb County at Macomb Community College!" (MCC, 2020, para. 1).

---

through dual enrollment and advanced placement courses. In framing articulation agreements with four-year institutions, community colleges must work for greater comparability among such agreements with their partners—and vice versa.

But the trend toward "seamless" transfer is becoming stronger. According to the Education Commission of the States (ECS), 33 states now "guarantee [that] students who are awarded an associate degree before transfer to a four-year institution can transfer all of their credits to the four-year institution and enter at the junior-standing level. The majority of policies state that students are not required to complete any further general education courses" (ECS, 2018, para. 1). Moreover, many universities choose to accept AA degrees "from out-of-state accredited community or junior colleges" as satisfying their general education requirements (Missouri State, 2020, para. 3).

Such efforts have benefited from the leadership of organizations such as the Western Interstate Consortium for Higher Education. WICHE has created a national network of two-year and four-year nonprofit institutions to discuss and agree on learning outcomes for general education attainment with the expectation that an "Interstate Passport" will facilitate more efficient transfer of students and their credits among participating colleges (Interstate Passport, 2020).

Even when there are policies that allow students to satisfy general education requirements with transfer credit, however, such policies may not ensure the acceptance of credits toward majors. For instance, some courses that may be taken for an Associate of Applied Business (AAB) degree may not meet curricular requirements for a Bachelor of Science in Business Administration (BSBA). At the University of Central Florida (UCF), for instance, "business majors are expected to complete their business coursework at UCF" (UCF, College of Business, 2020, Transient Policy). That is consistent with a requirement by program accreditor AACSB (2018) that schools or programs abide by policies that "ensure that the academic work accepted from other institutions is comparable to the academic work required for the school's own degree programs" (p. 38). While a community college student transferring to UCF may request that a course "be reviewed for equivalency with a College of Business course," credits for courses not deemed "equivalent" will not transfer. In that case, the student will be obligated to take the UCF course (UCF, College of Business, 2020, Course Equivalency Evaluation). In short, even when there are clear policies in place mandating the acceptance of transfer credits, the evaluation of such credits by the chosen major may still operate on a course-by-course basis.

Convenient, full-value transfer agreements are a major convenience for students who seek to apply their associate degree to baccalaureate study. But there is the broader concern referenced in the "One Problem, Three Potential Solutions" sidebar on p. 72. In 2015 the data from the National Student Clearinghouse showed that while 80% of community college students indicate that they intend to attain a bachelor's degree, only 25% eventually transfer to a four-year college (Jenkins & Fink, 2015). And of those that *do* transfer, most (80%) do so without having been awarded an associate "transfer" degree (Jenkins & Fink, 2015). Why? The marketplace value of the "transfer" associate degree, with its liberal arts and sciences concentration, may fall below that of the workforce-oriented associate degree. In fact, some applied associate degrees may offer greater immediate rewards than some liberal arts bachelor's degrees (Backes et al., 2015). Clearly, the AA and AS need attention.

Making a Good Degree Better
That attention appears in a December 2018 joint publication by the American Enterprise Institute and Burning Glass Technologies, "Saving the Associate of Arts Degree: How an AA Degree Can Become a Better Path to Labor Market Success." The report analyzes different ways in which the AA degree underperforms relative to comparable credentials especially when it fails to offer a platform for transfer—which is far too often the case! Reinforcing the NSC data mentioned, authors Mark Schneider and Matthew Sigelman cite two studies (one tracking a 2003 cohort of beginning community college students, the other focused on a 2010 cohort) showing that roughly four of five students begin community college with the intent of proceeding to at least a four-year degree. Six years later, however, "only 9 percent had completed a degree at a four-year institution" (Schneider & Sigelman, 2018, p. 4).

That creates an obvious dilemma for students and the economy. Having prepared for transfer through a curriculum focused on "general" education rather than "marketable skills," AA recipients who do *not* transfer often "fare poorly compared to . . . graduates who are completing an associate degree in a technical field" (Schneider & Sigelman, 2018, p. 4).

What's the remedy? In addition to creating better pathways meant to encourage those pursuing the AA to proceed to a bachelor's program, the AA degree should itself be fortified with "marketable skills" many now lack. The report suggests several such approaches, including the addition of "skills-based courses" to the AA curriculum and the expansion of access to providers of industry certifications. If cognizant of labor market needs, such reforms could make the AA degree "more valuable than it is today" (Schneider & Sigelman, 2018, p. 11).

The "Applied" Associate Degree

"Applied" degrees promise a direct path to employment by focusing more on career education and less on liberal education or general knowledge. Such degrees include the Associate of Applied Science (AAS), the Associate of Applied Business (AAB), and the less common Associate of Applied Arts (AAA).

SIDEBAR
Transfer in Reverse
Many students leave higher education after earning some credits but before earning a credential. As one means of increasing the rate of credential completion, "reverse transfer" enables a student who has transferred from a community college to a four-year institution prior to receiving an associate degree to qualify for that degree on the basis of credits earned at both the two-year and the four-year institution. More than 40 states now permit such awards, either by means of statewide policies or through agreements between institutions. "Reverse transfer" can also refer to students who choose to enroll in a community college after enrolling in a four-year institution, those who enroll in a four-year institution and a community college simultaneously (perhaps taking a community college course during a break), and those who have completed a four-year degree and enroll in a community college to obtain targeted skills.

Most students who undertake such programs do so with the intention of proceeding directly from classroom to career, and the list of careers available to recipients of appropriate associate degrees is formidable. For students aspiring to become paralegals, computer technicians, respiratory therapists, dental hygienists, veterinary technicians, or assistants in many health care fields (physical or occupational therapy, pharmacy, etc.) an associate degree offering the required professional preparation is the credential of choice.

But the quotation marks appearing in the subhead offer a reminder that more recipients now exercise the option of using their "applied" associate degrees to "apply" for further education. "Since the 1970s . . . a high proportion of students who complete vocational programs have been transferring to universities" (Cohen & Brawer, 2003, p. 32). Such AAS students may have to meet requirements that AS recipients will already have satisfied, but because more colleges and universities now welcome students who wish to transfer credits earned in applied degree programs, most recipients of an associate degree, whether "transfer" or "applied," should find it possible to gain access to further education. In particular, institutions engaged in state and regional efforts to develop pathways to careers are finding ways to assign credit to "vocational" coursework and to integrate it into bachelor's degree programs. To be sure, the process is not always smooth. Beyond facing general education requirements that their friends with AA and AS degrees may have already satisfied, those who have earned an applied associate degree may find that their preprofessional courses do not meet the requirements of their intended professional program. (We mentioned the influence of AACSB policy earlier in this chapter and gave the example of the University of Central Florida.)

There can be good reasons for such impediments. Preprofessional courses offered toward an applied associate degree may be very different in content and intensity from apparently similar courses offered within the major. But such differences should be subject to periodic reexamination. In the past, decisions as to what credits transfer and meet disciplinary requirements have usually been the purview of academic departments. The time may have come (a) for institution-wide attention to the evaluation and recognition of prior learning in all disciplines and (b) for leadership from specialized accreditors and professional associations with regard to transfer within their respective disciplines. In the meantime, students should be made fully aware of possible constraints on the transfer of associate degree credits. Academic advisors, particularly those advising students in associate degree programs, must have the necessary tools to do their job.

"Desirable—But Not Essential?"

Perhaps as the distinction between "transfer" and "career" (or "vocational" and "applied") continues to erode, appreciation for the multifaceted value of the associate degree will increase. But at present the differences may puzzle employers. Will the degree recipients be content with obtaining entry-level jobs or are they presenting evidence of potential for advancement within the organization?

The resulting uncertainty may help to explain why the associate degree can be regarded as "desirable" but not essential. For example, while a 2015 report by the San Diego Workforce Partnership expresses a positive view of the associate degree as an appropriate qualification for jobs that require "at least a high school diploma, but less than a four-year degree," the phrase "an associate degree *or less*" appears repeatedly throughout the report, and the report's concluding recommendations do not mention the associate degree at all.

SIDEBAR
The Associate Degree and Evolving Standards
Expectations concerning credentials within a discipline evolve. Once a nursing school diploma was sufficient for entry-level practice as a nurse. Then an associate degree became preferred or mandatory. A decade ago, the National Academies (2011) recommended that nurses either obtain a bachelor's degree or commit to secure one early in their careers in order to qualify for practice. The American Nurses Association (ANA, 2011) and the American Association of Colleges of Nursing (AACN, 2019) have since sought legislation state by state to require that nurses earn a bachelor's degree at least eventually. Recategorizing the associate degree as an interim rather than a qualifying credential need not diminish the value of AS programs but does underline the importance of secure, convenient, and efficient transfer pathways from associate to baccalaureate programs.

There are many employment opportunities for which the associate degree signifies appropriate preparation, but the San Diego survey of five health care careers cites only one for which the associate degree is required: respiratory therapist. For all others (nursing assistants, medical assistants, licensed vocational nurses, etc.) the "typical entry level education" is described simply as a "post-secondary non-degree award" (San Diego Workforce Partnership, 2015, p. 13).

What can be done? A lack of clear alignment between the competencies to which associate degrees attest and the requirements of specific jobs suggests a need for college-led initiatives to build trusted relationships with local employers (Deil-Amen & Rosenbaum, 2004). Community colleges in particular share an institutional obligation to interpret their programs and the competencies of their graduates in terms that will appeal to appropriate labor markets.

All of their students stand to benefit, but those who stand to benefit most are those who may otherwise lack access to the contacts and networks that can expand opportunities for employment. Because such graduates must depend almost exclusively on the credibility and value of the credential they have earned, they must rely on their institutions to speak powerfully on their behalf through promoting and clearly characterizing the associate degree. The challenge for community colleges is not only one of job placement. They share also a challenge—and an opportunity—to address inequity by promoting the value of their principal product.

Preferred Providers

Although the providers of associate degrees include for-profit providers and four-year institutions, the primary providers are community colleges, "the United States' unique contribution to higher education worldwide" (Trainor, 2015, para. 3). While there were junior and a few community colleges as early as the 1910s, in the 1960s new community colleges were opening at the rate of nearly one a week. No institutional category has grown more rapidly—and none is more closely identified with a particular credential. In 2016–2017, community colleges offered 549,000 certificates. An impressive number. But in the same period they conferred 840,000 associate degrees.

The value of the degree, like that of any credential, is closely related to the reputation of the provider. And most community colleges, as their names suggest, have earned solid reputations within their respective communities. George Boggs (2012), former head of the American Association of Community Colleges (AACC), has referred to community colleges as "democracy's college" because they "offer an open door to opportunity to all who would come, are innovative and agile in meeting economic and workplace needs, and provide value and service to individuals and communities" (para. 1).

But there is the problem hinted at in the analysis of San Diego hiring. Notwithstanding their undisputed success in expanding access to affordable education, in creating a better educated workforce for employers, and in offering services to communities, community colleges may still encounter uncertainties concerning the credentials they award. Some questions may arise from genuine confusion as to the meaning of the associate degree. But there is a more subtle and insidious concern: Because they laudably serve high numbers of low-income students through open access policies (Dougherty et al., 2017) community colleges may appear to occupy a lower rung within a "tiered" system of postsecondary education. By this thinking, they educate the less well qualified for positions that are undemanding and less competitive. Beyond its inaccuracy, such hierarchical thinking ignores and thus perpetuates inequities.

A proper defense of the associate degree might begin with a generous appreciation for both the advantages and disadvantages inherent in the increasingly complex community college mission. With "no traditions to defend, no alumni to question their role . . . [and] no statements of philosophy," there has been nothing to prevent "their taking on responsibility for everything" (Cohen & Brawer, 2003, p. 3). Beyond offering traditional associate degrees in the two broad categories mentioned, community colleges have developed new credentials in new fields, provided educational services to underserved constituencies, and served as a cultural resource for their communities. Many offer noncredit programs that enroll as many students as their credit programs. Such programs include short-term training programs in a wide range of fields and avocational programs that address community interests (AACC, 2020). Entrepreneurial, efficient, and responsive to emerging challenges, community colleges, in the words of one national journalist, have "been at the forefront of nearly every major development in higher education since their inception" (Trainor, 2015, para. 2).

Appreciation for the public responsiveness of community colleges surely enhances respect for the associate degree. The "institutional charter" implicit in the close relationship between colleges and their communities helps to inform public trust in the credentials they offer. Yet, paradoxically, as the roles played by the community college have increased, so, too, have the risks that the credential most closely associated with the college will be less well understood and valued.

Hence, while all institutions should consult with their stakeholders, community colleges should be particularly attentive to doing so. Employers within their respective service areas, who may hire many of their graduates, should be given regular opportunities to weigh in on graduate preparedness and on emerging needs for new programs. Partnerships with social service agencies should be developed to ensure that institutional outreach to the community is well coordinated and that students receive needed support. And there must be close working relationships as well with both K–12 schools and the four-year institutions that welcome the college's transfer credits.

A Credential Whose Time Is Now

None of the questions raised with regard to the associate degree will surprise either providers or recipients. Savvy administrators, advisors, and faculty members will take them seriously and seek to address them. But given the advantages of the associate degree for students, employers, and institutions they will do so from a position of strength.

First, thanks to several possible economies, associate degrees can often be *less expensive* to develop. For applied degrees, especially, faculty members often may be recruited from the practitioner community the degree is meant to serve. Staffing costs tend to be lower as well in that community college faculty are more likely to focus on instruction and agree to teaching loads higher than those standard in four-year institutions. A second economy can sometimes be found in facilities costs. Programs meant to serve a specific industry (or even a particular corporation) may be able to negotiate for on-site space and to seek donations of instructional equipment.

Second, community colleges place a priority on identifying and *responding promptly* to emerging needs of the regional economy. And while community colleges respect faculty governance, their processes for curricular review and new program development are often more streamlined than those at four-year colleges.

Third, associate degrees often invite *active collaboration* between providers and employers that can draw on and leverage expertise within the business and industrial organizations. Such expertise can inform program development and review and thus help to ensure a program's continued currency and relevance to industry needs. A degree program that offers hands-on experience and that remains current by drawing on real-world expertise will capture many advantages—increased student motivation, greater curricular efficiency, and a more direct path from the classroom to full-time employment. Colleges that take their local labor market connections seriously will both seek and maintain such collaboration.

Finally, the associate degree can offer a unique degree of *flexibility* for providers and students alike. Allowing for its broad spectrum, from the breadth of "transfer" credentials to the depth of "career" credentials, the degree can be offered through a wide variety of scheduling options (full-time, part-time, Monday–Friday, weekends), means of delivery (in person, remote, hybrid), and locations (on campus, remote instructional facilities, corporate sites). Rather than allowing a virtue (flexibility) to become a liability (confusion), administrators, faculty members, and academic advisors should consider how best to enable their students to make wise decisions among clearly communicated options (Bailey et al., 2015).

Four Advantages, Two Recommendations
These four advantages of the associate degree justify two recommendations.

The first, directed to community colleges, suggests that they take the opportunity offered by an environment of change to scrutinize their offerings.

Are all of their programs current in the competences they develop, cognizant of employer needs and likely future demands, and responsive to an increasing preference for online nonsynchronous programs accessible at the convenience of the student?

The second recommendation (in two parts) is directed to four-year institutions. Most importantly, they should pursue with their neighboring community colleges a more vigorous commitment to transfer—not only to provide an efficient and generous "onboarding" process, but also to make associate degree recipients feel welcome. Given their conspicuous commitment to freshman orientation and freshman experience programs for first-year students, four-year institutions might well give equivalent attention to a no less vital cohort, those who arrive with associate degrees. Further, four-year institutions might consider awarding associate degrees to students who meet degree requirements on the way to their bachelor's degrees. One motivation is that of providing "at least something" to students who might drop out before completing a bachelor's program. But a far stronger motive may be that of providing an intermediate goal to students as a source of motivation prior to or in conjunction with their work within a major. Simply offering the associate degree would be a missed opportunity. Savvy colleges will align the award with inviting and well supported paths to the baccalaureate!

One other strategy for enhancing the perceived value of the associate degree is to enable recipients to avoid transfer issues or a physical change of venue by proceeding from the award of the associate degree to applied and technical baccalaureate programs within their community colleges. Such "applied bachelor's degrees" may fill a need that neither associate degrees nor traditional bachelor's degrees address. Authorized in 24 states as of May 2021, such degrees may be structured to include both technical courses associated with an applied associate degree and courses that fulfill general education requirements. Such "general education" courses may even add breadth in ways that depart from traditional requirements in the liberal arts (e.g., they may add up to a management capstone).

While such programs have raised concerns about community college "mission creep," program duplication, and quality, they may be able to provide an effective response to issues of access, affordability, and workforce needs (Fulton, 2015). In most instances, the community college retains its identity as a two-year institution while offering a limited number of such degrees. But in some states, with accreditor approval, community colleges may become bachelor's degree–granting institutions while continuing to offer mostly associate degrees. (See the sidebar for one example.)

SIDEBAR
Maui's Program Mix
Once a community college that offered only associate degrees and certificates, Maui College of the University of Hawai'i within the past decade has introduced a few carefully chosen baccalaureate programs. Here's the message: "Pursue a bachelor of applied science degree in emerging industries like Sustainable Science Management, Engineering Technology, and Applied Business and Information Technology, or an associate degree or certificate from over 20 other programs" (University of Hawai'i Maui College, 2020, Programs of Study).

It is important to acknowledge that most community colleges engaged in this transition "are not trying to be just like the four-year postsecondary institutions." Typically (though not in every case) the bachelor's degree is offered as an *extension* of an associate degree program. "Students earn the associate degree first to become eligible to apply for the bachelor's program." Moreover, such degrees usually are limited to those offering direct access to the workforce. "In keeping with the long-standing tradition of community colleges to raise up a new generation of work-ready adults, these programs are designed specifically with a profession in mind" (Chen, 2020, What's Different About Community College Bachelor's Degrees?).

In Sum

The many advantages offered by the associate degree—most especially to students, to their community colleges, to their employers, and to their communities—deserve to be more broadly acknowledged and appreciated. At first an innovative offering inviting a few marginal students to undertake a college education, the degree has become a staple for millions, a firm foundation that can lead both to lifetime learning and to satisfying employment.

Takeaways

- If your institution is a primary provider of the associate degree, affirm that all (or most) two-year programs offer access to further education while making clear the priority of each: immediate career readiness or seamless transfer to a four-year curriculum.
- Provide students who plan to transfer to a baccalaureate program at a four-year college or university with detailed advice on transferability.

Students who choose to pursue applied degrees also should receive advice concerning options for transfer. They may choose to continue their learning.

- Recognizing that many students who earn "transfer" associate degrees *will not transfer to a baccalaureate program*, AA and AS providers should (a) improve the pathways that encourage transfer while (b) fortifying these programs with "marketable skills" that will enhance the employment opportunities of graduates.

- Four-year institutions with a broad service mission (metropolitan and urban universities, regional colleges, etc.) that award few associate degrees (or none) should expand their transfer and articulation agreements with community colleges. And community colleges can invite cooperating four-year institutions to use space on their campuses to disseminate information, to offer assistance with transfer, and to provide instruction.

- Four-year institutions might consider awarding associate degrees to students who have completed coursework equivalent to associate degree requirements while working toward the baccalaureate. Likewise, two-year colleges may consider strategically adding applied bachelor's degrees in fields where there is labor market need and where they already offer two-year degrees as part of four-year pathways.

5

THE BACHELOR'S DEGREE

The most frequently awarded academic credential, the bachelor's degree, signifies preparation for a profession, provides a platform for possible graduate study, and, at best, confirms a readiness for enlightened citizenship. The American contribution to this historic degree has been general education, study in breadth, across a variety of disciplines, meant to complement the study in depth offered by a "major." But concerns about the quality and relevance of the degree, expressed principally by employers, have prompted both a rethinking of the traditional degree and the emergence of variations such as the "applied" baccalaureate now offered by some community colleges. This 700-year-old degree has become a platform for innovation.

A s early as the 13th century, the "scholar's" degree (precursor to today's "associate" degree) was awarded to signify eligibility for study toward a bachelor's degree, the keystone of collegiate education. In many ways, the bachelor's degree continues to represent just such a keystone— both an achievement in itself, meant to qualify the recipient for a successful career and a satisfying life, and a qualification offering possible access to further education leading to "mastery" or even to the student's becoming a "doctor."

The Degree of Choice

A 2019 analysis of numbers of first-time graduates by credential type shows that the bachelor's degree remains the credential of choice for many. In 2017–2018 nearly twice as many bachelor's degrees (1,495,720) were awarded as were associate degrees (National Student Clearinghouse Research Center [NSCRC], 2020). Perhaps even more surprisingly, while the period under review (2012–2013 to 2017–2018) shows a decline in awards of both degrees, the decline in associate degrees was far greater in all age categories except that for those under 25. In the 25–29 age group, for instance, the decline in associate degrees was 13.8% while the decline in baccalaureate degrees was 4.2%. Other age categories showed more dramatic disparities. (Note, however, the findings of Credential Engine [CE]: While the number of degrees awarded may have declined, the number of "unique" credentials awarded has in most instances increased.)

It is true that not everyone needs a college degree; other pathways to professional competencies can prepare individuals to fill critical roles. It is true also that designating the bachelor's degree as a prerequisite for employment may not always be justified in terms of actual on-the-job requirements. Recall the concern with "credentialism" introduced in chapter 1, i.e., unexamined deference to credentials qua credentials. Still, the bachelor's degree remains for many good reasons—some of which may be relevant to hiring requirements—the most widely sought and most readily recognized award among postsecondary credentials (NSCRC, 2019). And that status makes it all the more critical that bachelor's degree programs offer meaningful and well-documented value to recipients.

What Is a Bachelor's Degree?

The ingredients in most U.S. bachelor's degree programs are general education (otherwise known as a core curriculum, distribution requirements, or liberal learning) and the major. And virtually all U.S. colleges and universities and their accreditors define the bachelor's degree as one offering both breadth and depth. Even the most recent incarnation of the degree, the "applied" bachelor's degree offered by community colleges in nearly half of the states, promises both dimensions. But if general education in some form and the major should be synergetic in all bachelor's degrees, carefully aligned for a balanced baccalaureate education, they are offered far too often as discrete programs—a sequence rather than a continuum.

SIDEBAR
Dispense With the Degree?
At a spring 2021 summit convened by the *Wall Street Journal,* several prominent CEOs agreed that routinely requiring a bachelor's degree for corporate employment could act as a "structural barrier." The CEOs of Merck & Co. and of IBM urged their counterparts to reconsider hiring criteria so as to diversify their candidate pools and thus offer greater opportunity to "unconventional candidates" who may not have had access to traditional educational opportunity (Cutter, 2021).

What's the Difference Between a BA and a BS?
As we explained in the introduction to Part Two, the simple answer is that there isn't one. The medieval differentiation between "arts" and "science" degrees is now most often used to suggest career tracks (e.g., a BA in psychology may lead to graduate study in counseling, while the BS more often leads to a career in research) but there is no agreed upon standard. Hence the important question to ask would be "What does *your institution* mean by the BA and BS?"

What a Bachelor's Degree Signifies

There is a considerable consensus as to what a bachelor's degree should mean—both for graduates and for the employers who hire them. The *Essential Learning Outcomes* (Association of American Colleges & Universities) and the *Degree Qualifications Profile* (Lumina Foundation) both agree that a baccalaureate education, regardless of major, should teach at a minimum (a) knowledge of cultures and of the physical world, (b) intellectual skills such as quantitative literacy and critical thinking, (c) an awareness of and commitment to ethical reasoning and civic responsibility, and (d) an understanding that different disciplines will require different intellectual approaches. Given the familiarity of these resources, there would be little value to summarizing them in detail, but it is worth acknowledging that despite modest differences in nomenclature they offer complementary answers as to what the degree *means*—or should. What's the difference between the two? They address different questions. The ELOs ask, *What are the liberal learning objectives that represent broad requisites for effective degree programs—and that all students should be enabled to achieve?* The DQP asks, *What learning—specifically—should degree recipients be able to demonstrate? And how should they demonstrate this learning?*

Of course, even as they seek to enable their students to achieve the "essential" learning outcomes and to demonstrate their mastery along the lines suggested in the DQP, institutions may define additional outcomes consistent with their culture, their identity, or their mission. Wheaton College (IL) promises "a strong foundation in moral virtue." Embry-Riddle's 27 BS degrees all offer an acquaintance with the culture and priorities of the aeronautical industry. Julliard's 23 bachelor's degrees all focus on the fine arts. But all three institutions, all regionally accredited, express a commitment to the familiar balance between highly specialized professional education and broad liberal learning (Embry-Riddle Aeronautical University, 2020).

General Education

As suggested, strong bachelor's degree programs integrate general education and the major. General education, often defined as "liberalizing" or "liberal" learning, enables growth in the knowledge and skills important for any major.

It enables students to understand the "essential" building blocks of a baccalaureate education and to navigate the complex curricular structure that leads to the degree. In turn, every major, even as it provides focused preparation for a career or further study, demonstrates the value it attaches to general education by sustaining and building on the skills and knowledge developed there. Indeed, the value that students, faculty members, and academic advisors place on general education inevitably reflects the quality expectations of those who most directly rely on its effectiveness, faculty committed to their respective majors.

From one perspective, the essentials of that quality lie deeply within the past. Indeed, defining the principal components of a liberal arts education has challenged educators since Plato. Efforts in the Renaissance to specify the requisite disciplines of liberal learning (recall the *trivium* and *quadrivium*) have had a direct influence on the United States—as Emerson's 19th-century education at Harvard makes clear (Richardson, 1995).

But to offer that quality in the 21st century requires an appreciation for the complexity of modern colleges and universities, the diversity of their students' goals, the variety of their institutional missions, the conventions that govern their academic structure and curricula, the needs and expectations of employers, and the sources of external oversight and quality assurance. It's complicated! But there are a few basic principles common to institutions that offer effective general education programs:

- They share a clear vision of what they seek for their students. That vision is clear in the design of the general education program and in clearly defined learning outcomes.
- Their general education program reflects the distinctiveness of their institutional mission—which itself is clearly defined.
- They affirm that essential learning is by its nature experiential, "real-world" learning, and they offer "high-impact practices" (e.g., undergraduate research, cohort learning) to enrich student accomplishment and experience.
- They place a priority on and celebrate the value of an inclusive and diverse academic community.

The Many Forms of General Education

Successful general education programs can take many forms. On the one hand there are "laissez faire" programs that assign the responsibility for coherence and continuity to individual students, who presumably will confer closely with academic advisors. On the other there are compact "core" curricula that offer all students at the institution a shared experience. There is no single "best" approach. Any can succeed if its objectives are clear, if the paths toward the accomplishment of these objectives are coherent (the students value the courses they take), and if there is continuity (students experience incremental learning) from start to finish.

- General education "programs" with no explicit requirements beyond the "hours" required by accreditation can offer coherent and cumulative learning through careful planning and advising. Students make thoughtful choices of courses that either complement or *contrast by intent* with their specialized study.
- Faced with broad distributive (large menu) programs, students choose courses from categories offering many options. Although the result may be far too often an unfathomable mélange, students who receive expert guidance can find the benefits of synergy among their carefully chosen courses.
- Finding a rewarding direction often can be easier in narrow distributive (limited menu) programs as students choose from categories offering a carefully selected and regularly monitored range of opportunities. But even so there must be a logic to the choices that are made.
- In hybrid programs, students take one or more courses to fulfill common requirements (e.g., verbal and oral communication, quantitative reasoning, scientific knowledge) before choosing their remaining general education courses from broad or narrow categories. The goal, not always realized, is a thoughtful alignment between the core and the other courses.
- In a broad core curriculum, all students share a common experience prior to choosing among concentrations or tracks.
- Finally, a narrow core curriculum in which all students take the same courses to meet their general education requirements can ensure a degree of coherence to the extent that the curriculum as a whole reveals alignment between general education and the majors.

Each of these categories offers pros and cons. Student individuality and autonomy must be weighed against both the benefits of learning in common (inspired student discussions arise when students are reading the same books) and the appeal of a "signature" curriculum. And each category offers opportunities for innovation. But the question raised by every category is the same. Does the curriculum for the bachelor's degree embody a clear alignment between general education and the major?

General Education and the Major

Although there has been progress toward the definition of clearer learning outcomes, there is much progress waiting to be made. When administrators, faculty members, and academic advisors regard general education and the major as discrete academic fiefdoms and students speak of "getting general education out of the way" prior to entering a major there clearly is more that needs to be done.

The "consensus" resources that have been described, the ELOs and the DQP, can be useful tools for those seeking to address the challenge, in that neither limits itself to general education. Both consider how institutions might document student accomplishment of important curricular goals through both general education and the major.

As an example, consider the goal of "broad and integrative knowledge." As defined by the DQP, this goal includes both the breadth of general education and the focus of specialized study. Students demonstrate their pursuit of the goal by producing "an investigative, creative or practical work that draws on specific theories, tools and methods *from at least two core fields of study*" (Lumina Foundation, 2014, p. 15).

Similarly, an institution might refer to AAC&U's Essential Learning Outcomes (ELOs) to affirm that "quantitative literacy" is essential to the award of every bachelor's degree. A question then would follow: Does the curriculum provide for the "extensive practice" of this "intellectual and practical skill . . . across the curriculum, in the context of progressively more challenging problems, projects, and standards for performance"? (AAC&U, 2019).

The bottom line is that institutions seeking to strengthen the bachelor's degree should question any curriculum based on the juxtaposition of two discrete programs. To create an educational continuum "takes a university"— faculty members who make a priority of general education, those focused on major programs, and those who share both commitments—all working together in the interest of their students.

A Basic Template for Curricular Strengthening

The challenge of seeking greater synergy between general education and the major can be daunting. But there are priorities found in most successful approaches.

1. Define the baccalaureate offered by the institution in terms of the learning outcomes their degree recipients—all of them, regardless of their discipline—should be able to demonstrate.
2. Delineate and document the *respective* contributions that both general education and their majors are expected to make toward assuring the accomplishment of these outcomes.
3. Build from the ground up a curriculum to ensure the accomplishment of both broad and specialized learning outcomes. Students should choose among clear, inviting, and motivating learning corridors that offer continuity between general education and the major.

SIDEBAR
Curriculum Mapping
To determine the extent to which a curriculum enables students to accomplish the institution's clearly defined learning outcomes, map the institution's degree-level learning outcomes to the outcomes of courses offered both in general education and in the majors. If gaps appear (e.g., there are institutional learning outcomes addressed in neither the general education or major programs) there's work to be done. The National Institute for Learning Outcomes Assessment (NILOA) offers "a toolkit of resources" at www.learningoutcomesassessment.org/ documents/Mapping%20Learning.pdf.

Educationally effective institutions typically balance respect for faculty experience and expertise with recognized good practice and clearly understood student priorities. One measure of success, certainly, lies in the enthusiasm and persistence of students. A company once advertised a simple formula, "better ingredients, better pizza." It's the same with the bachelor's degree. Savvy students prefer institutions that enable them to understand and pursue clear learning priorities and that provide visible means for accomplishing these priorities. Generalizations about the advantages of a liberal arts education or particular majors may be attractive, but only institutions that enable their students to achieve such advantages through a curriculum focused on results will serve them well.

The Major

Strengthening the academic major, the most widely understood element in baccalaureate education, also represents a priority—one long overdue. Why overdue? While it has become obvious that critical issues rarely conform to disciplinary boundaries, many colleges and universities continue to operate according to a traditional academic structure. Chemistry departments teach chemistry majors. History departments teach history majors. Marketing departments teach students aspiring to careers in marketing. And the bachelor's degree for the most part remains resolutely "academic," long on classroom learning, short on practical experience.

There are salutary examples to the contrary—institutions that emphasize active, problem-based, cross-disciplinary learning and that require an internship or similar real-world experience of all of their students who seek the bachelor's degree. But as employer surveys suggest, such institutions are the exception. As a result, over time the bachelor's degree has become less reliable as an assurance of career readiness. Employers who report dissatisfaction with the college graduates they hire tend to question in particular their ability to address complex problems, to work collaboratively toward solutions, to communicate effectively, and to make effective use of computation.

Career-Ready Competencies

In an effort to create a more systematic definition of career readiness, the National Association of Colleges and Employers has created a list of eight competencies. These correspond in some ways with those that appear in the ELOs and the DQP, but they do so in language that expresses employer expectations more directly. In addition to critical thinking, oral and written communications, the ability to "leverage existing digital technologies ethically and efficiently," and "global/intercultural fluency," they include the following:

- *Teamwork/collaboration* (e.g., the ability to work well with others in achieving results and resolving differences).
- *Leadership* (e.g., a capacity for self-discipline and organization that enables motivation and effective delegation).
- *Professionalism/work ethic* (e.g., the development of values such as reliability, personal integrity, and a capacity for ethical reasoning.).
- *Career management* (e.g., the individual can pinpoint priorities for further education that would lead to appropriate opportunities.) (NACE, 2020).

When NACE conducted a survey with respect to these criteria, employers' misgivings were clear. Only 43% of those surveyed shared a positive evaluation of graduates' work ethic. Only 42% expressed a positive view of their ability to communicate effectively (NACE, 2018).

But there was an even more disquieting subtext, that "employers see skills gaps in key areas where college students don't believe gaps exist." For example, while 89.4% of the students surveyed expressed pride in their work ethic, just 42.5% of employers would agree students share a work ethic that would justify such pride. And while 79.4% of the students thought themselves proficient in oral and written communications, just 41.6% of employers agreed. As a final example, three of four students (70.5%) thought themselves proficient in leadership, while only one third (33%) of employers would concur.

SIDEBAR
Toward Improved Career Readiness
Founded in 2016, the QA (Quality Assurance) Commons focuses on student employability through a certification process that encourages and enables institutions to become more effective in preparing their graduates for the workforce. The QA Commons does not restrict itself to disciplines that are obviously career preparatory. It "believes all disciplines need to prepare students for employability" and has defined eight "Essential Employability Qualities" that all students should achieve: communication, thinking and problem solving, inquiry, collaboration, adaptability, principles and ethics, responsibility and professionalism, and learning. More information is available at https://theqacommons.org/.

These figures clearly point to a structural discrepancy between what the bachelor's degree is said to signify and what it often delivers in terms of student competencies. While the employers' concerns should prompt institutional attention to both general education and the major and to the alignment between them, there is a front line in this campaign and it is the major.

Making "Major Decisions" and Implementing Promising Reforms

There are promising initiatives concerning the major under way that span a considerable spectrum, from readily achievable reforms to highly challenging ones. They tend to fall into the two categories captured by Bianca Quilantan (2018): You can "let them go" or you can "soup them up."

Eliminate, Recast, or Reorganize Majors

Responding to declining enrollments by eliminating majors—an all-too familiar recourse—may be readily achievable in comparison with more ambitious reforms, and sometimes there is no feasible alternative. Some disciplines become obsolete. Advances in artificial intelligence may reduce the demand for translators. Regional programs in mining engineering decline as coal mines close. In order to introduce or grow programs showing increasing demand, an institution may be forced to reduce or close programs showing declines.

But closing programs may not be the only way for a college to expand its opportunity fund. Some savvy colleges have undertaken a graduated approach through savings made possible by restructuring. For instance, rather than maintaining separate departments of French, Spanish, and Italian, they may instead create a department of romance languages. Instead of a French major, they may offer a major in romance languages with a concentration in French.

SIDEBAR
The Lessons of "History"
Faced with a decline in both the number of history majors and undergraduate enrollments in history in general, the American Historical Association (AHA) took on the challenge of reforming its discipline. The goal was that students would be better able to appreciate how a carefully structured history curriculum can offer effective preparation for a myriad of career opportunities. By taking part in a national initiative called the "Tuning" process, the AHA (2021) sought "to articulate the disciplinary core of historical study and to define what a student should understand and be able to do at the completion of a history degree program" (para. 1). Notably, the work of defining the degree clarified its potential "real-world" applications and encouraged a more explicit curricular focus on them. The association's "History Discipline Core" offers a good model for disciplines seeking to clarify their means and ends.

Similarly, departments of physics and chemistry joined in a department of physical sciences can offer attractive interdisciplinary degrees with a concentration in either physics or chemistry.

There are often virtues to be found in such necessities. A student studying French in a broader linguistic environment may become a more capable Francophone. One pursuing a concentration in physics while studying the physical sciences more broadly may become a more capable, adaptable, and employable scientist.

One example of a major recast in this mold may be found in the Bachelor of Science in interdisciplinary physics at John Carroll University (JCU; OH). In addition to pursuing "an in-depth study of the core areas of physics," the student takes "a selection of courses from the departments of biology, chemistry, psychology, and mathematics and computer science" (JCU, 2020, para. 1). The university describes the credential as ideal preparation for medical school. However, with the addition of selected courses in business, the major can offer access instead to completion of a five-year MBA program.

Create "Blended" Majors

In addition to enabling more students to choose double majors, some institutions may "prepackage" disciplinary combinations to provide convenient educational corridors to further study and to careers. We have already mentioned the "recombinant" degrees at the University of Illinois at Urbana-Champaign (UIUC) that offer "a strong grounding in computer science with technical or professional training in the arts and sciences" (UIUC, 2019, para. 3). Participating arts and sciences programs point to impressive gains. "In 2013, before the inception of the CS-plus-linguistics major, only 58 students were enrolled in linguistics. Four years later, the program has 152 students enrolled" (Quilantan, 2018, para. 10). Of these, 69 are enrolled in the blended major. Roxana Girju, the director of the CS-plus-linguistics major, adds, "We've realized that this kind of combination is much more appealing to these employers [Apple, Google, Amazon, Microsoft] than just doing individual degrees and trying to cobble them together" (Quilantan, 2018, para. 15).

A similar approach to blending creates "alloys" or "hybrids" that "emphasize commerce between other disciplines, particularly STEM or professional fields, and humanistic ways of thinking" (Williams, 2019, para. 2). Writing for *The Chronicle of Higher Education*, Jeffrey Williams describes a wide variety of such programs—environmental humanities, energy humanities, global humanities, urban humanities, medical humanities, food humanities, and many others that reveal a demonstrable alignment with employer priorities. One characteristic common to many such programs is their willingness to look beyond academe "to explain their research . . . drawing on lessons from journalism, public relations, and marketing" (Williams, 2019, para 8). Having looked into the associations backing such programs and the programs themselves, Williams concludes that they're not a fad. "They're here to stay."

A different approach to "blending" involves the splicing of undergraduate and graduate programs to create a more expeditious path to a graduate credential. Programs enabling students to enter law school or medical school after three years of undergraduate study have existed for many years, of course. In most, the student completes the requirements for a bachelor's degree in the first year of professional study. More recently, this principle has been adapted to offer a five-year master's degree in academic subjects. At California Polytechnic State University (2019), for instance, students may apply for admission to a blended program at the midpoint of their undergraduate career. If accepted, they may take graduate-level courses (provided that they have satisfied the prerequisites) and earn credits toward a master's degree. Considered undergraduates until they have earned 180 "degree-applicable units," they then "transition to graduate status" and qualify for the award of a master's the following year.

How Majors Evolve

Examples of new fields and disciplines abound. Earlier (chapter 2) we mentioned several unusual new programs and have cited one of the most conspicuous of the new disciplines, cybersecurity. The list, growing longer by the month, raises the question as to whether there is a recognizable "evolutionary process" behind the trend.

A recent study by Santhosh Areekkuzhiyil suggests there may be. The processes that he describes probably do not exhaust the subject, but they can suggest questions that savvy administrators, faculty members, and academic advisors should keep in mind when scanning the environment:

- Two or more branches of knowledge merge and develop [their] own distinct characteristics and form a new discipline. Examples: neuroscience, biochemistry, geobiology.
- A professional activity emerges as an independent field of study. Examples: agriculture, social work, management.
- Changes in the sociopolitical scenario may result in the formation of new disciplines. Example: urban studies.
- New research and consequent developments and inventions can create new disciplines. Examples: nanotechnology, computer science (Areekkuzhiyil, 2017, Formation of New Disciplines).

It requires little imagination to project the possible emergence of further new disciplines. The more important issue concerns which possibilities might justify the investment of institutional time and resources. Here the approach should take advantage of an institution's most valuable assets: its faculty members, its academic advisors, the professionals in student services, and its students. An institution's faculty offers its best guides as to emerging fields—but there may be no guidance forthcoming unless administrators request it. Academic advisors, similarly, are likely to become aware before others of student interest in innovative majors found at other institutions. But few institutions have channels in place to ensure regular consultation. Employers, experienced observers, well-informed alumni, and others within the community also can provide a broad spectrum of advice but will do so in all likelihood only if asked.

When a possible opportunity is identified through any of these means, the next steps are the familiar ones of (a) assessing current and potential institutional capacity for developing and offering the degree, (b) surveying the current and potential competition, and (c) weighing potential costs and benefits, both to students and to the institution. These considerations should include also an awareness of relevant labor market data, particularly that which surveys online job postings to identify emerging occupational opportunities and the competencies employers are seeking for them. Cross calibrating such information with advice from employers, institutions can become more confident that they are considering a credential that could offer real value to their students.

Do you recall the sobering figures as to the success of new degree programs? (Turn back to the sidebar in chapter 3 summarizing a recent report from Burning Glass Technologies.) Given the frequent lackluster performance of new offerings, at least in the early going, and the risks involved in reallocation of resources from existing to untried programs, the value of a thorough needs analysis, clearly summarized, can hardly be overstated. Such an analysis, an essential management tool, may be essential to persuading all relevant constituencies—board members, faculty, accreditors, community supporters—that the undertaking is one of documented potential.

Develop Majors That Transcend Disciplines

James Madison University (JMU; VA) asks its undergraduates, "Do you want to chart your own path?" Qualified students who find this challenge appealing may pursue an independent scholar's BS or BA. Although entry to the program requires a competitive GPA (3.25 or higher) and intensive advising, a student admitted to candidacy "devises a curriculum, plans research and field study, and conducts independent research . . . in consultation with the IS faculty and a faculty mentor from another academic unit" (JMU, 2020, para. 1).

At Oberlin College (OH), similarly, qualified students in either the College of Arts and Sciences or the Conservatory of Music can create a personal major that "draws together the strongest courses and resources that Oberlin has to offer into a curricular plan that is stronger than any of its parts" (Oberlin, 2020, para. 2). Continuing consultation between the student and at least two advisors is required both for the initial development and approval of an individual major proposal and then throughout the student's undergraduate career.

Thoughtfully developed curricula should embody clear intent and conspicuous logic in order to serve all students well. However, colleges and universities should recognize also a complementary commitment, that the baccalaureate curriculum of *every student* should express a clear, efficient, and logical rationale. Students are capable of creating degree programs that engage different disciplines in creative but intentional ways but cannot do so without robust institutional guidance.

Encourage More Students to "Double Major"

Persuading more students to pursue a second major can offer clear benefits for both the student and the institution. Even if the institution's complement of majors remains unchanged, having more students pursuing double majors can offer those students the benefits of a cross-disciplinary perspective while challenging faculty members to consult with colleagues in other disciplines. Some adjustments in program requirements or in the academic calendar may be necessary if double majors are to be completed within a four-year college career, but major curriculum reform should not be required.

An exercise: Select two disciplines at random and imagine the singular advantages of exploring both. History and accounting. Mathematics and art history. Management and musical performance. It is difficult to imagine a juxtaposition without potential!

Offer Degrees With a "Special Added Ingredient"
As chapters 8, 9, and 10 will show, nondegree credentials have become attractive options for many students—less expensive to obtain (usually), less time-consuming (usually), and more directly aligned with employment opportunities (usually) than degrees. But such credentials need not be an either/or alternative. Savvy institutions will consider a both/and approach. There's no reason students should not be encouraged to obtain a certificate or certification in the course of their progress toward a baccalaureate degree. That encouragement is the focus of the Workcred project we describe in chapter 2. One way to "soup up" a major? Add a certification! Any opportunity through which a student may apply their learning and gain real-world experience should add value to the degree and make the recipient more competitive. In the words of the redoubtable Goldie Blumenstyk (2019b), it's a "no-brainer."

In sum, institutions that offer the bachelor's degree less as a traditional platform for courses and credit hours and more as a scaffold for linking innovative approaches to documented learning will be well positioned to guide their students to the options most appropriate for them.

End College Majors as We Know Them
What if we were reinvigorate the bachelor's degree by upending the major? In a powerful commentary, Jeffrey J. Selingo, the author of *There Is Life After College: What Parents and Students Should Know About Navigating School to Prepare for the Jobs of Tomorrow* (2016), argues that the major "as we know it" has outlived its usefulness. "The problem," he says, "is that the taxonomy of academic majors that broadened significantly over the past hundred years can no longer keep pace with the churn of knowledge needed to compete in nearly every profession." Given the documented shortfall between what students are accomplishing and what employers need, Selingo believes that the college curriculum should offer students experience with a broad spectrum of disciplines (Selingo, 2016).

That is in one sense unrealistic, of course. No student can study *all* academic disciplines. And Selingo does not suggest that we bar students from studying intensively in a discipline. He believes rather that students should undertake a "T-shaped" education: "The vertical bar of the T represents deep understanding of one subject (the current conception of the major) [while] the horizontal stroke . . . allows people to work across a variety of complex subject areas with ease and confidence." In the best of circumstances, a "T-shaped" education would embrace the learning outcomes of the thoughtfully designed general education program we describe earlier in this chapter as well as broad peripheral vision enabling an awareness of their roles within a complex but finally coherent educational environment.

Such majors would not be "majors as we know them." They would be continually cognizant of related disciplines. Problem based, they would require students to question, to think creatively, to synthesize. Through such an approach the advantages of the individualized degrees offered at JMU and Oberlin would become available to all. By this perspective, what Selingo proposes is a profound reform *at scale*. As a "special advisor" to the entrepreneurial president of Arizona State, Michael Crow, Selingo shares with his boss a creative skepticism with regard to traditional departmental structures. "Grounding knowledge" will remain essential, he says, but the job of the university is to offer its students a variety of "pathways for learning" (Selingo, 2018).

Schedule More Creatively
Through the Bologna Process, European postsecondary educators have replaced a complicated quilt of competing degree options with a standardized template organized around a three-year baccalaureate. In so doing, they have in effect challenged U.S. educators to justify the four-year bachelor's degree.

Several institutions have risen to this challenge by introducing a three-year option—but with mixed results. The requirements of such programs are in general meant to be commensurate with those of four-year programs, but they typically require substantial advanced placement (AP) credit, demonstration of proficiency, or summer study. Table 5.1 shows a few examples of how colleges and universities make three-year degree programs "work" without lowering degree requirements.

Having reviewed some of the problems evident in bringing three-year degrees to scale, Paul Weinstein (2018) offers advice to institutions that consider expanding such degrees:

- Take advantage of opportunities to reduce "unnecessary electives" and other course requirements not clearly related to defined learning outcomes.
- Encourage students to study abroad—independently.

- Invite students to declare majors *as they enter*, "with, of course, the choice to change."
- Drop "unethical and misguided" restrictions on acceptance of AP and international baccalaureate (IB) credit.
- Incentivize the option by reducing tuition fees by 25%.

Other scheduling options, such as single-course terms (e.g., at Colorado College and Cornell College [IA]), are receiving another look. Or consider Knox College (IL), at which students take three courses in each 10-week trimester. Or Spalding University (KY), which offers seven six-week sessions. For-profit institutions in particular continue to explore opportunities for making postsecondary education as convenient as possible through multiple points of entry. Institutions that continue to offer only the traditional fall and spring semesters with (or without) a summer session might want to consult their students to determine whether traditional scheduling remains their preferred option. If not, institutions may want to consider increasing the options they make available.

Consider an Expansion in Online Education
Rather than awaiting the necessity for another abrupt escalation of online learning, as experienced by many institutions in 2020, undertaking a thoughtful and deliberate expansion of online learning now could offer several advantages—more flexibility for resident students, greater access for remote ones, and more engrossing pedagogical approaches for everyone.

Institutions already committed to and invested in online learning found themselves at an advantage during the pandemic when others were suddenly forced to migrate their programs virtually overnight. Those that had

TABLE 5.1
Five Approaches to a Three-Year Bachelor's Degree

Institution	*Adjustment or Accommodation*
Ashland University (OH)	Summer study
Thomas More University (KY)	Summer study or extra course work during semesters
Purdue University (IN)	Two summer sessions
New York University	More two credit-hour courses, enabling 18-hour semesters
University of Massachusetts, Amherst	Assumes "considerable" AP or IB credits in high school

offered online degrees exclusively, such as Western Governors University, Empire State College (NY), and American Public University, required little or no transition. Others, such as Southern New Hampshire University and the University of Phoenix, were already focused on serving their considerable online enrollments. And those serving both large on-campus and large online enrollments (e.g., Arizona State and the University of Washington) were able to navigate the sudden transition more readily than many others. But for most institutions, the lessons learned in managing an emergency should sustain their continued attention to the advantages in greater reliance on online learning, advantages of particular relevance to the bachelor's degree: more conspicuous intentionality in the shared pursuit of explicit learning outcomes, more creative expectations as to undergraduate research, more flexible and accessible scheduling, and the like.

Distance learning has always required the defining of clear learning outcomes—for every degree, every course, every lesson. But baccalaureate programs offered on campus have often operated according to more relaxed standards. To the extent that we accept that the "intentionality obligation" should define in-person as well as online learning, an important gain will have been realized. More to the point, bachelor's degrees that embody that gain are likely to be those that will thrive.

What Success Looks Like

In its 2019 list of colleges that are "best and worst" in awarding bachelor's degrees in computer science and engineering to women, *The Chronicle of Higher Education* reports enormous disparities from one institution to another. Doubtless many demographic, economic, and geographical factors are relevant, but what different institutions choose to *do* appears to make the greatest difference (CHE Staff, 2019).

At Salisbury University, a state university located on Maryland's Eastern Shore, women in 2016–2017 earned 35.9% of all bachelor's degrees awarded in computer science. By contrast, at Central Connecticut State University, women earned only 6.7% of the computer sciences degrees awarded in the same period. Or consider engineering. In 2016–2017, at Eastern Washington University, women earned only 4.1% of the bachelor's degrees in engineering, while at North Carolina State, women accounted for 29.2%.

These disparities raise many more questions than can be addressed here, but Salisbury's emphasis on undergraduate learning and student research may offer a clue. At the top of a web page titled "Emphasizing Hands on Learning," a woman student (or young faculty member) is shown in a laboratory, standing in front of a bank of colorful flasks. The accompanying copy emphasizes a campus priority.

> SU is known for its undergraduate and graduate research along with self-directed learning opportunities. Home to an annual student research conference and two-time host of the National Conference on Undergraduate Research, students in all majors are encouraged by accomplished faculty-mentors to take inspiration beyond the classroom and share their own connections and discoveries. (Salisbury University, 2019)

Similar lists for other disciplines would reveal different disparities. The point is not to draw invidious comparisons between institutions, because an institution with low enrollments of women in STEM fields (or of minorities in health care or of men in nursing) may be able to point to impressive diversity in other programs. The concern rather is that broader access to degrees in all fields for all students should become a priority, region by region, discipline by discipline.

In Sum

While we may acknowledge that a "build it and they will come" approach is insufficient to ensure equity of access and support for success so far as any credential is concerned, improving access to and support for the bachelor's degree could create postsecondary education gains notable for their impact. As this chapter suggests, there are many salutary examples of innovation so far as the bachelor's degree is concerned. The question is why more institutions have not embraced the opportunities such innovations offer. When students fail to gain access to pedagogies, schedules, and structures shown to enhance learning, colleges and universities miss out on opportunities as well.

Takeaways

- Inventory enrollments in all disciplines so as to document significant gaps in participation. If it appears that gender, racial, and economic constituencies are not equitably represented in all disciplines, identify priorities for redress, consult best practices, and pursue explicit targets for improvement.
- Define clearly easily understood and demonstrable learning outcomes for the bachelor's degree irrespective of discipline, measure the extent to which the curriculum assures their accomplishment, and address any gaps that appear.

- Develop a "signature" general education program that offers students both broad knowledge and critical skills with obvious relevance to their specialized study in the major.
- Ask the employers that hire your students whether the students are meeting their expectations and undertake remedial actions to address the most often voiced concerns.
- Review the list of opportunities for creative approaches to the major, including (a) redefining or merging underperforming majors, (b) initiating blended majors, (c) developing degrees in emerging disciplines, (d) developing majors that transcend traditional disciplines, (e) promoting double majors, or (f) replacing traditional majors with concentrations or specialization hubs and consider pursuing any that would benefit your students.
- Consider whether alternate academic scheduling might serve some (or all) of your students more effectively than your current scheduling.
- Determine the extent to which the institution is prepared for a future abrupt transition to increased or exclusive reliance on online learning and take any remedial actions that may be indicated.
- Seek qualitative parity between online and in-person learning. While accreditors expect that online learning be equivalent in content and quality to in-person instruction, in-person instruction should become as focused as online learning on assessing accomplishment relative to explicit learning goals.

6

THE MASTER'S DEGREE

Despite an "identity crisis," the master's degree has gained new life in an economy where advanced knowledge and professional-grade skills are at a premium. Students seeking an accessible but highly competitive credential may find the master's degree particularly appropriate. But without guidance they may not choose wisely. Risks abound. The costs of some master's degrees far outweigh the probable returns.

What Is a Master's Degree?

The "identity crisis" of the master's degree began in the late 19th century, when the credential became more desirable and more widely available. That crisis has now become more evident. The problem is one not of a lack of identity, but one of too many identities. While any credential may support multiple applications (an associate degree may signify both employment readiness and preparedness for baccalaureate study) there's no list of potential applications to compare with that for the master's degree, which, for instance,

- may be awarded as an interim credential to a graduate student who will proceed to a doctoral program;
- may be awarded as a terminal degree to a graduate student who chooses not to proceed to doctoral study;
- may entitle a K–12 teacher to qualify for employment or, more frequently, for tenure and increased compensation;
- may serve as a respected qualification for professional practice in fields such as speech pathology, social work, library science, and psychology;
- may enable artists to identify themselves as accomplished performers— or rather as educators or administrators;
- may offer those already employed a qualification entitling them to promotion;

103

- may enable a student who has earned a bachelor's degree in one field to change direction by developing competence in a different field; and
- may qualify a recipient for a faculty position at a community college.

That the master's degree may serve in all of these circumstances (and in many more) speaks well for the many values it can offer. But such variation also complicates any understanding of the degree's distinctive place within the hierarchy of credentials.

SIDEBAR
The "Honorary" Master's
Although master's degrees in the United Kingdom and Ireland are in general similar to those awarded in the United States, there are three universities (Oxford, Cambridge, and Trinity) that grant a Master of Arts degree simply on application five to seven years after the award of a bachelor's degree. Unlike other master's degrees awarded at these and other universities, this MA does not signify the completion of additional study beyond that required for the baccalaureate.

As we suggest later in the chapter (see "Defining the Degree") one effort to define the value of the master's degree relative to the bachelor's degree can be found in the Degree Qualifications Profile (DQP). But because that useful guide has not yet informed public awareness on a wide scale, master's degree providers can find it a challenge to explain how a master's degree *should* point to knowledge and experience *beyond that provided by a baccalaureate education*. Many master's degrees may appear simply as incremental (i.e., "bachelor's degrees on steroids"). And colleges that offer upper level courses serving both graduate students and advanced undergraduates can compound the confusion.

There are many reasons to value this credential, but if we are to do so credibly, we must attempt to agree on what it signifies.

An "Endangered Species"?

Goldie Blumenstyk once observed that a precipitous decline in the market value of a particular online program provider had prompted it to reconsider its focus on the master's degree. During its first decade, the company had contracted with higher education institutions to deliver online master's programs—for a price. But the proliferation of other online options, creating "a new reality in the marketplace," had prompted the company to shift its focus to bootcamps and other nondegree credentials. Blumenstyk (2019a) concluded this might be another indication "that interest in the traditional master's degree is dwindling."

A subsequent report from EAB (a provider of research, technology, and services) reinforced Blumenstyk's concern. EAB found that the increase in the award of graduate certificates in 2007–2012 had outpaced the increase in master's degree awards sixfold. For the master's degree to remain a viable and attractive option, it seemed clear that colleges and universities would have to become more creative in developing a wider variety of formats, program lengths, and prices. Was that likely? Blumenstyk's (2019a) answer: "I suspect, not very. At least not yet."

In December 1919 and February 2020, two different analyses of the master's degree for *Inside Higher Ed* prompted nearly identical headlines. The first, covering the degree in general, asks "Has the Master's Degree Bubble Burst?" The second, focused on only one form of the degree, asks "What Happens After the M.B.A. Bubble Bursts?"

Marc Rubin, a long-time professor of accounting at Miami University (Ohio), echoed the warning concerning the MBA in particular. Citing an October 2019 survey by the Graduate Admissions Council, he identifies "declining interest in what was once the silver-bullet credential for those interested in business careers." Having listed familiar factors in the decline such as program costs, a strong job market, and employer-provided training, he considers whether his discipline is prepared to undertake a fundamental rethinking of what students and employers need. He might easily have echoed Blumenstyk: "I suspect, not very. At least not yet." But what he says is more direct: "I've yet to see any truly bold proposals" (Rubin, 2020, para. 3).

As these cautionary perspectives suggest, while cyclical variability in the demand for particular degrees and disciplines has long been evident, there are reasons to suspect that the current decline in master's degree enrollments may signal more than a periodic ebb.

That may not be altogether regrettable. The pursuit of the master's degree simply to secure an additional advantage in a labor market crowded with baccalaureate degrees may not prove cost effective for students who incur considerable additional debt without significantly increasing their competitiveness. Later on in this chapter, we refer to a recent, particularly striking example of cost *ineffectiveness*. But extreme cases are not required to suggest that responsible administrators, faculty members, and academic advisors must guide students toward considering return on investment as one important ingredient in judicious curricular decisions—even if that consideration should lead some students to consider alternatives to a master's. Some may find greater value in nondegree credentials attesting to specific industry related skills. The University of California (UC) Berkeley Extension (2020) program has an inviting pitch for its certificate: "With employment of advertising and marketing managers projected to grow 8 percent from 2018 to

2028, you could find yourself in demand in less time, and at less cost, than [if you were to earn] a master's degree" (para. 1).

Inroads on the master's degree from the other end of the scale may be found in professions, especially ones in health care, that now prefer—or demand—the professional doctorate instead of the master's. You will learn more about this trend in the following chapter, which focuses on the doctorate. In the meantime, when next you pick up a prescription, you may want to realize that your pharmacists probably have earned the PharmD. Should you address them as "doctor"? That's the subject of an interesting debate we won't touch!

One last issue for the master's degree arises from the fact that some of the long-standing incentives for the degree—such as the salary bump and increased job security traditionally provided to K–12 teachers who earn a master's—are no longer as widely available. And those that remain are being questioned. A study by the National Council on Teacher Quality (NCTQ) found that within its polling sample 92% of large school districts offer additional compensation to recipients of an advanced degree. However, given the average cost of earning that degree, a teacher may have to work at least eight additional years before enjoying that advantage.

Perhaps more damagingly, the NCTQ research found "that teachers with master's degrees are rarely more effective than teachers without them" (Nittier, 2019, para. 1). Scholars and commentators have in general not been kind. A recent assessment by Grace Gedye (2020) in *Washington Monthly*, provocatively headlined, "Masters of None," begins with the challenging subhead: "Teachers across the country earn grad degrees to get raises. Turns out those degrees don't improve student learning—they just fatten universities' bottom lines."

So if the master's degree is to remain a viable credential, it would seem that the "truly bold proposals" called for by Professor Rubin are overdue.

Life Support for the Master's Degree

Concerns regarding the viability of the master's degree should prompt exploration of opportunities for innovation. But the value of any initiative must be found in its benefits for the student. Resourceful providers will increase their likelihood of success by observing what may be learned from the following two initiatives.

Utah: Identifying an Unmet Need

An initiative introduced during the 2019–2020 academic year by the University of Utah, a master's degree in business creation (MBC), illustrates several good practices. First, administrators and faculty members identified an unmet regional demand that was both urgent and likely to prove sustainable—entrepreneurial business creation. Second, they determined that a master's degree would be an appropriate response—more focused and professionally demanding than a baccalaureate program but not as expensive or as time-consuming as a doctoral program. Third, they established a business plan based on the recruitment of small cohorts of highly motivated students. And they determined that they would model in their program precisely the qualities they would seek to teach: a continuing awareness of the environment and a readiness to respond "entrepreneurially" to changing circumstances.

Those principles were tested almost immediately. While the adjustments made necessary by the pandemic early in 2020 would have threatened many new programs, they proved "a perfect test for the fledgling MBC" (Kelling, 2020, para. 3). The program faculty agreed on "being entrepreneurial and managing the program like a startup" (Kelling, 2020, para. 6). Although one would not wish for another such crucible, there are two important principles to learn from Utah's response. First, there has been a commitment to learn from experience and to apply lessons learned to program improvement. Second, both the learning and the improvement processes were in collaboration with students and nonacademic experts. The Utah determination to embrace emerging opportunities through a new program and their confidence in the systematic development of that program even at the height of a pandemic may suggest one way out of the degree's "identity crisis."

Lumina Foundation: Defining the Degree

If the master's degree is to maintain its viability, it must be more clearly defined. Of course, there are important details that each institution must provide about its own programs. How much time do they require? How much do they cost? How successful are the recipients? But if each institution were to define only its own master's degrees, we would be little better off.

The unasked question is critical: What does a master's degree mean, regardless of institution and regardless of discipline, when compared to a bachelor's or doctoral degree? We must be able to explain that in a way that students, employers, faculty members, and the public will find useful. Armed with a cogent explanation of the degree's value, providers and recipients alike would be better able to explain that value to employers or graduate institutions.

In chapter 5, we described how the DQP can support definition of the bachelor's degree. Its usefulness in defining the master's may be of even greater moment. As it differentiates among three of the four degrees we consider, the DQP can be particularly useful in explaining how the master's degree, regardless of the subject in which it is earned, differs *both in kind and in degree.* The focus of the DQP on student learning and its "demarcation of increasing levels of challenge as a student progresses from one degree level to the next" are meant to "correct the tendency to view the credential as an end in itself, independent of the learning it is meant to represent" (Lumina Foundation, 2014, p. 8).

As we have mentioned, differences among degrees are organized according to five categories. The first is "specialized knowledge" relative to the field in which the degree is earned. The other four—broad and integrative knowledge, intellectual skills, applied and collaborative learning, and civic and global learning—all transcend the chosen field so as to define the degree *qua* degree. Because defining the master's degree may prove essential to its revitalization, the practical advice of the DQP could hardly be of greater moment.

Table 6.1 addresses a single question: What should the recipient of a master's degree know and be able to do *beyond the expectations appropriate for the recipient of a bachelor's degree?*

TABLE 6.1
Three Differences Between Two Degrees

	Bachelor's Degree	*Master's Degree*
Ethical reasoning	Identifies and elaborates key ethical issues present in at least one prominent social or cultural problem, articulates the ways in which at least two differing ethical perspectives influence decision-making concerning those problems, and develops and defends an approach to address the ethical issue productively	Articulates and challenges a tradition, assumption, or prevailing practice within the field of study by raising and examining relevant ethical perspectives through a project, paper, or performance
Civic and global learning	Develops and justifies a position on a public issue and relates this position to alternate views held by the public or within the policy environment	Develops a formal proposal, real or hypothetical, to a nongovernmental organization addressing a global challenge in the field of study that the student believes has not been adequately addressed

	BACHELOR'S DEGREE	MASTER'S DEGREE
Specialized knowledge	Investigates a familiar but complex problem in the field of study by assembling, arranging, and reformulating ideas, concepts, designs, and techniques	Articulates significant challenges involved in practicing the field of study, elucidates its leading edges, and explores the current limits of theory, knowledge, and practice through a project that lies outside conventional boundaries

In each case, relative to the holder of a bachelor's degree, the recipient of a master's degree should be able to demonstrate a broader sense of the field in its relation to other fields, a stronger sense of command in the formulation and solution of problems, and a clearer commitment to ethical and responsible practice. Such distinctions are meant to be as applicable to a master's in history as to one in business administration, the fine arts, or biology.

While defining the degree may not appear to be a "bold" reform, it can be a significant and constructive one through its clarification of degree-specific learning objectives in terms that faculty members can pursue, that academic advisors can explain, that students can embrace, and that employers can value. Expressed in terms of how students should be able to *demonstrate* their knowledge and abilities, learning outcomes encourage continuing monitoring of the extent to which the "means" of the curriculum align with and ensure the "ends" sought by those who earn it.

Pros and Cons of a "Discretionary" Degree

In chapter 2, we introduced a metaphor for credential programs as "islands separated by broad straits" and called for convenient bridges among them to encourage student mobility. That metaphor is particularly useful in understanding the status of the master's degree. Students considering graduate study must have a realistic expectation that if they invest the time and money in earning a master's degree they will achieve the advantages they seek. And institutions must be transparent about both costs and benefits so that students can make wise choices. After all, as we observed earlier in this chapter, the cost can be considerable—especially when added to that of a bachelor's degree. For the approximately 60% of master's degree recipients who graduate with debt, the average is a whopping $66,000 (NCES, 2018).

SIDEBAR
Competing Internationally
Individuals not interested in the international labor market (or in working for an international firm) may question whether the eventual return on a master's degree will justify the time and money spent in obtaining it. For others it becomes more complicated. In Europe, where the three-year baccalaureate is standard, students often proceed to a master's degree. Clifford Adelman's 2009 prediction that the master's would become "the preferred exit point for [European] 'undergraduate' education in virtually all fields, academic and occupationally-oriented" was prescient (p. 203). While the proportion of students continuing to this "exit point" within a year after earning the baccalaureate differs from country to country, "in around half of the countries, most first-cycle graduates (50% or above) undertake a second-cycle programme within one year of graduation and, in some of these countries, according to the European Commission, Education and Culture Executive Agency, & Eurydice, the proportion reaches 75% and above" (EC/EACEA/Eurydice, 2018, p. 125). To an increasing extent, U.S. baccalaureate recipients will find themselves competing with European students who have earned the master's.

In July 2021 the *Wall Street Journal* found examples in USDE data that far exceed even this formidable figure. The most outrageous example was offered by film students at Columbia University who were taking on education debt above $180,000 to qualify for positions likely to offer less than $30,000 per year (Korn & Fuller, 2021). In general, some programs in the arts offered by private institutions appear to be frequent examples, but Kevin Carey observes that such programs are not alone. He points to health care programs that ask students to borrow "doctor money" in order to earn "therapist wages" (Carey, 2021).

What can be done? Carey's view is that the imbalance has become so conspicuous that "two policy responses" are likely. Legal limits on borrowing and loan forgiveness for graduate school might be imposed to discourage would-be students from making calamitous investments. And regulations that would disqualify high cost/low return programs from eligibility for federal aid should prompt providers to question master's degree programs that fail a cost-benefit analysis (Carey, 2021).

But an even more accessible solution may be found within institutions themselves. There are two elements. The first is that institutions should reexamine the conventions—course scheduling, modes of instruction, disciplinary pigeonholes—that may contribute to the high costs of graduate study. While working to improve their quality through defining and assuring explicit learning outcomes, savvy institutions should also seek to make degree programs more efficient and cost-effective. The second element to the solution is the one we have already asserted, that responsible administrators, faculty members, and academic advisors must guide students toward considering return on investment as a critical ingredient in curricular decisions.

There are practical steps that can and should be taken.

At the level of the discipline, faculty members, advisors, and professional associations should encourage bachelor's degree recipients to weigh seriously the advantages they might find through earning a master's degree. Considering costs vs. benefits is critical. So is distinguishing more clearly between the bachelor's and master's degrees so as to identify the incremental gains students will achieve.

At the institutional level, continuity and convenience represent complementary priorities. One particularly inviting pathway to the master's degree enables students to complete both the bachelor's and master's degrees within five years. Through an approach such as that offered by Brown University, students may begin their graduate work as juniors, complete the baccalaureate in the first year of the master's program, and qualify for the master's in their fifth year of study. "Up to two courses of the eight required for the master's degree may be completed while the student is an undergraduate" (Brown University, 2020).

There are of course impediments to this innovation that may also deserve attention. Traditional academic calendars, rigid curricular structures, lengthy time to degree, and high program costs can discourage students. And because more than half of all students take more than four years to earn a bachelor's degree, and one fourth take more than six years to graduate (NCES, 2020), it should not be surprising that most recipients of the bachelor's degree choose to take their chances on the job market without spending more time in college.

For many that may be a wise decision. Even if a master's degree may eventually prove useful, gaining some experience prior to undertaking further study may prove more advantageous than proceeding directly from one level to the next. As we have noted, some master's programs require on-the-job experience as a prerequisite for admission.

But that recognition should not obscure the need for systemic change. Academic calendars and curricula *can be* modified to enable students to complete a baccalaureate degree within 36 months with no compromise in programmatic rigor or depth. Baccalaureate program objectives as a matter of course *can* include preparedness for graduate study and awareness of its potential advantages. And broad and convenient bridges *can* enable students for whom the master's makes sense to proceed directly to graduate study.

Introducing Innovative Alternatives

Defining the master's degree more clearly and compellingly and facilitating the transition from baccalaureate to master's programs would sustain and strengthen the credential as traditionally provided. Increasingly, however, alternatives to traditional master's degrees may prove even more appealing. Here are four approaches.

"Netflix" Programs

Joshua Kim has argued that traditional master's programs offered by regional institutions to on-campus students face-to-face in classrooms are becoming the academic equivalent of Blockbuster Video—an obsolete protocol for doing business. He recommends as an alternative the "Netflix" model, low-cost online master's programs available through a variety of virtual modalities (Kim, 2019). As an example, Kim cites "the $21,384 iMBA from the University of Illinois on the Coursera platform." Highly regarded institutions that take the lead in developing similar low-cost programs "at scale" will prosper, he believes, while regional institutions still offering relatively expensive on-campus programs will be making "the same mistake as Blockbuster" (Kim, 2019).

A review of available online master's degrees will suggest that many institutions have been competing to develop just such "Netflix" programs. Now, as a result of their recent experience of "total immersion" in online and hybrid learning, many more institutions are considering how they might expand master's enrollments (and revenues) through expansion of online offerings. Such initiatives are to be found even in disciplines that might appear to be defined by the relationships, challenges, and personal satisfactions associated with face-to-face learning. Thus Ohio University offers an online Master of Social Work, while Boston University offers the Master's in Music Education. Our Lady of the Lake University offers a 100% online Master of Arts in Counseling!

Such extraordinary initiatives should prompt the concerns with quality and equity we will explore in chapter 11. But ignoring the opportunities for program growth through innovation would be to confront the existential questions that institutions still committed to Kim's "Blockbuster" offerings may face. Innovative online delivery represents one such opportunity. But there are other options as well:

- Expand "hybrid" master's programs that combine online instruction with limited but efficient on-campus experience. Regional institutions, especially, share the advantage that a majority of their students and potential students live in their region. Such students are uniquely positioned to benefit from occasional, limited access to in-person learning that complements their work online.
- "Merged" programs can offer students both a master's degree and a career-ready certificate or certification. What can be an enhancement for baccalaureate programs may offer an even clearer competitive advantage for master's degree programs.
- "Bracket scheduling" can offer both the advantages of intensive face-to-face learning and the convenience of distance learning. A variation of "hybrid" offerings, courses in such programs meet on campus for a week or so at the beginning of the term and again for a few days at the end. In between the two, students work online with other students and their instructor.

The "MicroMasters"

The offering of an incremental path to *candidacy* for a master's degree program appears in "MicroMasters" programs. What's on offer is not a miniature version of the master's degree, as the name might suggest, but online courses that may enable a student to qualify for entry to a master's degree program. The idea arose in tandem with the early (c. 2012) enthusiasm for MOOCs. In 2016 that enthusiasm resurfaced in an announcement by 14 prestigious universities. They would offer MicroMasters modules, "a series of graduate level courses from top universities," that would enable sufficiently assiduous students to complete about half of the work required for a master's degree.

Yet for many students, the MicroMasters courses may suffice, in that certificates of course completion in a MicroMasters program may themselves entitle the recipient to career advancement. As Adam Gordon observes in a 2018 article for *Forbes*, "It's apparent most students won't pursue the full degree. They'll walk with the MM." One reason lies in a close affiliation of employer sponsors. As of spring 2018, there were 40 such sponsors, including IBM, WalMart, Ford, and Microsoft. The program thus offers a compact linking students, institutions, and employers.

But students who earn certificates through "online, examined and graded, credit-eligible graduate-level courses" (Gordon, 2018, para. 3) need not "walk." They may apply the MicroMasters certificates toward the requirements of a full degree at a participating university thereby gaining access to "an accelerated and less expensive Master's Degree" (edX, 2020, MicroMaster's Programs Are a Pathway to Today's Top Jobs). As of 2020, participating institutions (Massachusetts Institute of Technology [MIT], Columbia, Penn, Georgia Tech, and 19 others) were offering 58 programs in such fields as entrepreneurship, bioinformatics, information systems, accounting, and international law.

One recent development should be kept in mind, a decision by MIT and Harvard to sell their EdX platform to a for-profit provider, 2U. The June 2021 move (awaiting approval by the Massachusetts attorney general as this book went to press) elicited considerable criticism. For instance, a strong denunciation by Jefferson Pooley, "MIT and Harvard Have Sold Higher Ed's Future," appears in the July 23, 2021, issue of *CHE* (pp. 34–35). The case for the move can be found at https://news.mit.edu/2021/mit-harvard-transfer-edx-2u-faq-0629.

Gordon predicts that the increasing popularity of the MicroMasters will over time "take a huge bite" out of the market for traditional and executive master's programs in business. That seems possible. But there are other career-focused disciplines that should be paying attention as well. If the challenges facing institutions do not prompt them to make their master's programs more appealing and competitive, the opportunity to do so may not return. None of the closed Blockbuster Video stores has reopened for business.

A Mini-Master's

Actually, it's a mini-MBA, or in our example, a portfolio of mini-MBAs offered by Rutgers University. There are other mini-MBA programs, such as those at Pepperdine and the University at Buffalo (SUNY), but the variety of subdisciplines on offer at Rutgers, the convenient format (10 "modules," each covered in three-and-one-half hours), and the program's relative affordability (about $5,000) make it well worth mentioning as an alternative to the "Blockbuster Video" MBA offerings competing for declining enrollments.

Within the Rutgers portfolio there is a mini-MBA in biopharma innovation that "teaches life sciences experts key business management theory," one for engineers and technology managers that invites students "to expand your contribution beyond technical solutions," and another in social media marketing that encourages a "deep dive into topics specific to what you do every day [that] will take your game to the next level." Other programs are offered in data-driven management and in business essentials (Rutgers Business School, 2020).

The Professional Master's Degree

Analogous to both the applied baccalaureate and the professional doctorate (see chapters 5 and 7), the professional master's degree differs from other master's degrees in that it is meant to serve not as a stepping-stone to further education but directly to employment. Master's degrees with this focus are not entirely new, of course. The MBA and Master of Fine Arts are familiar. So-called "terminal" master's programs may be found also in fields such as engineering, public administration, public policy, the arts, public health, education, and social work.

But the professional master's degree is aimed specifically at liberal arts students who discover that their undergraduate preparation may not offer reliable access to a career. While such students might otherwise be disinclined to pursue graduate education, they may benefit from supplementary education that prepares them for the world of work.

The so-called professional master's programs that have emerged so far can be divided into two types, those with a social science or humanities focus and those emphasizing the sciences. Both reflect a 1995 undertaking by the Council of Graduate Schools responding to growing interest in graduate programs with a stronger vocational focus. Grants in 1997 from the Alfred P. Sloan and William M. Keck foundations funded startup costs for pioneering programs that would blend technical courses in STEM disciplines with practical experience aimed at developing skills sought by employers.

Georgia Tech is one of the institutions that has picked up this ball and run with it—a cliché prompted by a university web-page photo of recent professional master's degree graduates shown overlooking the end zone at Bobby Dodd stadium. The featured programs are the professional master's in applied systems engineering (PMASE) and the professional master's in manufacturing leadership (PMML), both of which "are targeted at working adults looking to advance their careers or become more marketable in their fields." The programs are designed to emphasize experience rather than research (Georgia Tech Professional Education, 2016).

Flip the Curriculum!

We noted Marc Rubin's warning concerning "declining interest" in the MBA and his disappointment in the scarcity of "truly bold proposals" that might restore the standing of what at one time was regarded as a "silver-bullet" degree in the business world. He offers a bold proposal: "Remove majors altogether" from undergraduate business education so that graduates learn to "think critically, creatively and conceptually," to "understand coding and computational work," to "communicate effectively," and to "thrive in a constantly changing environment" (Rubin, 2020, para. 5). Thus prepared, undergraduates would choose among highly focused certificate programs and "specialty master's degrees."

Rubin's proposal of a "flipped" curriculum could apply to many disciplines. The idea is that undergraduate students whose majors now educate them narrowly for employment in specific fields might instead develop through their majors the broad knowledge, skills, and aptitudes required for more intense, focused study in a master's degree. The bachelor's degree in business that Rubin has in mind would better prepare students for the unpredictable economies that continue to develop, while the master's degrees he envisions would enable a graduate student to develop highly specialized and thus highly competitive and mobile skills. Rubin's colleagues in the sciences, the humanities, and the fine arts might want to pay attention.

In Sum

Rubin's proposal offers a useful coda to this chapter on the master's degree by suggesting that degrees cannot and should not be regarded in isolation from one another. Despite the question pursued here—whether the master's degree can be strengthened so as to offer greater value for students who choose to pursue it—the overriding question is whether the postsecondary education spectrum as a whole is as effective, as efficient, and as economical as possible. If the answer to that question were affirmative, there would be little reason for this book.

The master's degree is by no means a lost cause. To the contrary, if the academy were to define clearly what the degree means, regardless of discipline, and make it available in formats and in specialties that respond to present and future needs, the master's degree could again emerge as a singular opportunity for both institutions and for students. But the clock is ticking. The Blockbuster stores are long gone.

Takeaways

Reviving the master's degree will require the concerted and collaborative attention of academic advisors, faculty members, and administrators. Advisors share valuable perspectives on how baccalaureate students might be more effectively enabled to understand and consider the possible advantages of study at the master's level. Faculty members should understand more fully than anyone the distinct value of a master's degree relative to baccalaureate and doctoral degrees. And administrators should be able to identify competitive advantages awaiting responsibly entrepreneurial institutions. There are some initiatives that appear particularly worthy of attention.

- Determine the value of the institution's current master's degree offerings—both for students and for the institution. Document those which are profitable for students and for the institution. Focus on those that benefit both.
- Consider whether the offering of a master's degree is the most effective way of meeting student and employer needs. In the post-pandemic era, a tranche of courses leading to the award of a graduate certificate might more readily enable a student to qualify for available employment.
- Identify master's programs that may be closely comparable to programs offered by an institution's neighbors or peers. Are there ones that can be made more distinctive and, thus, more of a competitive asset? If a program appears inessential to institutional mission and of limited potential for growth through innovation, its reorganization or termination might free resources for the development of programs more responsive to documented needs.
- Pursue a "zero-sum" analysis of institutional strengths and emerging demands to identify opportunities (e.g., an English department that has become a magnet for creative writing students might weigh the benefits of initiating an MFA degree). Similarly, a university serving a community with increasing opportunities for underwriters might weigh the costs and benefits of introducing a master's degree in actuarial science.
- Consider the potential advantages in serving more fully those seeking more limited and more focused credentials such as graduate-level certificates and certifications.
- Understand that such initiatives depend for their success on a strong collegial collaboration among administrators, faculty members, and academic advisors. If not all contribute to the discussion, the results are likely to be unsatisfactory.

7

THE DOCTORATE

At one time the most clearly defined of all academic credentials, a final destination on the educational pathway, the doctorate has now become another ambiguous credential in a volatile environment. There are now many more opportunities to earn a doctorate. And many more doctorates. And considerable confusion as to what that means.

Seeking the Superlative

Superlatives tend to become more superlative. The uncritical use of "excellent" in the 1980s to express approval gave way to "great" in the 1990s and 2000s. "Let's schedule a meeting," someone suggests. Your heart sinking, you would respond, "Great!" Now the process of escalation would appear to have developed as far as possible. You order a grilled cheese sandwich. Your server approves. "Perfect," she says.

The same kind of escalation appears in credit cards. Gold offers more prestige (and costs more) than green. Platinum costs more than either. Airline hierarchies? Because qualifying for the silver level at United Airlines will no longer guarantee you a comfortable seat, go for the gold! Some frequent flyers schedule discretionary lengthy trips in November and December to earn the miles needed to maintain or improve their "status."

Platinum-Level Credentials

A similar phenomenon, attributable to two distinct sources, can be observed in higher education credentials. To be sure, the prompts tend to be more practical than those behind contemporary slang—though not always that much more practical than frequent flying.

First, as we have seen in the example of nursing, increased expectations of a profession can necessitate increases in the standards required for practice.

That evolution has led to both a research degree (a Doctor of Philosophy in nursing) and a practitioner degree (the DNP, or Doctor of Nursing Practice). In audiology, increasing expectations for clinical practice and for collaboration with other health care providers first prompted a transition from the master's degree to the professional doctorate, the AuD, then to the PhD.

Second, practitioners of different specialties within a discipline have found it expedient to distinguish themselves more clearly from one another. The PhD is routinely awarded *in a particular discipline*, whether that be political science, biology, French, or, for that matter, philosophy. In that sense, a PhD is no less "vocational" than a "practitioner" doctorate such as the AuD. But there is (or should be) a significant difference between the two in that a PhD traditionally signifies not only command of a discipline but also a deep grounding in and respect for knowledge in general, a command that enables the holder to contribute to the expansion of that discipline and to the store of knowledge. "Philosophy," after all, combines the Greek words for "love" and "wisdom." But doctoral degrees that are meant to signify both research proficiency and vocational focus—such as the EdD (Education), the Doctor of Management (DM), and the Doctor of Business Administration (DBA)—complicate the distinction.

To an extent, requiring advanced credentials for practice, licensure, or employment tends to reflect expanded responsibilities, heightened expectations, more exacting standards. But the principle that superlatives tend to become more superlative also may be at play. One discipline after another, rather than strengthen its bachelor's or master's programs, has chosen to undertake a transition to the professional doctorate. The three "Rs" apparently offer compelling justification: recognition, respect, and remuneration. But there may also be at work the desire of the "gold level" frequent flyer not to be outstripped. In the credentials environment, the doctorate is platinum.

The Familiar Paradox

No harm done? That is a more difficult question. As the doctoral degree functions more and more often as an entry-level credential in an increasing range of professional roles, its once clear eminence as an academic pinnacle has become less clear. In comparing a recipient of a Harvard MBA to a recipient of a Doctor of Management degree from a less prestigious institution, what criteria will the employer apply? A century ago, recipients of the doctorate were entitled to the respect reserved for those exercising disciplinary leadership grounded in persistence, initiative, and breadth of

TABLE 7.1

Doctoral Degrees: Similarities and Differences

The Doctoral Degree		
All doctoral degrees represent capstones, either for a discipline (PhD) or for preparation for practice (DVM). All confer recognition for leadership within a discipline or specific level of practice, and all include an obligation to research or to remaining informed about research.		
A Continuum of Doctorates		
Emphasis on Research	**Balanced Emphasis on Research and Application**	**Emphasis on Preparation for Practice**
The PhD	*Applied Research Doctorate*	*Practitioner Doctorate*
• Admission to program typically requires 5–6 years prior study (bachelor's degree and master's or equivalent)	• Admission to program requires 5–6 years prior study (bachelor's degree and master's or equivalent)	• Admission to program may require 4 years prior study (bachelor's degree)
• Research dissertation typically required as contribution to scholarship	• Applied research (e.g., review of scholarship) or alternate exercise required	• Internship, research experience typically required
Typical Program Length	*Typical Program Length*	• Other requirements possible
3–4 years	2–3 years	*Typical Program Length*
Examples	*Examples*	2–3 years
PhD in political science	EdD (education)	*Examples*
PhD in biology	DMA (musical arts)	MD (medicine)
PhD in nursing	DBA (business administration)	JD (law)
PhD in audiology		DDS (dentistry)
PhD in musicology	*Institutionally Defined*	*More Recent Examples*
PhD in history	• Admission requirements set by institutions, accreditors	DPT (physical therapy)
	• Requirements set by institution: applied research, practicum, internships, etc. may be required	AudD (audiology)
		DPM (podiatry)
	Typical Program Length	
	• Variable, depending on program and institution	

Note: While this chart offers a descriptive overview of the principal categories of the doctoral degree and of characteristics typical to these categories, it cannot indicate every possible variation of admissions standards, program requirements, and so on.

knowledge. Now, the question is *which* doctorate? And what was required to earn it? The list of doctorates grows longer year by year.

Our familiar paradox thus arises again: greater opportunity on the one hand, greater risk of misunderstanding and confusion on the other. Consider the queries that abound on search engines. What's the difference between a nurse who has earned the doctor of nursing practice (DNP) and a doctor of medicine (MD)? Should one call one's pharmacist (or audiologist, physical therapist, etc.) "doctor"? What about the writer of an op-ed who encouraged a First Lady who had earned an EdD to renounce the title of "doctor"? Of course, it didn't help that Joseph Epstein, once an editor of *American Scholar,* addressed her as "kiddo" (Treisman, 2020). At a time when doctoral-level skill and expertise of all kinds are critically important, the current level of confusion as to how to regard and respond to the many varieties of "doctorates" is a challenge well worth addressing.

A Simple Chart Is Not So Simple

The point of the chart included in this chapter is not to reassert a hierarchy or to understate the value of specialized credentials at a time when physical therapists and audiologists and DNPs are meeting critical needs, when many PhDs are finding opportunity in the corporate world, and when some professionals pursue hybrid programs (MD/PhD) in order to bring a commitment to research directly into practice. But we should take the opportunity to reconsider a credential that now appears in often misunderstood variants.

We will first consider the broad continuum of the degree through an "environmental scan." That will offer an opportunity to consider how all doctoral degrees may be alike and to glimpse how remarkably unlike some different categories of the doctorate can become. Then we will separate the categories for more focused analysis.

The Doctorate: A Broad Enviornmental Scan

The Integrated Postsecondary Education Data System (IPEDS) maintained by the U.S. Department of Education's (USDE) National Center for Education Statistics (NCES) offers an overview of a complicated landscape. (See a helpful guide to using the system at https://datainventory.ed.gov/HowToSearch.) Table 7.1 offers a simpler (but complementary) picture, one that divides doctorates into four categories, two of which offer some degree of clarity.

The Research/Scholarship Doctorate

The USDE defines the research doctorate as a credential that "requires advanced work beyond the master's level, including the preparation and defense of a dissertation based on original research, or the planning and execution of an original project demonstrating substantial artistic or scholarly achievement." In addition to the PhD, which is now awarded in an increasing number of disciplines, the "research" category includes doctorates in fields such as education (EdD), musical arts (DMA), and business (DBA). In comparison with programs leading to the PhD, those programs are more likely to maintain but modify requirements for research and may substitute practice focused expectations for traditional ones. They appear in the chart in a separate box along the continuum from an emphasis on research to an emphasis on practice.

But the presumption of the research category as a whole is that such degrees, despite their differences, include elements that may be considered characteristic of any research/scholarship doctorate: mastery of the discipline, awareness of its relation to related disciplines, a capacity for leadership, and a strong commitment to research—if not to performing research, at least to maintaining awareness of it. (As Table 7.1 indicates, the PhD *nearly always* requires research leading to a dissertation or other contribution to knowledge, while other research doctorates may allow instead a demonstration of research awareness.)

The annual National Science Foundation (NSF, 2020b) "Survey of Earned Doctorates" identifies research doctorates according to somewhat more restrictive criteria that require "completion of an original intellectual contribution in the form of a dissertation or an equivalent culminating project (e.g., musical composition)." The list of such degrees has been constant at 18 since 2008 (NSF, 2020a).

The "Professional Practice" Doctorate

As the name suggests, this doctorate is awarded by programs that provide "the knowledge and skills for the recognition, credential, or license required for professional practice." This broad category includes such familiar credentials as the JD (law), the MD (medicine), the DVM (veterinary medicine), and the DDS (dentistry). But it includes also credentials that have emerged largely within the past 20 years. The total time required to earn such a degree (including both preprofessional and professional education) must be "at least six full-time equivalent academic years."

The NSF (2020b) Survey of Earned Doctorates excludes such programs because they are "primarily intended as a degree for the practice of a profession." To be sure, one might argue that any graduate degree is in some sense "primarily intended" to lead to the practice of a profession. The difference lies partly in the assumption that professional practice enabled by a professional or practitioner doctorate may *preclude* original research. Clear? Not so much as it might seem. There are recipients of professional doctorates who conduct important research!

The "Other" Doctorates

Rather than a discrete category, the third column is meant to accommodate "other" degrees that do not correspond closely to either of the other two categories. For example, an institution may classify its EdD degree as *neither* "research/scholarship" *nor* "professional practice"—perhaps somewhere in between. As we shall observe later, that is one of the issues the EdD raises. "Other" doctorates are awarded relatively infrequently.

Such categories, broad as they are, may offer some clarity, but IPEDS data rarely appears at breakfast tables—even academic breakfast tables! And even those who familiarize themselves with the categories may still find themselves confused. As a Council of Graduate Schools (CGS) whitepaper observed 10 years ago, IPEDS definitions are not organized according to "the structure of graduate schools and graduate education." Moreover, "IPEDS allows institutions to determine how doctorates are categorized." And, alas, "similar degree programs may be reported in different ways by different institutions" (Bell, 2010, p. 3). That has not changed.

The Trend: Pros and Cons

Degrees described as "doctoral" may be difficult to assign even to the broad categories meant to describe them. Most criteria appear permeable. These days, there are more doctorates—and more kinds of doctorates—than one can shake a mace at. Seeking real confusion? First, focus on the health care disciplines that once designated the baccalaureate or master's degree as the qualification for licensure and professional practice but now prefer or require a doctoral degree. Now consider disciplines that have rebranded a PhD as a *practitioner's* degree. Some degrees that once qualified for inclusion in the NSF census no longer do!

Two in One

Further confusion arises from the fact that some disciplines otherwise similar to those now requiring the doctorate have chosen to retain the master's as the qualifying degree. In fact, two disciplines within the same professional organization, the American Speech-Language-Hearing Association (ASHA), have taken different paths. Those seeking to practice as licensed audiologists now earn the AuD or the PhD, while speech pathologists most often qualify for practice by earning an MS, MA, or MEd.

Inexorable? Or Not?

Is the trend toward a "universal doctorate" inexorable? The answer appears to be "not necessarily."

Within the fine arts, it began at one time to appear as though the MFA degree, long regarded as a capstone credential for practicing artists, had joined the endangered species list. It seemed likely that the doctorate would in time eventually replace the MFA (Berrett, 2012). One prompt was the European practice of awarding the doctorate to advanced arts students who could demonstrate a commitment to both scholarship and creativity. The other arose from the practical concern that recipients of the U.S. master's degree might suffer by comparison with more highly credentialed European colleagues—or, for that matter, with their domestic colleagues seeking promotion and tenure within "doctoral" disciplines.

Where do we stand now? It appears that the challenge for such a doctorate may lie in maintaining a differentiation between the creative and scholarly paths in the arts while requiring the "original contribution" that justifies a research degree. As Berrett (2012) observed, "People on both sides of the debate are trying to sort through how a dissertation in their discipline can best meet the expectation that doctoral-level scholarship will contribute new knowledge to a field while also remaining true to the act of creating art."

Since Berrett's 2012 report, the number of U.S. fine arts practitioner doctorates has increased. But the increase has not been dramatic, and there are signs of a pushback. One reason may lie in a disinclination on the part of some practicing artists to undertake the scholarship required for a doctorate. A more powerful reason may lie in the continued credibility of the MFA as a talisman for accomplished creative practitioners. It is the credential for *artists*. By this perspective, the recipient of an MFA affirms a career track clearly different from that of a scholar in fields such as art history or art therapy.

Notably, a relatively recent perspective on the subject offered by the board of the directors of the College Art Association (CAA), a 2015 "Statement on Terminal Degree Programs in the Visual Arts and Design," seeks a judicious balance, affirming on the one hand that "the Master of Fine Arts (MFA) *is the terminal degree in studio art practice*" (para. 1), while recognizing "the existence [of doctoral degrees] that incorporate art and/or design practice" and "the unique prospects such programs offer for research-intensive study in the visual arts and design" (para. 3).

In one way or another, every discipline that offers graduate degrees has confronted or will confront the issue of the doctorate. But the terms of that confrontation differ from one discipline to the next. There are challenges concerning the EdD, for instance, that are very different from those related to practitioner doctorates in health fields. And there are challenges even within health fields that are particular to one provider but not another.

The Doctoral Degrees and the Questions They Prompt

Given the institutional prerogative (within limits) to categorize doctoral programs, attempting to account for every variety would be unrealistic. The result of this prerogative is that there are more than 50 research doctorate categories (some with multiple designations) and more than 30 professional doctorate categories. But because a few prominent categories account for most doctoral degrees awarded, considering these categories can suggest some questions—and perhaps a few answers.

The PhD

As the IPEDS categories suggest, three factors have contributed to the necessity for greater clarity concerning the research doctorate.

- Because institutions may characterize their doctoral degrees more or less at their own discretion, any consensus about what defines a PhD is rickety. Most institutions distinguish the "applied doctorate" from the PhD, but the PhD is now awarded by some institutions in applied disciplines (*applied* mathematics, *applied* developmental psychology, *applied* life sciences). Such degrees will not appear in the NSF census of research doctorates, but the graduates of such programs receive diplomas that read "Doctor of Philosophy."
- The proliferation of practitioner doctorates in fields as distant as law and physical therapy has led to inexplicable variations. It is an irony of history that those who have earned a research PhD—the original "doctorate"—may be denied use of the title of "doctor" so that it may be reserved exclusively for physicians who have earned practitioner degrees.
- Many research PhD programs prepare students for employment in nonacademic sectors, an increasingly popular option given the overall decline in academic tenure-track positions and the apparent overproduction of doctorates in fields such as the biosciences.

Close—but No Consensus
A discussion conducted by the Council of Graduate Schools (CGS) in 2016–2017 (with support from Lumina Foundation) considered whether participants might reach agreement on at least a few clear learning outcomes that would define the 21st-century doctorate in general and the research PhD in particular. Could a summary comparable to how the master's degree is defined in the DQP be achieved?

The potential advantages of such an agreement were clear enough. For example, explicit outcomes could

> help doctoral students from diverse backgrounds weigh the costs and benefits of their educational investments, or help universities specify the learning goals of graduate assistantships. Doctoral outcomes can also help programs more purposefully prepare their students for a variety of career paths. (CGS, 2017, p. 1)

Elements of a consensus emerged during the discussion, but differences in perspective among participants representing diverse institutions finally made it impossible to affirm them in a statement offering some practical advantage. The final report by the CGS (2017) on the project reiterated the "evident" benefits of outcomes but voiced skepticism as to whether a "degree of consensus" might be found even *within* institutions—one of "many unanswered questions."

A Rather Recent Muddle
This lack of a consensus is of fairly recent vintage. As recently as the 1970s, most PhD programs required a working knowledge of one or more second languages (on the premise that meaningful research would be international in scope), significant independent research under faculty guidance, and the completion of a dissertation that could claim to offer a meaningful contribution to knowledge. Although a "meaningful contribution" remains essential for a research doctorate as defined by the NSF, many PhD programs now disregard some of these requirements and provide workarounds for others.

What Can Be Done for the PhD?
In challenge may lie opportunity. In fact, recognizing that the academy may be losing its role as the principal employer of PhDs could be a good thing for doctoral recipients, for the economy, and for the university. But for that to happen, as Leonard Cassuto and Robert A. Weisbuch (2020) have said, "We need a PhD that looks outside the walls of the university, not one that turns inward" (para. 7).

To this end, Katrina L. Rogers (2020) has proposed several constructive steps to improve graduate education that would improve doctoral education in the humanities in particular. She suggests an increased emphasis on career preparation, an expansion in the definition of scholarship, stronger partnerships between programs and current and potential nonacademic employers, courses that teach the application of research skills in the marketplace, the celebration of doctoral alumni who have succeeded in nonacademic appointments, and increased recruitment to doctoral study of the historically underrepresented (Rogers, 2020).

Some of these steps are suggested even more recently by the February 2021 report from a "Humanities Doctoral Education Advisory Working Group" at Yale University. It begins by acknowledging some hard facts. For instance, while most students who enroll in Yale's Graduate School of Arts and Sciences aspire to an academic career, "fewer than half . . . obtain tenure-track jobs" (Yale, 2021, p. 5).

The report calls for greater flexibility overall, for expanding the criteria for "acceptable dissertations," and for inviting students to propose alternate paths to meeting requirements (e.g., obtaining a command of coding might satisfy a language requirement). The number of those admitted to programs might be aligned more closely with the employment prospects of graduates, and pedagogical training might be given more prominence. One of the most striking of the report's recommendations asks faculty members to place greater emphasis on advising—to collaborate with other faculty members in offering guidance, to take the initiative in scheduling advising appointments with students, and to work with the university's career office so as to encourage students to consider and prepare for a wide range of employment possibilities (Yale, 2021).

But beyond managing the PhD more resourcefully, there's also the need for institutions that award more than one kind of doctorate to make it clear that the research PhD, unlike applied doctorates and "practitioner PhDs," is a *graduate* degree, a capstone credential that signifies both mastery of a body of professional knowledge and a readiness to provide leadership. Professional doctoral programs that focus on practical knowledge and skills should be more clearly defined in terms of the entry-level practitioner competencies they represent.

The need for such consensus has become more urgent at a time when respect for expertise has been undermined by facile misrepresentations and groundless conspiracy theories—that is, by lies. These days, a clear appreciation for the "expert's" degree is of greater importance than ever. Might the discussion summarized in the report on the CGS project offer a point of departure for a follow-up discussion?

The EdD

The most familiar alternative to the PhD as a capstone degree, the *Educationis Doctor,* or EdD, occupies an uncomfortable position between the PhD, with its research emphasis, and the professional doctorate, with its vocational emphasis. That amorphous "other" category in the IPEDS listing might have been created specifically to accommodate certain EdDs. But the position of the degree in the educational spectrum has been imprecise from the start.

The intent behind the creation of the EdD was reasonable. A doctorate *in education* would offer advanced professionals—system superintendents, principals of large schools, instructors in schools of education, and the like— a pragmatic alternative to the PhD. Students would develop relevant expertise without having to meet requirements of questionable usefulness to them. But what may have seemed reasonable in theory embodied an unfortunate distinction in practice, one between the achievement of intellectual distinction through a contribution to knowledge (the PhD) and the strengthening of educational leadership through study within the field (the EdD). That distinction can be and should be difficult to make.

There have been robust efforts to defend the EdD and there are many distinguished recipients, including the First Lady of the United States. Many of those who have earned the EdD doubtless would vouch for its distinctive value. But an increasing inconsistency in how the degree is defined and awarded has compounded the structural defect some have perceived to lie at its heart.

As Arthur Levine observed in a scathing 2005 report, *Educating School Leaders,* the EdD

> is reserved by some institutions for practitioners, but others award it to academics and researchers as well. The PhD is by contrast defined as a degree for scholars, but some institutions award it to practitioners. Some universities award only one of the degrees. Some offer both. The rules for awarding EdDs and PhDs sometimes differ even among departments within the same university.

Levine concludes that the EdD has outlived its usefulness.

A symptom of the enigma may be found in the difference between how the degree is typically marketed—as an educational capstone for experienced, mature administrators—and how it is often described, namely, in terms of what it is *not.* An EdD degree program does *not* emphasize or require independent research. It does *not* require an original contribution to knowledge on the part of recipients. It does *not* demand the cultural depth (second language competency, broad liberal learning) that the PhD has traditionally signified.

Defining the degree becomes particularly complicated when an institution awards both the EdD and the PhD *in education*. An explanatory web page for Northeastern University's graduate school of education quotes Joseph McNabb, "a professor of practice" who makes a valiant effort at defining the difference. According to McNabb, "With a PhD, [students are] reviewing the research, seeing a gap in the literature, and generating new knowledge based on a theory or hypothesis [while] conversely an EdD student starts with a problem of practice and [works to learn] the skills it will take to resolve that complex problem of practice" (O'Connor, 2019, para. 5). There is one other difference at Northeastern. The Doctor of Education degree has a residency requirement. The PhD in education does not. But the difference sits uneasily atop a tenuous distinction now a century old.

Clearer (but no more reassuring) is the suggestion that the two degrees may be differentiated according to who chooses which. An EdD is for "those pursuing educational leadership roles" while a PhD in education is "designed to prepare graduates for research and teaching roles" (O'Connor, 2019, para. 4). Might not the recipient of a PhD serve as an educational leader? Must an EdD recipient avoid research?

Perhaps there remains an opportunity to define the EdD as a credential particularly well suited for an environment that sorely needs leadership concerning educational standards, opportunities, and risks, particularly with regard to K–12 schools. If colleges and universities were to redefine the EdD in terms of rigorous, relevant education concerning school leadership, pedagogical reform, instructional technology, and the like, they might develop a competitive opportunity for themselves, for their students, and for society.

But it may be time to consider whether the credential currently on offer should be maintained indefinitely. Arthur Levine's (2005) view of programs in school leadership as "a race to the bottom" continues to reverberate. And it may be too late to recover the idealistic vision that prompted the creation of the *Educationis Doctor.*

The Professional Doctorate

We have described the prompts behind the recent development of additional professional doctorates—increasing complexity within the various professions, increasing demands on professionals, and an increasing need for cross-specialization collaboration. But we have not yet addressed the questions these new credentials have raised. To what extent have the changes been ones of nomenclature rather than of substance? Have the new professional doctoral programs in health care and other disciplines been developed to offer greater challenge and more advanced preparation than the master's (or baccalaureate) programs they have succeeded? Have they become in some ways different in kind?

It's confusing.

As we have noted, professional doctorates are *not* graduate credentials, at least not in the sense that graduate credentials imply *advanced* study within a discipline that leads to "a career in academia or research." For example, the Doctor of Physical Therapy (DPT) degree in the United States has replaced the master's degree as the basic qualification in the discipline. But the new degree, like the old one, simply enables recipients to seek a license that will authorize them to practice as physical therapists—not to teach the discipline or to contribute to its knowledge base. The distinction between a practitioner degree and a genuine graduate credential is made clear by programs that offer both. At The Ohio State University (2020), for instance, students aspiring to a career in physical therapy research or as an instructor in the discipline may apply to a "dual degree" program, the DPT/PhD.

Similarly, the MD, while a well-respected credential, is by definition a vocational degree that qualifies its recipient, once licensed, either to undertake general practice directly or, much more likely, to undertake an internship and eventually a residency under supervision in a specialty. By contrast, a related *graduate* qualification, the MD/PhD, enables the recipient (according to the Association of American Medical Colleges [AAMC]) "to experience the passion of solving a patient's medical struggles while pursuing research that may define the mechanism of that patient's disease and may ultimately translate into a clinical cure for the disease" (AAMC, 2020, para. 1). MD/PhDs become "physician-scientists."

Defining the Degree

For the most part, professional disciplines have taken seriously the challenge of defining preparation for the professional doctorate as distinctly more challenging, more thorough, more engaged with the practice and awareness of research, and more attuned to the obligations of professional leadership. Such commitments lie behind a constructive approach to defining the degree, a 2008 statement by the Association of Specialized and Professional Accreditors (ASPA). Following consultations with colleagues representing what was then known as NASULGC (the National Association of State Universities and Land-Grant Colleges, now APLU, the Association of Public and Land-Grant Universities), ASPA proposed "demonstrable end points of doctoral study that should characterize any professional doctorate" (ASPA, 2008, p. 1). Such "end points" include readiness for "professional practice appropriate to the stated purpose of the degree," an ability to make use of current research and "ideally" a readiness to pursue research of use to the profession, the capacity to work "in both an interdisciplinary and interprofessional manner," an "advanced level of communication, critical thinking, and problem solving skills," and a "demonstrated ability to identify and address population based issues affecting the health and well-being of society" (ASPA, 2008, p. 1).

The recommendations that follow add clarity to these broad "characteristics." "Optimally" a doctoral program will require "a minimum of three full academic years beyond the baccalaureate." Expectations as to the conduct and use of scholarship should be explicit. Programs must be given institutional resources and commitment appropriate to "a professional level program." And the efficacy of the degree in enabling recipients to secure professional appointments and "status" should be clearly documented.

Whether such credentials routinely enjoy the credibility their creators have sought may be a matter of concern in some cases. Consider (once again) audiology. Prior to the beginning of the 21st century, as we have noted, the qualification for practice most often was an MS. Then, early in the 21st century, the profession navigated a challenging transition to the "professional doctorate," the AuD. Now, roughly 20 years later, another transition appears to be taking place. If you consult the FAQ page of ASHA (2020) to ask, "How can I earn an AuD or PhD?" you will be directed to a web page focused exclusively on the PhD.

And therein lies another problem. If the PhD is itself offered as a "professional" or "practitioner" doctorate, distinguishing between the research degree and its more vocationally centered counterparts becomes even more difficult.

In Sum

As the "takeaways" will suggest, the confusion that has developed around the credential most directly identified with expertise represents a dilemma both for postsecondary education and for society more broadly. Institutions that educate themselves and their students to make meaningful distinctions among the doctoral programs they and other providers offer will serve their own advantage and benefit their students. But as doctoral degree recipients of all kinds increasingly find careers beyond the academy they will be serving the broader public interest as well.

Takeaways

In the absence of a national credentials framework (such as those in Europe or Australia) that would clarify what doctoral degrees at different levels signify, institutions must be as clear as possible about the credentials they award and recognize: their respective objectives and the professional opportunities to which they promise access. Administrators, faculty members, and academic advisors should do the following:

- Remain aware of current information, discipline by discipline, concerning their institution's capstone degrees—or those to which they direct their graduates. What has changed recently or is likely to change soon? What new opportunities are emerging? And how should they be appropriately categorized? What additional providers are entering the market? Are they attracting underserved cohorts to doctoral study or competing for the same students who otherwise would choose from traditional institutions? Such analysis should guide the institution's evaluation of any doctorates that it offers and its consideration of opportunities for the initiation of new doctoral programs.

- Encourage your sector association (APLU, AAU, AASCU, etc.) to consider sponsoring or collaborating in discussions leading to a credentials framework that would clearly define and categorize doctoral degrees according to explicit criteria.

- Respond to the shift taking place in the employment of PhD recipients as the trend away from academic hiring to opportunities in the private sector accelerates. Competitive PhD programs will prepare students for a broader range of employment. And savvy institutions will work with organizations that hire PhDs so as to align their programs more closely with a range of employer needs.

- Recognize challenges likely to arise when there is need to discontinue doctoral programs. When an institution's current offerings prove less appealing for students and less responsive to the needs of the economy than those the institution *might* be offering, some programs arguably should be terminated so that others may be initiated. But political opposition in such cases from faculty, alumni, and disciplinary organizations can be formidable, and the process of program closure can be lengthy.

- Provide straightforward information to candidates about the challenges likely to await recipients of the "liberal arts and sciences" PhD. Not even the most distinguished institutions can promise that their graduates will find academic employment. Too often, in the biosciences, for instance, doctoral recipients find themselves working in less well compensated postdoctoral fellowships for years in the hope of eventually finding an academic job (Iasevoli, 2015). On the other hand, competitive institutions that clarify the distinctive values of their programs and emphasize their quality can better prepare their students to meet increasing needs beyond the academy for individuals who have earned doctoral research degrees.

- Undertake an environmental scan to determine the need for further professional doctoral degrees. The startup costs for new programs in health care disciplines such as physical therapy can be substantial, but a doctoral program in occupational therapy (the OTD) may (as one example) fill needs no less urgent and prove considerably more affordable.

8

NONDEGREE CREDENTIALS

Certificates

Having examined the most familiar credentials, college degrees, we now begin to consider the alternate credentials that enable students not seeking degrees to develop functional skills and competencies aligned with labor market needs. Such credentials have recently become unprecedentedly popular. In this chapter, we focus on for-credit and not-for-credit certificates, the most familiar of such credentials. In chapter 9, we will examine certifications and other credentials such as occupational licenses, coding bootcamp records, and corporate qualifications that are likely to be less familiar to administrators, faculty members, and academic advisors. Finally, in chapter 10, we will discuss apprenticeships. The three chapters agree that savvy institutions will make appropriate NDCs available to their students through programs that encourage and enable their pursuit.

The Moment Has Come

"Alternative Credentials on the Rise" asserted the headline for Paul Fain's August 27, 2020, article that declared the "moment" had arrived for short-term, online, mostly "non-degree" credentials (NDCs). Fain (2020) explained that two principal advantages—"less time, less cost"—together with the added advantage of clearer focus on employable skills, had created "strong consumer interest."

A Trend Accelerated

Interest in NDCs has been growing for more than a decade. Although it is difficult to determine enrollments in such programs (the U.S. Department of Education tracks only for-credit certificates offered by Title IV providers), enrollments that have been documented make clear a notable expansion in the number and visibility of NDCs—a phenomenon that prompted the creation in 2018 of a research group based at George Washington

University. (The coauthors of this book have been members of the group since its inception.) But more recently the conspicuous advantages of these credentials—their promise of a direct path to employment through in-demand skills delivered through highly focused, short-term programs—have become more appealing. The most recent estimate for the award of noncredit credentials in a single year: 3.7 million in 2020 according to Opportunity America (Jacoby, 2021).

Acknowledging the influence of the pandemic, Fain raised two questions. First, are such credentials in fact living up to their promise of offering "alternative pathways to well-paying jobs?" Second, would degree programs regain the competitive advantage they had enjoyed before the 2020 shutdown or would continued growth in the NDC share of the educational market be likely (Fain, 2020)?

The advantages of these credentials—and the particular importance of certain advantages for those considering them—point to the likelihood of a sustained phenomenon. A Strada Education Network study in June 2020 showed that characteristics of NDCs align with the educational priorities of many. For 38% of those considering an NDC, "relevance" was a first priority. Other students identified efficiency (28%), value (24%), or stackability (10%) as priorities. Of course, such priorities are not entirely discrete. Value, for instance, may emerge from relevance and stackability. But none of these advantages is likely to become less appealing in a post-pandemic world (Strada Education Network, 2020).

New Opportunities, New Partnerships

One indicator of sustained interest in nondegree programs appears in new institutional partnerships, such as the two most notable in 2020, that between the University of Arizona and Ashford University (for-profit, online) and that between the University of Massachusetts and Brandman University (nonprofit, predominantly online). Such alliances may offer large universities a faster track to an expanded presence in online education in general and to the delivery of nondegree programs in particular.

An alternate fast track to the offering of NDCs for some other institutions may lie instead in their making greater use of the knowledge and experience available in their continuing education divisions. Entrepreneurial by definition, continuing education leaders often are able to be more flexible in terms of program scheduling (creating calendars responsive to student needs), student services such as clarifying pathways or offering career guidance (where available), and access (resolving prerequisite issues, tailoring programs to specific constituencies). Continuing education professionals are also likely to have developed close relationships with the employer community.

SIDEBAR
What's a "Microcredential"?
We have avoided this familiar term in favor of NDC. Both terms point to career-focused credentials other than degrees, but NDCs may or may not be "micro." Some certificate programs require as much as three years' study. Credential Engine (2021) defines a micro-credential as "an online educational credential that covers more than a single course but is less than a full degree" (p. 18). To make matters even more complicated, providers are using different terms for the credentials they offer. Udacity offers "nanodegrees," Coursera, "MasterTrack certificates," Swayam, "diploma programs."

The most significant constraint so far as NDCs are concerned has arisen from a limitation on federal financial aid. Currently, only students enrolled in undergraduate degree programs at accredited institutions have been able to qualify for Pell grants to support pursuit of an NDC. Although it is risky to predict Congressional priorities, discussions of Pell funding for short-term offerings (Kreighbaum, 2019) have suggested the possibility that such aid might eventually be extended to cover students not enrolled in degree programs who are seeking an NDC. In April 2021, recommendations for just such an extension attracted considerable attention. The argument was that extending such grants to students seeking efficient pathways to employment would benefit the recipients, their eventual employers, and the economy in general.

There are skeptics, to be sure, who argue that such a move could paradoxically *exacerbate* the very inequalities it is meant to address (Bustillo & Laitenen, 2021). Given such funding, hiring organizations may benefit through avoiding training costs, but entry-level workers may find themselves in low-paying, dead-end jobs with high turnover rates (Loprest & Sick, 2018).

But what seems clear is that savvy administrators, faculty members, and academic advisors should pay attention to NDCs as an attractive option for many students, either as an alternative to degrees or as a supplement before, during, or following degree programs. Some NDCs may be worth considering as in-program options. Others (such as certifications) must be found outside academic institutions. But the particular advantages of particular NDCs should be understood and weighed carefully by anyone in a position of academic leadership.

Opportunities in a Complex Environment

We have observed the confusion that can arise from the wide assortment of degrees. The chaotic environment of NDCs can make that of degrees appear well-ordered by comparison! But it is nonetheless important to decipher that environment. Employers need to know which credentials offer the most reliable indicators of competency for hiring and advancement. Advisors want to offer reliable counsel as to which credentials are most worth pursuing. Policymakers may want to consider allocating funding to support solutions to workforce needs. Educational institutions should consider which NDCs not yet on offer might provide their students with timely opportunities. Most important, individuals need to know which programs are most likely to lead them economically and efficiently to the accomplishment of their goals.

But all of these challenges are far more difficult than they should be! Just as college degrees emerged in the United States prior to the development of institutional accreditation, so, too, has the proliferation of NDCs outpaced the development of platforms for quality assurance. If on-the-job performance by recipients of these credentials represents the most reliable measure of credential quality, it is by no means clear that existing oversight mechanisms are adequate to the job. Judicious decision-making both by institutions and by students will become more likely only as data gathering on the value of NDCs (i.e., their return on investment) begins to keep pace with their growth in number and variety. We are not yet to that point.

To understand these challenges and opportunities more fully, we should begin by separating the several major types of NDCs: certificates (for-credit and not-for-credit), our focus in this chapter, and those we cover in chapters 9 and 10, such as certifications and apprenticeships. The distinctive features of each are summarized in the Workcred chart (Figure 8.1).

We should begin by acknowledging that some characteristics are common to all NDCs. Nearly all are occupationally focused. Some provide broad preparation for career entry and advancement, while others signify a highly focused skill or set of skills, but NDCs can be found across all occupations at all educational levels—undergraduate to graduate to postgraduate—as an alternative to college degrees. Most may be earned in less than a year—often in much less time. Most (not all!) are less expensive than degrees. Compared to degree programs, a high percentage of NDCs are available entirely online.

However, as the chart indicates, the differences between the NDCs are as significant as their similarities. Some are offered in conjunction with an academic or occupational program. These include many certificates, most badges, and some apprenticeships. An individual receives instruction from a provider and earns a credential from that provider. By contrast, while certifications require some form of preparation, either academic or vocational, they are awarded apart from that preparation and the institution or organization that has provided it. In most cases certifications signify satisfactory performance on a third-party assessment, which may be written, oral, or performance based.

Figure 8.1. How do credentials differ?

	CERTIFICATE*	CERTIFICATION	DEGREE	LICENSE
Awarded by	Education and training providers, employers, labor unions, and industry associations	Industry certification bodies	Education institutions	Government agencies
Awarded for	An exam at the end of a training or education course or a one-time assessment	Third-party, independent competency assessment	Course of study	Meeting requirements of an occupation
Indicates	Education/knowledge/ skills	Skill mastery/ competencies	Education, successfully passed courses	Legal permission
Time to complete	Variable, generally less than 2 years	Variable	Variable, generally 2 years or more	Variable
Time and renewal requirements	Often no time limit, no renewal requirement	Time-limited, includes recertification	No time limit, no renewal requirement	Time-limited, renewal generally required
Revocation process	Cannot be revoked	Can be revoked for incompetence or unethical behavior	Cannot be revoked	Can be revoked for incompetence or unethical behavior
Examples	CNC Machinist, Zurich Insurance Apprenticeship	CompTIA Cybersecurity Analyst, Certified Energy Auditor, Medical Laboratory Scientist, MLS(ASCP)^{CM}	Bachelor of Science in Engineering, Associate of Arts in Business Administration	Electrician, Professional Engineer, Registered Nurse
Standard for accreditation	ANSI/ASTM E2659-18, a globally recognized American National Standard	ANSI/ISO/IEC 17024:2012, an international and national standard	National, regional, or programmatic	State law defines scope of practice

* There are many types of certificates. Some examples include: certificates of participation, certificates of achievement, certificates of completion for apprenticeship, and assessment-based certificates.

Many certifications also have codes of conduct/ethics that must be observed if certification is to be maintained. Both certifications and state licenses are time limited and must be renewed periodically.

This mix is one that, properly understood, can serve well the diverse needs of learners, because in addition to the "just-in-time" needs of that market, there are many "just-for-me" advantages of NDCs. PhD recipients may seek an NDC to make a career shift. Students pursing a baccalaureate degree may enhance the competitiveness of their degree with an NDC. Those not attracted to traditional postsecondary education may find NDCs a welcome alternative.

Because many such credentials may align with and enhance other credentials, including degrees, they offer not only different paths to entering the workforce, but also platforms leading to further learning, career advancement, and career change. For individuals with a bachelor's degree, an NDC can lead to an earnings premium (Ewert & Kominski, 2014; Markow et al., 2017). For those without a degree, short-term credentials may offer access to employment or to additional study leading to the award of a degree. For instance, while someone who has earned Automotive Service Excellence (ASE) certification should qualify for an entry-level position as an automotive technician, one who proceeds to add a certificate in marketing may become a service manager. Similarly, while medical assistants who earn the medical assistant certification may be able to choose from attractive positions in health care, an advanced certification that qualifies them for academic credit could lead to the award of an associate degree and to even more desirable appointments.

Instead of a predetermined order for such opportunities (a recognizable hierarchy or fixed "stack") NDCs can connect with other credentials in multiple ways. This may be our final opportunity to mention the analogy to Lego bricks, which differ in terms of the number of studs they have. More studs? More potential for connections!

It is also worth mentioning that some students initially reluctant to pursue a degree may find in the successful pursuit of a NDC the confidence to enter a degree program leading to even greater returns. "Even roundabout individual pathways can produce positive economic outcomes" (Coffey et al., 2019, p. 7).

Advantages and Applications

There is an impressive variety of nondegree credentials. Although it is important that students understand the differences among them and limit their choices to programs offered by reliable providers who can document student success, it is also important that they appreciate at the outset the advantages NDCs can offer in combination with other programs.

Adding Value With NDCs

A former Australian vice chancellor makes the point that students completing a liberal arts degree "may gain quite a bit by completing a . . . course that focuses on specific technical, practical skills and provides hands-on specific industry experience" (Temmerman, 2019, para. 12). "Hybrid" programs that enable a student to earn both a degree and a certificate can offer that student "a competitive edge when applying for a post" (Temmerman, 2019, para. 14).

That perspective from Down Under applies no less to the United States. While some students will find NDCs an alternative to traditional associate or bachelor's degrees, others will earn an NDC *while pursuing a degree* so as to increase their competitiveness. Brandon Busteed, the president of Kaplan University Partners, has introduced the term *credigree* for hybrid programs that enrich degree programs with certifications and certificates. "To be both broadly educated and specifically skilled is a graduate's ideal outcome" (Busteed, 2020, para. 2).

One advantage for institutions of blended programs is that most require little restructuring, curricular retooling, or significant investment in additional infrastructure. There are exceptions, of course, but many institutions can offer such blends simply by (a) endorsing (and documenting) their value, (b) offering degree seekers a choice of appropriate nondegree credential programs (not all of which must be provided by the institution), and (c) enabling advisors to guide students to combinations likely to serve their needs.

Because of their already established priority on career preparation, community colleges have a particular advantage. While they may offer NDCs as alternatives to the associate degree, their workforce-oriented associate degree programs may incorporate NDCs such as certifications. Students thus can earn both a degree and an industry qualification. For example, Ivy Tech Community College in Indiana incorporates industry certifications into its information technology associate degree programs. Students can prepare for certification exams as part of their coursework (ITCC, 2020). But community colleges also can offer discrete programs designed specifically to prepare students for certification exams. For instance, the Community College of Philadelphia offers a 225-hour course that "will prepare you for the Cisco® CCNA 200-301 exam" (CCOP, 2020).

Finding Pivot Points in NDCs

Hybrid degrees may appeal largely to students already pursuing a degree, while standalone NDCs are more likely to attract students seeking alternatives to degree programs. But employees experiencing volatility in the labor market are likely to find both options appealing. An economy that values adaptability and opportunity above job security and employee loyalty encourages continued learning leading to fresh marketable skills. Earning a certificate or certification may extend a career for some, while others may earn an NDC to find a bridge to a different organization—or a different career. Of course, for this to happen NDC programs must be visible, accessible, and economical. Because many employees have little or no connection with an institution of higher education, institutions must find ways to reach out to them.

Colleges and universities are not starting from scratch. While traditional degrees may remain the most widely acknowledged credentials, there are already many students benefiting from the alternatives we have described (Brown & Kurzweil, 2017). Indeed, data from the 2016 Adult Training and Education Survey (USDE, 2018) indicates that of the 58% of the workforce holding some postsecondary credential, approximately one third had earned an NDC. Regardless of the strength or weakness of an economy, when the pressing needs of employers are going unmet, a heightened commitment to NDCs would appear to be a priority.

Finding a Safety Net in NDCs

For increasing numbers of students, NDCs may offer a satisfying initial experience with postsecondary education. However, there are many other students who will find an academic lifeline in NDCs. Those who enroll in college without clear goals may find themselves struggling. If poor grades, a lack of motivation, or a loss of financial support should prompt them to withdraw, they may leave with considerable debt without having anything to show for their effort. For the 36 million who fall into this category, earning a nondegree short-term credential may offer ready access to employment—a vital "recovery."

Others know they do not want to pursue a traditional degree program (at least not within the near term) but are unaware of alternatives that can offer access to opportunity. Reminded that most individuals with *no* postsecondary credentials face a profound limitation on their lifetime earnings, students may find that an NDC can offer a practical, realistic portal to remunerative employment. Moreover, students who gain confidence through earning an NDC may discover an aptitude for further education. No credentials (we repeat) need be "terminal."

Finally there are those who are part of the 18% of the workforce holding both a postsecondary degree and an NDC. As we have noted, both students pursing a more competitive degree and degree holders seeking a career change are ideal audiences for hybrid degrees.

What's the downside? NDCs may offer a lifeline, but there is also a concern that the lifeline could in some circumstances perpetuate workplace inequalities by dropping recipients into low-wage, deadend positions. Few credentials of any kind come with guarantees. Because NDCs can prepare people for a particularly wide range of occupations with particularly disparate economic outcomes, recognizing and understanding which NDCs are more likely to lead to well-paying jobs or to promising career pathways is particularly critical. Hence we should endeavor to guarantee that all students and prospective students receive both relevant information and well-informed advice. Otherwise, a lifeline can become a snare.

Certificates: The Familiar Standard

The term *certificate* covers a wide range of meanings, from a document distributed to recognize participation in a day-long community seminar to a credential attesting to significant learning gained over many months (perhaps more than two years) that qualifies the recipient for employment or advancement. There is a wide range of educational providers as well, including professional associations, for-profit storefront operations, accredited colleges, and corporate employers. It is "more familiar" for two reasons. First, many (though not all) postsecondary institutions offer some type of certificate. Second, certificates are similar to degrees in that they document learning and do not require periodic renewal. (See Figure 8.1 for more details.)

For-Credit Certificates

For more than a decade, for-credit certificates at the sub-baccalaureate level have been touted as "the most direct path to college completion and career success" (Complete College America [CCA], 2010, p. i) and a particular benefit to "those with less formal academic preparation" (Carnevale et al., 2012, p. 36). These advantages have been repeatedly reaffirmed—in presidential debates and State of the Union addresses, in foundation initiatives, and in Congressional action. The result has been a modest increase in the award of for-credit certificates and a modest uptick in online certificate programs. The advantages of such credentials are compelling:

- **There is a considerable variety**. Because they differ widely in length and in the commitment required, from programs of one semester or less to those requiring more than three years, students may choose options that reflect their career aspirations without incurring unwanted financial obligations or neglecting other priorities.
- **They serve many purposes**. Recent high school graduates can earn a certificate as an efficient path to employment or as first step toward a college degree. Professionals may earn a certificate as preparation for certification or licensing. Employees seeking a change or experiencing layoffs may find that certificates enable them to qualify for other opportunities.
- **They can provide pathways**. Most for-credit certificates are offered at the sub-baccalaureate level. Credits earned may apply to requirements for associate or bachelor's degrees if institutions create pathways that invite their acceptance.
- **They are especially useful within a few fields**. Although the range of fields where certificates can be useful is increasing, at present they tend to be concentrated in a few areas (Markow et al., 2017) such as health care. The home health aide certificate appears to be the most commonly awarded, followed by certificates in paralegal work, phlebotomy, and medical billing and coding.

- **They are economical**. Although students not enrolled in a degree program may be ineligible for federal financial aid, students who *are* pursuing a degree may qualify for federal assistance as they also pursue a certificate. When compared to associate and baccalaureate programs in the same or similar fields, certificates typically cost less, require less time for completion, have fewer academic requirements, and offer greater scheduling flexibility.

In addition to sub-baccalaureate certificates, there are graduate certificates available in a broad variety of fields (e.g., web design, creative writing, health sciences, education) that may appeal to students who "decide to forego a master's degree but still want a competitive edge" (Northeastern University, 2019, para. 3). A typical graduate certificate requires 12 to 14 credit hours and can be earned in one year or less. Some of these certificates may correspond to certain master's program requirements and may be accepted for credit toward a master's degree, but graduate certificate students ordinarily do not qualify for federally guaranteed financial aid. (By the way, U.S. graduate certificates should not be confused with international certificates such as the GradCert awarded as alternatives to the bachelor's degree.)

Factors Bearing on Certificate Value
Remaining fairly constant have been four important factors bearing on the value of certificates: the institution awarding them, the field in which they are earned, the location or region in which they are earned, and how substantial the program appears to be, which is often a function of its length.

Institutions that are accredited by USDE-recognized accreditors and are authorized by the USDE to offer Title IV federal student aid may enable their students seeking degrees and for-credit certificates to qualify for aid. "Non-Title IV" credentials include those awarded by institutions without such authorization and those offered by Title IV institutions through their noncredit or continuing education divisions. Quality programs and credentials may be found on both sides of the "Title IV" divide, but credentials from Title IV institutions are likely to be more affordable (given consideration for federal financial assistance), more widely recognized, and more often accepted by other Title IV institutions for transfer.

The value of certificates, like that of degrees, depends heavily on the field. That's common sense. Competencies in high demand bring greater rewards. Hence administrators, faculty members, and academic advisors should remain aware of workforce data showing important differentials so as to make that information available to students—while recognizing that some students may find their greatest satisfaction in fields that are not among the most highly remunerated.

Location matters. The value of any certificate—or of any credential, for that matter—will depend in part on employer demand in the context of local and regional economies. For that reason, it is important that administrators, faculty members, and academic advisors remain aware of the earnings potential of graduates awarded specific credentials in their areas. States may cite national figures. In 2020, for instance, the Department of Higher Education in Ohio shared a bellwether study on earnings potential by the Georgetown University Center on Education and the Workforce showing that certificate recipients (a) earn an average of 20% more that recipients of only a high school degree, (b) become "more employable," and (c) may find themselves on "stepping stones to college degrees." But the more important point for Ohioans would be that such findings are reflected in their own access to success.

Length matters. Most for-credit certificates may be completed in *less than one* academic year, but some require *more than one but less than two* academic years and others may require *more than two* (but less than four) academic years. Even though current growth in certificate enrollments favors short-term programs, returns on educational investment appear to favor recipients of long-term certificates.

"Appear" is an important qualifier, however. For one thing, federal reporting required for IPEDS does not ask institutions to distinguish shorter (300–600 clock hour) programs from longer (600–900 hour) programs. For another, "some colleges award very short-term certificates only on a non-credit basis or make them available on a non-credit basis as well as on a for-credit basis" (CCA, 2010, p. 3). The data might be more reliable. But there remains a clear bottom line. A 2016 study by Di Xu and Madeline Trimble (2016) analyzing the "positive impact of attaining a long-term certificate on an individual's probability of employment and earnings" found that, in general, a greater investment of time and resources in the pursuit of a certificate typically leads to significantly greater returns. In short, many students in a highly competitive field are likely to find the additional cost of longer programs a wise investment.

Noncredit Certificates

Some noncredit (continuing education) certificates may document a workshop lasting only a few hours. Others, often in combination, may signify the acquisition of skills and knowledge essential to a demanding job. Given the variety of such credentials—Credential Engine (2021) estimates that there may be more than 40,000 different noncredit certificates—and the fact that NCES counts only for-credit certificates, it is difficult to measure the growth in this sector with any reliability.

But it is reasonable to surmise steady growth if we understand that community college enrollments in noncredit programs tend to be nearly as high as those in for-credit programs (AACC, 2020) and then observe the documented increase in for-credit certificates from 21% of all credentials in 2011–2012 to 23% in 2017–2018 (NCES 2019a). If there are 6.8 million credit enrollments, we may assume there may be as many as 5 million noncredit enrollments—especially if we include certificates awarded by the military, professional societies, credentials earned in coding "bootcamps," and badges attesting to proficiency in technical skills. These can provide access to a career pathway or advancement within one year (Van Noy et al, 2008).

They *can.* But it can be risky simply to assume that they will lead to employment or to increases in earnings. Those who earn a *for-credit* certificate in a competence that is in demand are likely to enjoy a greater positive impact on their earnings than those who gain some work experience but no additional education (Jepsen et al., 2014). Those who earn a *noncredit* credential documenting skills closely aligned with employer needs also may gain advantages, but because of a lack of data, it is especially important that those considering such credentials seek evidence of likely positive outcomes before proceeding.

One such positive outcome might well be a pathway to for-credit programs. As one example, a two-year advanced manufacturing pathways program offered by Delaware Technical Community College offers a non-credit certificate to students who gain employment skills while still in high school. But in addition to offering access to employment, the certificate also can qualify a recipient for up to 13 college *credits* at Delaware Tech—a running start toward a postsecondary degree (National Council for Workforce Education [NCWE], 2020).

There can be significant challenges to making good on this potential. Recent analyses across nine community colleges in different states show that students who seek to apply noncredit certificates to credit-bearing programs may face an uphill climb. Over half of such students, often those most in need of an advantage, drop out (Xu & Ran, 2019). And those who persist may learn that the noncredit certificate they have earned leads neither to employment nor to further education. The advice that students should attempt to assure themselves in advance as to the potential usefulness of the noncredit certificates they may be considering is thus worth repeating.

Administrators, faculty members, and academic advisors who see in noncredit certificate programs an opportunity to serve students well (and increase enrollments) should consider, at a minimum, four criteria. First, these programs should reflect current employer needs as determined through regional economic analyses and consultation with employers. Second, as we suggest in chapter 2, such programs should align with career pathways leading from noncredit to for-credit programs. Third, those encouraging students to follow such pathways should be aware of likely impediments to success—inexperience with college-level work, obligations to outside employment, and financial stress—and suggest workarounds. Finally, leaders should persuasively affirm the value—for the institution, for students, for the economy, and for society—of programs that extend opportunities specifically to challenged students even as they offer potential advantages to all.

Just as there are for-credit graduate certificates, there are also graduate level noncredit certificates that may be offered through an institution's continuing education or extension departments. Available to individuals who already have a bachelor's degree, such certificate programs may enable students to complement their for-credit education with skills in areas such as public relations, digital asset management, and business communications.

The spectrum of noncredit certificate offerings is thus a broad one—and it is growing broader by the month, in part because the offerings of educational institutions are supplemented by those of a broad spectrum of alternate providers that includes, for example, directors of education in professional societies, Armed Services educators, and for-profit trainers.

Harbingers of Change

As new credentials are introduced to meet the demand of emerging disciplines, it can be difficult to keep clear the important distinctions between certifications, for-credit certificates, and noncredit certificates. But it is important to do so for the sake of coherent institutional planning—and for the sake of students. Two recent certificate variations deserve attention.

Career Certificates

Google's new "Career Certificates" program may attract some who are also pursuing or possessing degrees, but Google advertises them as an explicit alternative. Adam Weinburg (2020), the president of Denison University, puts it succinctly: "Google is starting to act like a university." In addition to teaching "job-ready skills to start or advance your career in high demand fields," Google (2020) provides some of the services once associated solely with traditional institutions, such as placement assistance in the form of links to employers and guidance with "job search and interview preparation."

The programs are offered online, they require neither a degree nor prior experience, and the learning is entirely asynchronous. Set your own pace and timeline, Google (2020) urges. If brought to scale through multiple offerings in multiple fields, a scenario easy to imagine given Google's massive resources and worldwide influence, the delivery of Career Certificates could have a profound impact on postsecondary education.

Employers have been offering credentials for quite some time, to be sure. For instance, IBM's digital badging program, now nearly a decade old, has awarded nearly 4 million credentials. Cisco, Novel, and Microsoft have been offering IT certifications since the 1990s. But Google may deserve the attention it is receiving for offering credentials that are "different—and potentially transformational"—both as an alternative to a college education and as a complement to one. Hubspot, another recent innovator, works with colleges to make sure that the certificates it issues will align well with their curricula.

Conceived more broadly than earlier credentials focused on "proprietary technologies related to a given tech vendor," such initiatives "reflect competency or content mastery in specialized areas in the same way that traditional educational certificates and degrees do" (Gallagher & Zanville, 2021). If aggregated, such credentials can even offer access both to a college degree and to employment. "If this is a sustained trend, it may represent an especially exciting way that employers, higher education institutions, edtech startups and workforce intermediaries can partner to thoughtfully create new options for learners" (Gallagher & Zanville, 2021).

Bootcamps
A second kind of variation, distinctive less for its providers than for its intense short-term focus on a particular skill, typically computer coding, appears in "bootcamps." The term, borrowed (carelessly) from the Navy and Marine Corps, describes a noncredit certificate of course completion that can be earned primarily through online programs distinctive for their efficiency and single-mindedness. That intensity can be an advantage if the demand for coders is sustained, but the specificity of the education may not appeal to hiring organizations seeking employees with a broad skill set.

Endeavoring to evaluate bootcamps through interviews with employers "at the intersection of higher education and hiring," Sean Gallagher (2016) found "the jury is still out" (p. 149). A typical complaint against one for-profit coding bootcamp by three former students in May 2021 suggests questions that savvy students and educators may want to ask before enrolling or recommending enrollment.

- What percentage of those earning a bootcamp certificate have received well-paying jobs in the industry within six months of graduation?
- Are the qualifications of the faculty consistent with program quality as advertised?
- Have the instructional materials been developed by the provider or may they be found in the public domain?
- Are there professional advisors assigned to guide students through the program? Or does the provider require that its students mentor one another?

—Burke, 2021

The need for routine due diligence should not suggest that bootcamps in general should prompt suspicion. As Shalin Jyotishi (2021) of New America has concluded, "When executed strategically by a credible education provider and with the learner and employer needs in mind, bootcamps can maximize affordable training outcomes for busy learners." One exemplar might be a "unique, stackable, customized, and for-credit" bootcamp on cable harness wiring developed through the collaboration of Boeing Corporation and Mesa (AZ) Community College. Students who complete the 36-hour program—and the current completion rate is nearly 100%—earn an industry certification, three credit hours, and an interview with Boeing. All for $270, most of which is refundable (Jyotishi, 2021).

This example of a collaborative bootcamp joining corporate and postsecondary competences points to an opportunity administrators, faculty members, and academic advisors may want to consider, one created by a dearth (so far) of regulation and quality assurance. In this still evolving environment, established providers, with the benefit of both institutional accreditation and collaboration with industry, may find it opportune "to get into the boot camp game, connecting boot camps' accelerated and job-focused modes of learning with new or existing types of university credentials" (Gallagher, 2016, p. 150).

An alternate approach to translating autonomous study into recognized credentials may be found in some universities, U.S. businesses such as IBM and Cisco, nonprofits such as Linus Foundation, "and non-academic training organizations" that offer "academic degrees and microcredentials" to students that can present documented learning obtained through MOOCs and other modes of independent learning (CE, 2021, p. 18). Through direct assessment, students can earn credit for the ends of their learning irrespective of its means.

In Sum

Nondegree credentials, particularly short-term, highly focused ones, suggest an unprecedented range of opportunities offered by an unprecedented variety of providers and programs offset by an unprecedented range of risks for the ill-informed and the poorly advised. Administrators, faculty members, and academic advisors thus have an unprecedented opportunity on behalf of their institutions and students to bring greater transparency and reliability to a credentials environment rife with NDCs.

Takeaways

Two-year colleges have a particular opportunity in certificates, both for-credit and not-for-credit, one many of them are pursuing. But there are attractive options for four-year institutions as well, particularly so far as "embedded" degrees and postbaccalaureate NDCs are concerned. Savvy, entrepreneurial institutions will explore these options. They can expand choices for students, increase the likelihood of credential completion, and address the evolving needs of the economy. Strategies may include the following:

- Consider embedding noncredit certificate programs within explicit pathways linked to credit offerings—for-credit certificates and degrees, especially associate degrees. Build secure and inviting bridges between "continuing education" and credit offerings.
- Confront the misguided impression that certificates are a default for the underprepared by pursuing a balanced approach to "primary" certificates (offering direct access to employment without additional postsecondary education), "concurrent" certificates (earned in the process of pursuing a degree), and "post-degree" certificates.
- In the light of region-specific data concerning the returns on certificates and in consultation with professional associations and employers, offer a balance of short-term, midterm, and long-term certificates. In addition, following scrutiny of the labor market benefits of popular short-term credentials, consider discontinuing those that clearly are underperforming in terms of enrollment and student success.

9

NONDEGREE CREDENTIALS

Certifications, Licenses, and Other Options

Although certificates can offer important stepping-stones to career opportunity and to possible degree attainment, they now face increasing competition from a variety of other nondegree credentials. Some certifications (as well as some occupational licenses) may be obtained only following several years study and perhaps supervised experience. But they may offer access to lifetime careers. Some badges may be earned in a few weeks. A variety of other credentials in between can enable students to "stack" highly focused short-term credentials to qualify for employment or to pursue further education. Although an increasing number of students may find such credentials instrumental to their educational and career goals, they may not yet appear on the radar screens of many administrators, faculty members, and academic advisors. They should.

The Promise of Certifications

Although the terms *certificates* and *certifications* are often used interchangeably, *they shouldn't be*. As the Workcred chart (Figure 8.1 in chapter 8) indicates, the two differ markedly in terms of (a) who provides them, (b) how they are earned, (c) who "owns" them, and (d) how they function.

Unlike certificates, "occupational" or "industry" certifications are *not* awarded by institutions of higher education, but by third-party providers such as occupational groups, companies, or professional organizations. Such providers define the skills, knowledge, and experience essential to a career so as to develop examinations offering a gateway to practice. Unlike many providers of short-term, noncredit credentials, most certification providers share a commitment to quality assurance. In fact, some maintain "accreditation" from independent oversight groups such as the American National Standards Institute (ANSI) and the National Commission for Certifying Agencies (NCCA).

Applicants gain access to certification first by meeting any prerequisites (such as a bachelor's degree, required for more than half of certifications) and second by passing the examination administered by the certification provider. Students may also be obligated to document their experience, to pass a criminal background check, and to subscribe to a code of ethics.

A further important consideration concerning certifications is that they are "owned" by the certification body itself, not by the individuals who become certified. Hence, certifications typically are awarded for a specific length of time and must be renewed periodically. Such renewal may be contingent on additional study, documented professional experience, the observance of ethical standards, and satisfactory performance on an examination.

How Certifications Function

Certifications may offer access to a career. And because they may often be developed more quickly than institutional credential offerings, they can offer access to emerging as well as established careers. One example of such alacrity would be the certification awarded by the Society of Certified Senior Advisors (CSA) to those who can develop, document, and demonstrate their qualifications to advise seniors on decisions concerning family finances, home management, retirement options, and the like.

Other certifications may offer access both to an occupation and to advancement *within* that occupation. For example, the Joint Commission on Allied Health Personnel in Ophthalmology (JCAHPO) offers entry-level, intermediate, and advanced certifications. Individuals qualify to take the Certified Ophthalmic Assistant (COA) examination (190 multiple-choice questions) after preparing for it with a self-study program. Those later seeking certification as ophthalmic technicians must pass both a three-hour multiple-choice examination and a two-hour evaluation in seven skills areas. Further up the ladder, experienced allied health personnel "who have progressed through the COA and COT levels or are training program graduates" may qualify to become ophthalmic medical technologists. They must demonstrate through a multiple-choice examination and a performance test in multiple skill areas their "knowledge in 22 content areas that the ophthalmic professional . . . performs on a daily basis" (JCAHPO, 2019). There are subspecialty (surgical assisting, ophthalmic sonography, etc.) certifications as well.

Like certificates, certifications can enable the recipient to further an established educational commitment, undertake a change in direction, or qualify for additional responsibility and compensation. On the one hand, for instance, the "ladder" of certifications described previously enables the ophthalmic assistant to qualify for expanded professional responsibilities. On the other, a student graduating with a liberal arts bachelor's degree who then obtains a certification as a project management professional (PMP) may find in new skills learned an opportunity to leverage competencies already acquired.

And certifications also can enable skilled workers, even those in entry-level jobs, to validate their experience and further develop their expertise specifically in order to qualify for higher wages. Examples might be found in the Automotive Service Excellence certification mentioned in chapter 8, the CompTIA A+ certification, and the American Welding Society certification. Although there is as yet relatively little wage data on the impact of certifications, what there is indicates that those with industry certifications tend to receive higher wages than those who lack them (Markow et al., 2017; Prebil & McCarthy, 2018).

Although certifications remain concentrated in particular arenas, the number of occupations for which certification is available continues to increase. Information technology certifications, for instance, especially those related to cybersecurity, have become far more widely available and continue to emerge. Examples include the certified information systems security professional (CISSP) and the Cisco certified network associate (CCNA). Other certifications showing increasing demand include those in risk and information systems control (CRISC), in ethical hacking (CEH), and in information systems security (CISSP). The U.S. Department of Labor offers a search tool and database on its "Career One Stop" website, accessible at https://www.careeronestop.org/Toolkit/Training/find-certifications.aspx (USDL, 2021).

Pathways to Certification

Pathways to certifications are as varied as the fields in which they may be earned. In some instances, preparation may begin with coursework or a degree program offered by a postsecondary education institution that will qualify an individual to seek certification from the appropriate third-party provider. In such cases, the relation between an academic program and a certification may be *indirect*—in one of two senses. First, a student may determine the prerequisites of a particular certification program and proceed to complete them through the appropriate academic programs. Alternately, a student may be well along the path toward the award of a degree before considering the advantages of obtaining a certification. In many such cases, preparation for a certification examination may be largely independent of an academic program.

In other instances, the relation can be *direct*, one based on close consultation between a college or university and a certification organization.

For example, a "financial planning certificate program" developed and offered by Boston University (BU, 2019) in consultation with the Certified Financial Planner Board of Standards enables a BU student to "satisfy the coursework requirement for CFP certification." That credential involves the direct participation of the postsecondary institution in two ways. First, the Certified Financial Planner Board of Standards will allow individuals to sit for the certification examination only if they are recipients of a bachelor's (or higher) degree from an accredited college or university. Second, the CFB Board requires the completion of specific coursework it has defined as "addressing the major personal financial planning areas" (BU, 2019).

All of these approaches express the recognition that those who earn both a degree and a certification will often become more highly competitive in the job market than individuals offering one or the other. A cross-sector coalition (Workcred, APLU, the Coalition of Urban Serving Universities, and the University Professional and Continuing Education Association) invited educators and educational professionals to a series of meetings in 2018–2019 focused on just this issue, whether the embedding of industry certifications in bachelor's degree programs would typically enhance the value of those degrees. The project report revealed a clear consensus—yes!—and called for the development of further such programs.

Students with effective guidance should be able to take advantage of certification opportunities without falling victim to "potential confusion in the marketplace" (Gallagher, 2016, p. 28). One differentiating factor might be the "accreditation" status of the certifying body mentioned. Because consistent quality control cannot yet be assured so far as certifications are concerned, institutions, providers, and employers all have their respective obligations. Institutions must make well-informed guidance to students considering certifications. Providers must offer quality assurance, preferably through seeking recognition by a qualified third party. And employers must distinguish between credentials that attest to useful competencies and those that simply identify their recipients as good test takers who have relied for their instant learning on short-term bootcamps (Bartlett, 2004; Gomillion, 2017).

Occupational Licensure

Unlike certificates or certifications, a license is a legal document awarded by a state licensing board that allows an individual to practice an occupation or profession. Licenses almost always are required as a supplement to some other credential. An electrician may apply for a license following an apprenticeship. A physician who wishes to be licensed must first earn an MD degree. Aspiring lawyers awarded the JD degree still must pass a bar examination in order to be licensed.

A certification and an occupational license do have one thing in common, however, in that they are exclusionary. That is, they are meant to establish occupational boundaries and to protect the public from unqualified practitioners. By embodying clearly defined standards of knowledge and practice, licensure enables only those who have qualified for a career to ask for the confidence of those whom they are to serve.

Many occupations and professions require licensure. Barbers and cosmetologists, electricians and plumbers, and real estate brokers may offer the most familiar examples, but professionals like teachers, doctors, nurses, lawyers, accountants, and psychologists also must be licensed. In fact, Credential Engine (CE, 2020) estimates that there are 11,938 *different* licenses in the United States, many of which differ from state to state in their requirements. Requirements for a cosmetology license, for instance, tend to differ widely. A chart of such requirements state by state (Best Cosmetology Schools, n.d.) reveals, for instance, that while Arizona offers licensure for completion of a 1,450-hour approved cosmetology course, South Dakota requires that such programs be at least 2,100 hours in length. A workaround in South Dakota? Yes, an apprenticeship of 40 hours a week for 18 months.

Fortunately, the U.S. Department of Labor offers a website (https://www.careeronestop.org/toolkit/training/find-licenses.aspx) that supports searches for information on particular occupations in particular states. In addition, the National Conference of State Legislatures maintains a national licensing database. The NCSL (2020) estimates that over the last 60 years, the number of jobs requiring an occupational license, or governmental approval to practice a profession, has increased from about 1-in-20 to almost 1-in-4.

Given that licensure requirements are consistent across all 50 states for only 60 occupations, these resources that document the differences are essential references. But they can be only a part of the solution. While institutions may not be able to qualify their students for licensure in every state, they must clarify for their students those states where they will be eligible to practice—or to sit for the exam leading to practice—and those where they will not be.

There are initiatives toward greater consistency. For instance, the National Council of State Boards of Nursing has created a "compact" with 33 states participating in an effort to ensure more consistency from one state to another in that discipline. But because powerful interests in some fields in some states continue to interfere with such efforts, there is much work still to be done.

And it is important work both for individuals and for society. Differences in licensure requirements can inhibit mobility from one state to another. They inconvenience in particular those who have invested significantly in gaining credentials and experience in one state only to face a fresh series of hoops whenever they must move from one state to another. And such inconveniences tend to disproportionately affect those whose moves are not discretionary: electricians and plumbers hired by projects with limited life spans, the spouses of military personnel, and public schoolteachers who may have to move from states with declining enrollments to ones that are recruiting teachers.

How Licensure Standards Evolve, for Good and Ill

States are not the only actors so far as licensure standards are concerned. Occupational groups such as the American Association of Colleges of Nursing (AACN) can have a considerable influence on state requirements. As we have noted, while an associate degree still will enable nursing students in New York to sit for the National Council Licensure Examination (NCLEX-RN), recent legislation in that state, reflecting the influence of AACN and related organizations, now requires that newly licensed nurses obtain a bachelor's degree within 10 years of their initial licensure. While nursing shortages may delay the passage of such legislation, states in addition to New York are likely to take up the issue eventually.

In this instance, support for the requirement reflects both a recognition of the increasing complexity in health care delivery and a commitment to improved patient care. But not all licensure requirements can be justified by concerns for protection of the public. Some may reflect at least in part a desire to limit access to particular careers and professions (Freidson, 2001) through the creation of arbitrary barriers (Kleiner, 2011). By limiting the number of practitioners, such barriers may serve to protect a positive wage differential for the favored (Kleiner & Vorotnikov, 2017). Another possible consequence? Higher prices for patients, clients, and consumers. And a third? An inequitable society.

Of course, there can be good reason to scrutinize credentials awarded by unfamiliar providers. Hence state licensing boards seek to limit access to practice to the well qualified. By restricting such access to those who cannot meet their reasonable standards, they protect the public. And there are organizations in disciplines such as nursing or medicine that coordinate the evaluation of credentials awarded by international institutions that are not well known. As additional for-profit providers enter fields such as medicine formerly reserved for accredited not-for-profit institutions, the need for scrutiny both by state licensing agencies and by professional organizations becomes ever more evident.

No, the concern is not with prudent assessment and screening but with restrictions on licensure that may express expectations only tangentially related to actual professional competence. The impact of such restrictions may extend beyond individuals. For instance, they may prevent well-qualified immigrants from practicing a profession for which they have been well educated and thus relegate underserved regions to continued scarcity. There are far too many accounts of experienced pediatricians driving taxi-cabs or waiting tables because the labyrinth of U.S. licensing requirements prevents their finding opportunities in out-of-the-way rural communities.

Licensing and Academic Leadership

What are the implications of licensing for administrators, faculty members, and academic advisors? Administrators should understand whether their programs meant to lead to licensure do so effectively. That requires track-ing the success of students on licensure examinations both in state and out of state. Federal regulations require that institutions inform students about the likelihood of their success in seeking licensure, program by pro-gram, state by state, but even if that were not the case, institutions that make a priority of student success should make such information clear and widely available.

Faculty members who represent licensed professions and occupations may have—and if not perhaps should seek—the opportunity to weigh in on the expectations that regulate licensure. Their commitment to student success should encourage them to advocate for the closest possible alignment between requirements for licensure and standards required to protect the public from the poorly trained or incompetent.

Academic advisors share a responsibility to make certain that students understand the practical consequences of the information that they pro-vide. Advisors cannot be expected to know the regulations in every state and in every profession or occupation, but they should make available information as needed on a case-by-case basis. In addition, advisors should be aware of employment opportunities within licensed fields that do not require licensure. While the practice of law requires a license, there are many employment opportunities within the legal profession that do not. Washington University in St. Louis offers an online master's degree in legal studies for students who seek to develop knowledge of law without work-ing as lawyers. And one does not need to be a licensed architect to teach architectural history.

Two Other NDCs

Beyond certificates, certifications, and occupational licenses there is a variety of nondegree credentials (NDCs) that students may find instrumental to their educational and career goals. We will describe the two most frequently pursued with the proviso that new NDCs may appear at any moment—or at least in time for the second edition of this book!

Digital Badges

Although the 2020 count of credentials by CE shows more than 380,000 discrete digital badges (an increase of roughly 190,000 from 2019), a survey conducted in 2020 by CE and IMS Global Learning Consortium confirmed the impression that "few people have an understanding of digital badges."

Digital badges are not new credentials, exactly, but, as the name suggests, have emerged in their present form as a paperless, online form of documentation that both attests to the award of a credential and provides information about it. Any kind of organization may issue a badge, but the most competitive tend to follow the Open Badges standard developed by the IMS Global Learning Consortium. The standard "describes a method for packaging information about accomplishments, embedding it into portable image files as digital badges, and includes resources for web-based validation and verification" (IMS, 2021, para. 1). A compliant credential will "describe who earned it, who issued it, the criteria required, and in many cases even the evidence and demonstrations of the relevant skills" (IMS, 2021, para. 1).

Because they are "digital," badges can embed metadata in "digital backpacks" or "digital vaults" shared on social media (Catalano & Doucet, 2013). As the Open Badges standard suggests, such data can document both the substance of the credential and the competencies it is meant to mark (Casilli & Hickey, 2016; Shields & Chugh, 2017). Badges can also include institutional profiles, information on courses taken, qualified evaluations of completed work, and test scores (Gibson et al., 2015). In short, badges can "capture and show granular details that the broader view represented by a degree can't" (Bowen & Thomas, 2014, p. 28).

Such details may enable an employer to discriminate in minute ways among different levels of preparation, different skill sets, and different indicators of potential for further preparation. On the one hand, a badge might document the acquisition of a highly specific and limited skill, such as the *use* of a particular software program. On the other, it might attest to skills and knowledge that qualify the badge holder to *write* a software program. Some badges even attest to more broadly applicable skills such as critical thinking, problem solving, or digital literacy (Shields & Chugh, 2017).

Badges can sometimes be useful standing alone in qualifying their recipients to meet requirements for employment. But their greater significance may lie in their potential to document learning cumulatively and systematically, either in terms specific to the badge or in combination with more traditional credentials (Hickey et al., 2015). For example, the University of Maryland, Baltimore County, offers badges marking such skills as collaboration, communication, critical thinking, globalism, interculturalism, leadership, problem solving, and professionalism (UMBC, 2021), while the State University of New York (n.d.) has introduced short-term, narrowly focused credentials designed to promote "each student's success and the value of individualized learning."

By their capacity to validate learning experiences that might otherwise go unrecognized or apprehended only in part, badges can enable learners to qualify for opportunities that might otherwise appear inaccessible. Some have even suggested that badges could develop into a discrete credentialing system that would compete with traditional transcripts (Finkelstein et al., 2013). But so long as few people understand them, there's work to be done.

The Pros and Cons of Badges

The advantages badges offer suggest ways in which all credentials might be strengthened. When carefully conceived and thoughtfully aligned with specific employment needs, badges promise singular efficiency, immediacy, and cost-effectiveness—advantages every credential provider should have in mind. Properly presented, badges can stimulate conversations about learning and prompt curricular review and reform (Knight & Casilli, 2012).

A particularly appealing claim for badges, whether they are embedded in a degree program or not, is that they can increase motivation (Gibson et al., 2015). No wonder! The objectives of a well-designed badge should be transparent, the learning requirements should be pragmatic, and the evidence of student success should be clearly defined. Badges might well become an essential ingredient in related initiatives such as the Learning and Experience Records Hub (LER Hub) being piloted by the U.S. Chamber of Commerce's (USCOC, 2020) T3 Innovation Network.

There are concerns that overemphasis on the quid pro quo associated with a badge risks compromising the intrinsic value of learning (Rughini & Matei, 2013), but that risk can be ameliorated when badges are offered within a broader educational context. One such context might be a class or academic program in which badges document the attainment of specific learning milestones contributing to a more comprehensive credential.

Another might be the inclusion of badges in pathways that lead to the acquisition of both broad skills and specific competences (Mah, 2016). A pathway can provide both landmarks for progress and a narrative students can draw on to frame their learning achievements (Rughinis & Matei, 2013). And as universities move toward competency-based transcripts, badges may become more useful still.

What are the "cons"? The principal drawback of badges, as with some other NDCs, is inconsistent quality assurance. The Open Badges protocol prescribes standards for the description of what a badge signifies, but a more robust form of oversight may be needed to identify and regulate dubious providers. At one end of the spectrum, an aspiring software developer may "train to enter the field of information technology—one badge at a time" by following a curriculum offered by a reputable provider with direct links to employers (SoftwareGuild, 2020). But another student may suffer from a shoddy curriculum advertised by an opportunistic profiteer.

It should not be surprising, then, that perceptions of badges vary depending on the information they provide and on their design—including the visual design of the badge itself (Dyjur & Lindstrom, 2017). Clarifying the credibility of the credential represents an obvious priority in postsecondary education, but the challenge of doing so in terms that are "grounded in verified, quality judgements" may prove considerable (Grant, 2016, p. 98). A thorough market analysis of the ways in which employers assess and reward badges should include a comprehensive and systematic overview of which badges are valuable and which are not, which contribute to a sustained learning pathway and which do not, and which providers are trustworthy and which are not.

There is a trade-off here for administrators, faculty members, and academic advisors. Particularly in certain high demand fields, badges offered by nonacademic providers may offer students valuable complements to their academic programs. Coordination with such providers could enable an institution to electrify its curriculum with short-term, substantive credentials applicable to degree completion. But with such an opportunity comes risk. The fields in which badges are at present most prominent, notably information technology, are notoriously volatile. A badge developed to meet an emerging demand could easily miss the curve.

As we have noted, some traditional institutions (e.g., Purdue, the University of Arizona) have allied themselves organizationally with former for-profit independents in the expectation that they will become themselves more agile and entrepreneurial. That too can prove opportune—or risky, as further proliferation of badges may result in confusion about their meaning and skepticism about their use. But the opportunities that badges promise may justify the risks, especially as they are aligned with and offered within broader contexts such as degree programs and other curricular pathways.

Diplomas

A term once reserved principally for the award given high school graduates, "diploma" now also designates two categories of postsecondary certificates—one at the sub-baccalaureate level, the other at the graduate level. (We have waited until now to mention them because they are decidedly "less familiar" as collegiate credentials.)

An example of the first category appears in a diploma offered by Minnesota State (2020) to recognize completion of "an academic program generally of 30 to 72 credits intended to provide students with skills leading directly to a specific job" (para. 5). Highly specialized postgraduate diplomas, the second category, are available through programs offered by the School of Professional Studies at New York University, where the term was chosen at least in part to differentiate new certificate programs from underperforming ones (Gallagher, 2015).

Making Sense of NDCs

We have yet to consider an increasingly prominent NDC, the apprenticeship. We will do so in chapter 10. But we can take stock of the remarkable variety of NDCs we have considered so far, both the familiar and the unfamiliar. As we have seen, NDCs tend to share several characteristics.

- Most document competencies relevant to occupations. The most competitive reflect consultation with employers and address industry and occupational standards directly.
- Most promise increased efficiency arising from a focus on employment requisites. Even the most demanding certificate programs (and most certifications) require less time to completion than most baccalaureate degrees.
- They are *typically* less expensive than degree programs—even though at present those not enrolled in a degree program may not qualify for federal student aid. (That may change.)

But the range otherwise is broad. On the one hand, it includes short-term credentials such as the CNA (certified nursing assistant) that qualify a recipient for an entry-level occupation open to those without a college degree and in some cases to those without a high school diploma. On the other hand,

NDCs include also occupational licenses for demanding technical employment or prestigious professions necessitating extensive preparatory study. In between lie the many others we have considered.

In general, the more rigorous the requirements, the more advantageous the credential for the recipient. But the alignment between requirements and potential advantages is not always clear or systematic. That is in part a reflection of differing levels of demand for the skills to which different NDCs attest. But that can also be an advantage, as both college sophomores and experienced PhDs may find themselves attracted to the same certificate or preparing for the same certification exam. It is the remarkable variety of learning and professional pathways associated with the remarkable variety of the credentials themselves that emphasizes the necessity for administrative awareness, faculty engagement, and advisor guidance.

Another important variation lies in the depth and complexity of the preparation that the credential signifies. In some cases, the skills documented by the NDC should track the evolving understanding of the competencies needed for an occupation. For example, while it may still be possible to obtain work as a medical assistant without being certified, the increasing competitiveness of the profession provides an increasing incentive to become certified—a process usually requiring graduation from an accredited medical assisting program and the passing of an exam.

Additionally, while NDCs are often understood primarily in terms of access to entry-level positions, we have noted how they may play a broader role in enabling career advancement within an occupation or organization. For example, credentialing as a CCNA (Cisco Certified Network Associate) may enable an information technology technician to gain an entry-level position. But earning an advanced certification such as the CCNP (Cisco Certified Network Professional) might win the technician a promotion.

At what point did such complexity begin to create confusion? As we have seen, the grounds on which NDCs may be awarded varies widely. For certifications assessment through examination is meant to measure demonstrated competency—but there may be prerequisites. For many certificates, successful completion of a program will earn the NDC—but the credential may or may not prove to be of value. For licensure, both the completion of a program and successful performance on an examination may be needed. And passing a licensure exam in one state may not satisfy the requirements in another. Such differences are likely to reflect another difference, whether preparation takes place in a classroom (e.g., certificates), as the result of an academic program (some certifications, some licenses), on-the-job education and training (apprenticeships), through independent learning, or through some combination.

There's still more to consider. The providers of NDCs differ widely, from community colleges to Ivy League universities to certification associations to major corporations to coding bootcamps operating from indeterminate locations. This list also includes the federal government, state governments, and organizations such as industry associations, employer groups, and unions.

For administrators, faculty members, and academic advisors, what are the implications for responding to this challenging environment? First, institutions must assure the quality of the NDCs they award themselves by documenting both the currency of their programs and the success of their students. Second, every institution should have at least one staff member who will maintain command of the NDC spectrum—a task requiring considerable patience, an eye for opportunity, and a nose for risk. Third, even if a department offers no NDCs, faculty members in that department should remain aware of those that bear on their disciplines. For instance, faculty in a department offering a bachelor's degree in criminal justice should learn about the many NDCs current within the field, some of which may be *required* for some openings as complements to degrees. For example, to become a candidate for sheriff in some jurisdictions, a law enforcement officer must present at least an associate degree in criminal justice *and a certificate in jail management*. Academic advisors have the most challenging responsibility, that of becoming aware of the NDCs available in every field for which they offer advice and of being willing to acquaint advisees with the full range of NDC opportunities *even when students will find some of these opportunities only outside the institution*.

As we have noted, one particularly promising strategy requiring the collaboration of administrators, faculty members, and academic advisors appears in the incorporation of NDCs into current academic programs. Some of the most appealing options include the following:

- Bachelor's degree programs that include a professional certification in a field related to the primary discipline. (We have examined in particular the report on Workcred's effort to encourage just such initiatives.) An alternative? A B+C program, in which the award of the bachelor's degree qualifies the recipient to pursue examination for certification.
- "NDC to degree" pathways, through which a student applies learning gained in earning an NDC to the partial satisfaction of requirements for an associate or bachelor's degree.
- The "academic apprenticeship" program, in which a student combines academic study toward an associate degree with on-the-job mentored experience in an industry or profession. More on this in the next chapter!

In Sum

The less familiar NDCs we have discussed are unlikely to remain so. Interest that was developing prior to the pandemic accelerated when the restrictions on traditional forms of higher education encouraged a renewed interest in short-term credentials, many of them NDCs, available through distance learning. By all indications, that growth—of opportunity, to be sure, but also of risks—is likely to continue.

Takeaways

Increasing their offering of NDCs is an obvious option for two-year colleges, one many of them are exercising. But there are options for four-year institutions as well, particularly so far as "embedded" degrees and postbaccalaureate NDCs are concerned. Savvy, entrepreneurial institutions will explore these options. Successful undertakings can expand choices for students, increase the likelihood of credential completion, and address the evolving needs of the economy. Strategies may include the following:

- Consider enabling students to embed certifications within their degree programs.
- As with certificates, confront the misguided impression that NDCs are a default for the underprepared by pursuing a balanced approach to "primary" credentials (offering direct access to employment without additional postsecondary education), "concurrent" credentials (earned in the process of pursuing a degree), and "post-degree" credentials.
- Create a process for the evaluation of prior learning represented by noncredit NDCs, assign and articulate credit where appropriate, and apply such credit to program requirements where possible.
- Revise institutional attainment goals to reflect an increased commitment to NDCs and track the completion of such credentials as one measure of institutional performance.
- Undertake or support the gathering of better data concerning NDCs. Who offers which? How successful are the recipients? What other quality indicators should be sought? What disciplines are becoming overcrowded? What opportunities are emerging?

APPRENTICESHIPS

A Special Case

The distinction between "students who work" and "workers who study" has outlived its usefulness. Balancing academic preparation and practical experience now represents an increasing priority for many if not most students. Now conveived more broadly, apprenticeships offer a powerful expression of this balance. They merit their own chapter because they incorporate many of the elements other credentials should embrace: classroom learning, on-the-job experience, exacting assessment, and preparation for leadership. Those who believe apprentices are to be found only in a few familiar trades are living in the past.

An Ancient Paradigm Reinvented

Apprenticeships are the most enduring of credentials. Before there were professors teaching students seeking academic degrees, there were cobblers, carpenters, masons, sculptors, and other masters of trades offering apprentices a quid pro quo—training in exchange for labor. Experienced craftsmen found needed assistants while apprentices who passed muster found their footing at the beginning of a secure career path. To this day, the paradigm of apprenticeship may be discerned in the many professions (law, medicine, higher education) that oblige newly credentialed individuals to work under supervision, to prove themselves, and eventually to have their growth acknowledged through partnership, recognition as a fellow in a specialization, or the award of tenure. The principle appears as well in co-op programs offered by academic institutions in collaboration with employers that are a mainstay in institutions such as the University of Cincinnati—which began offering such programs in 1906!

But there are now many more kinds of apprenticeships leading to careers in fields such as insurance, engineering, health care management, and quality management auditing. Offering access to an increasingly broad spectrum of opportunities, a 21st-century apprenticeship can create inviting paths to success. Some apprenticeships are designed for talented youth who begin supervised "earning while learning" as high school students. Other students may apply for registered apprenticeships (RA) following high school—a well established model we describe later. And still others may want to keep in mind industry-recognized and other "nonregistered" apprenticeship programs. But the principle remains the same: learning while earning, earning while learning.

A Brief Account of a Lengthy History

The "lengthy history"—longer than that of any other credential—stretches back to the Code of Hammurabi (c. 1754 BC), which mentions apprenticeships, but we begin instead with the economy of the U.S. colonies. As the U.S. Department of Labor (USDL, 2018b) points out, colonials educated as apprentices include George Washington (surveying), Benjamin Franklin (printing), and Paul Revere (silversmithing). "Thousands of others - carpenters, masons, shipwrights - did their part in developing and supporting the economy of our young nation and making the United States what it is today."

But the arc from that day to this has not been smooth. The replacement of skilled craftsmen by machines during the Industrial Revolution created a conflict between labor unions seeking to protect workers' wages and industries seeking to reduce labor costs. "The fall of American apprenticeships began as a compromise between labor unions and business executives over how much to pay young workers-in-training" (Ferenstein, 2018).

In the early 20th century, when corporations found it more difficult to obtain skilled labor, there emerged "a desire to return to old conditions" (Bureau of Statistics of Labor, 1907) and a renewed interest in apprenticeships. But the remedy, new federal funding for vocational programs, at first proved ineffective. "America's upwardly mobile, working-class families flat out rejected any second-tier vocational track that presumed their children should not even attempt to go to Yale or Harvard" (Ferenstein, 2018). It became clear that some more formal means of recognition and regulation would be necessary. It was time to fortify the apprenticeship.

The "Registered Apprenticeship"

The approval by Congress in 1937 of the National Apprenticeship Act (known also as the Firzgerald Act) authorized the secretary of labor

> to formulate and promote the furtherance of labor standards necessary
> to safeguard the welfare of apprentices, to extend the application of such

standards by encouraging the inclusion thereof in contracts of apprenticeship, to bring together employers and labor for the formulation of programs of apprenticeship, [and] to cooperate with State agencies engaged in the formulation and promotion of standards of apprenticeship. (USDL, 2018b)

The standards developed by the secretary for the recognition of Registered Apprenticeships (RA) would prove remarkably durable (Apprenticeship .gov., n.d.).

- Apprentices participate in on-the-job learning that provides both financial compensation and a structured curriculum combining experience and training. (A contract between the student-employee and the employer spells out the terms.)
- The structured curriculum is delivered at least in part through classroom teaching offered by the provider or a partner.
- The compensation of apprentices increases as their experience, skill, and knowledge develop.
- Apprenticeship programs are regularly evaluated by the federal government relative to clear standards.
- Those who complete apprenticeship programs receive a credential recognized by industry. While four out of five apprentices in a typical apprenticeship program find employment with the sponsors of their programs, the credential is meant to be "portable."

SIDEBAR
Other "Apprenticeships"
Some apprenticeships are neither "registered" nor "industry-recognized." These "unregistered" and unregulated programs can be difficult to pinpoint and to count, but CE (2021) cites estimates there may be "many thousands of employers [that] support apprenticeship-like programs" outside of either system (p. 28).

The legislation did not prompt an immediate expansion in apprenticeships. Public opinion, public policy, and public funding continued to privilege academic degrees throughout much of the 20th century and to stigmatize vocational education. Not even a *registered* apprenticeship would win acceptance as the equivalent of an academic degree. As Scott Carlson (2017) observes, "After years of policy makers seen as pushing 'college for all,' students and their families might perceive apprenticeships as something less prestigious than a college education." And while the quality of the internship experience would continue to be supported by the requirements announced in 1937, it also appears to be the case that these requirements may have discouraged some organizations from implementing apprenticeships.

A Favorable Environment

These are good years for the apprenticeship in all its forms. As college tuitions have increased along with employer concerns about the job skills of graduates, the apprenticeship has gained increasing favor with policymakers, educators, and economic development leaders. New programs (which may be initiated by a college or university, labor organization or industry association, or even a single employer) are appearing, new legislation supporting their growth is being enacted, and an alternate form of the apprenticeship has come onto the scene.

No longer limited to careers in a few traditional trades, the apprenticeship now offers a model for efficient, effective learning leading to a wide spectrum of careers. The apprenticeship once again can be seen as "the closest thing to a guaranteed pathway into the middle class" (McCarthy, 2019) for learners of all ages.

Those who offer and pursue apprenticeships still benefit from the ancient quid pro quo: productivity in return for education. What has changed—partly in response to compelling European models—is that for many well-qualified students today's apprenticeship programs may be *preferable* to traditional college degree programs. An ancient arrangement can become a route of choice for exceptional individuals seeking a direct path to "a successful career . . . without racking up debt" (USDL, 2018a).

An Interruption—and a Prompt to Innovation

Throughout its long history, the essential elements of the apprenticeship have remained remarkably constant. But changing circumstances such as the rise and fall of union influence, changes in workforce needs in established industries, and even the impact of events such as the Great Depression or the 2020–2021 pandemic, have prompted its continued evolution.

We can take the pandemic as the most recent example of "changing circumstances" by observing that it raised a question that otherwise might not have been asked. Given that "hands-on" learning has been seen as essential to apprenticeships for centuries, would it be possible for students to make progress without the oversight provided by mentors present in person?

Writing for *Inside Higher Ed* in June 2020, Madeline St. Amour described one effort to explore that possibility by Apprenti, a tech apprenticeship program that had "quickly pivoted to online education" to teach content while "working with companies to help apprentices continue their on-the-job training at home."

Not surprisingly there were skeptics. Eric Seleznow of the Center for Apprenticeship and Work-Based Learning at Jobs for the Future has expressed concern about the limitations of online instruction in teaching both the "soft skills" (respecting workplace expectations, working well within teams) and the "hands-on skills" (the operation of machinery, the mastery of process) essential to apprenticeship learning. Mentors may offer coaching online, monitoring work performed in front of a laptop camera, but there appeared "the possibility that it would not be done as well without in-person interaction" (St. Amour, 2020). In addition, industries *pay* apprentices because they contribute to the company's productivity. If apprentices are unable to contribute, how do they justify compensation? Hence a double whammy.

But necessity prompted invention. Even as the irreplaceable value of closely mentored hands-on experience has become more apparent, increased acquaintance with online learning demonstrated how some practical elements of the apprenticeship (in addition to content learning) may be acquired online. In one example, Southwest Tennessee Community College (STCC; Memphis) adjusted its apprenticeship program in information technology to provide "both in-person training and virtual engagement." By working with the University of Memphis, industry partners, and trade groups, the college was able to develop a "highly customized IT apprenticeship model" aligned with both employer needs and the public health restrictions then in place (STCC, 2020). So-called "hybrid" experiences, combining online and hands-on learning, may now appear as a viable option more often.

History Still Being Made

Some lingering misconceptions—that RAs are a recourse for underprepared students, that they lead only to a narrow range of trades, or that they offer little potential for advancement—die hard. And there are some legitimate issues worth keeping in mind. While the compensation apprentices receive is becoming more generous, it generally remains lower than that of regular employees doing the same job. And some apprentices may find themselves assigned to menial tasks that offer little significant experience or potential for growth. But the possibility of such problems simply emphasizes that individuals considering apprenticeships should choose carefully among the programs they are considering—exercising the same level of scrutiny that anyone should exercise before enrolling at a college or accepting a job.

In the remainder of this chapter, we will show how apprenticeships are *making* history. As part of a broader educational continuum, apprenticeships may now be uniquely well suited to offer the "occupational competencies and employability skills such as communication, teamwork, the ability to efficiently allocate resources, problem-solving, reliability, and responsibility" that have become critical necessities for a wide range of industries (Lerman, 2018). So what's the problem? As Robert I. Lerman (2018) has observed, "the scale of U.S. apprenticeship is minimal not just compared with Austria, Germany, and Switzerland, but even Australia, Canada, and the United Kingdom."

The issue, as Lerman and others have acknowledged, has little to do with questions of program quality. To the contrary, as a rule

> apprenticeship programs improve the learning process (as students directly apply what they learn), encourage student engagement, increase incentives for students to perform well in academic courses, improve the match between workers' skills and labor market demands, encourage employers to upgrade their mix of jobs, and widen access to rewarding careers for workers who prefer learning-by-doing over traditional classroom education and the four-year college model. (Lerman, 2018)

The issue, as Lerman says, is one of scale.

"Scaling" Apprenticeships

For more than 80 years, the registered apprenticeship has supported both those seeking careers in the crafts and trades and employers attempting to recruit well-qualified employees. Today, the apprenticeship can be described as "the country's most effective education and employment model" (McCarthy, 2019). But apprenticeships remain "vastly underused, poorly coordinated, nonstandardized, and undervalued by students, parents, educators, and policymakers" (Jones, 2011).

Despite recent expansion in apprenticeships, U.S. programs even now prepare just a small fraction of those seeking employment for a still narrow range of opportunities. According to data from the USDL (2016), apprentices in 2016, roughly 500,000, were preparing for only 2% of the 23 million employment opportunities available. And that includes apprenticeships offered by the armed services. By contrast, as Lerman has noted, apprenticeship programs in Germany and Switzerland prepare *more than half* of their nation's youth for a wide spectrum of employment opportunities.

There would thus appear to be a significant opportunity for expansion. That opportunity is the subject of a 2017 report by Joseph B. Fuller and Matthew Sigelman on behalf of Burning Glass Technologies and the Harvard Business School, *Room to Grow: Identifying New Frontiers for Apprenticeships.* The essentials of the argument are that the bachelor's degree offers only an oblique "proxy" for the kinds of knowledge and skills that employers are seeking. By contrast, an apprenticeship can be tailored closely to the demands of a trade, the expanding capacity of an industry or profession, or even a particular employer's expectations, thereby providing a more efficient and cost-effective path. "Instead of accumulating debt, students get to 'earn while they learn'" (Fuller & Siegelman, 2017). Both job seekers and employers benefit.

Focusing on skills specified in advertised employment opportunities in 2016, the study's authors determined that the number of occupations served by apprenticeship programs could increase "from 27 to 74" and that job openings for those completing apprenticeships could be "multiplied eightfold" (Fuller & Siegelman, 2017). Moreover, many of these openings would offer access to higher paying occupations, in part because apprenticeships can prepare candidates for openings "employers find difficult to fill" (Fuller & Siegelman, 2017).

The four most conspicuous barriers to upscaling the apprenticeship are well summarized by Lerman. The first is underinvestment (i.e., "a failure to try") on the part of the federal government. "The British budget for advertising its apprenticeship programs exceeds the *entire* U.S. budget for apprenticeship." The second is the "complex administrative structure" of the RA system leading to bureaucratic delays and inadequate quality assurance. The third is opacity. Information about apprenticeships is not widely disseminated, and the assistance that may be needed for the development of programs is not widely available. Finally, government funding reveals an "asymmetric" preference for enrolled students taking for-credit courses over those engaged in apprenticeships (Lerman, 2018).

Four solutions that align well with the "barriers" identified by Lerman and that incorporate many of his "elements" appear to be emerging. Three that are closely related—a rethinking of the apprenticeship in the context of a changing economy, the development of "early start" programs that enable students to begin apprenticeships while in high school, and the expansion of the spectrum of apprenticeships to include many "white-collar" professions—are already well under way. The fourth, an alternative to the RA known as IRAPs (Industry Recognized Apprenticeship Programs), attracted some interest toward the end of the previous decade but appeared to be still in an exploratory stage as this book went to press.

SIDEBAR
Ten Steps on a "Scale"
Lerman (2018) lists ten "elements" needed for "a high-quality apprenticeship system" at scale: (a) more effective marketing, (b) more compelling incentives for start-ups "among private and public employers," (c) more frequently updated occupational standards, (d) more public funding for the instructional component of apprenticeships, (e) improved evaluation of programs and program completers, (f) "certification bodies to audit programs and issue credentials," (g) systems enabling employers to track apprentices' progress, (h) improved "counseling and screening" for potential apprentices, (i) improved training for apprentice mentors, and (j) "research, evaluation and dissemination."

Revitalizing the Apprenticeship

Apprenticeships arguably offer the single most direct, efficient, and focused approach to long-term employment. But these advantages can in some cases camouflage limitations. Occupationally centered programs may not always serve well those who will experience a rapidly changing economic environment. Writing for *Inside Higher Ed,* Steven Mintz, a history professor at the University of Texas-Austin, endorses "skills-based, outcomes-focused education" but argues that preparation "ought not to be limited to skills-training." "A professional is not a technician," he says (Mintz, 2019).

Similarly, Carol Geary Schneider, former president of the Association of American Colleges & Universities (AAC&U), commends "practical career preparation in programs that offer compensation and clear job prospects." But she adds that apprentices are also "citizens who will have lives beyond their careers and professional roles." Like students enrolled at a traditional college, "[apprentices] should have the opportunity to explore their civic responsibilities, the ethical dimensions of their callings, and the place of their career or profession in society." Finally, Schneider says, "Since lifelong learning has become a necessity both at work and in life, their programs should lay a foundation for continued and self-directed learning as well" (Schneider, 2019).

If some apprenticeships are no longer focused solely on entry-level skills, some remain so. And while some link to programs that expand the breadth of the post-secondary experience, many don't.

A Step Along the Way

That may be changing for the better. As Diane Auer Jones (2011) has observed, "apprenticeship programs should be considered as a step along an educational continuum rather than a dead end." Many community colleges have now accepted the challenge to collaborate with industry and other employers in designing programs balancing classroom education (provided by the college) with on-the-job training (provided by the employer). A point made by New America (2019) is that apprenticeship programs, which may offer some an alternative to college, can lead others to qualify for college credentials—"an affordable path to and through college."

The idea has been developing for 30 years. Congress in 1990 approved a "Tech Prep" amendment to the Perkins Act calling for formal links between high school vocational curriculums and postsecondary programs. Three years afterward, Jeffrey A. Cantor (1993), in *Apprenticeship and Community Colleges,* acknowledged an emerging trend, "a move towards a trainee earning college credit for the hands-on portion of the program towards an Associate degree" (p. 38).

That move would make possible "a prominent role in apprenticeship" for community colleges, Cantor predicted, one that could include technical training, the recruitment of candidates, the development of faculty, and the providing of specialized facilities to meet training needs. Cantor was prescient, in that many of the apprenticeship programs initiated within the past 30 years have in fact involved community colleges, with the result that apprenticeships increasingly serve as paths not only to a career, but also to mobility. New America (2019) has observed that these programs

- enable workers to prepare for career change and enable companies to "upskill their current workforce";
- serve the cause of increased equity by enabling program participants to address familiar barriers to employment "such as lack of work experience or credentials"; and
- meet potential employees where they live. Rural young people can stay close to home while qualifying for remunerative careers.

That an increasing number of RAs are requiring or encouraging the completion of an in-tandem associate degree suggests that the apprenticeship has become both a path to skilled employment and a "stackable" credential that can lead to further education.

Enabling a Running Start

Why should qualified high school students with a strong career interest wait until after graduation to apply for an apprenticeship? The Partnership to Advance Youth Apprenticeship (PAYA), which includes the National Governors Association Center for Best Practices (NGA Center), New America, and several other national and state organizations, offers an answer: They shouldn't. The vision is that what is now a selective opportunity for a few students can become a broad educational and economic initiative through the expansion of "affordable, reliable, and equitable pathways from high school to good jobs and college degrees" (PAYA, 2019).

An initiative undertaken in spring 2019 by the NGA, New America, and other national organizations expresses this broader view. In promoting the extension of "high-quality" apprenticeship opportunities to high schools, the NGA (2019) partners call for connecting secondary schools and employers with "most often a community college." Quality must be assured through "ongoing assessment against established skills and competency standards." Both "a portable, industry-recognized credential" and postsecondary credit must be awarded at program completion (NGA, 2019).

Similarly, just prior to the pandemic outbreak, nonprofit CareerWise Colorado had announced plans to recruit high school students to a new "binocular" vision of the apprenticeship, one that would provide both access to a solid middle-class career and a potential path to further education. The model borrows from the Swiss approach to open-ended apprenticeships. One student completing an apprenticeship might "step directly into a bookkeeper position," while another might "start as an apprentice and end with a PhD" (CareerWise, 2019). The Colorado model appears poised for further growth.

Apprenticeship Maryland seeks to enroll high school students in the summer or fall of their junior or senior years in a program offering "at least 450 hours of work-based training under the supervision of an eligible employer and at least one year of related instruction." The focus of this program is on "high-demand occupations" in the sciences, technology, engineering, and mathematics (i.e., the STEM disciplines). What was a 2015 pilot in two local school systems has developed into a statewide program aimed at expanding partnerships between industry and education (Maryland State Department of Labor, 2019).

Wisconsin's Youth Apprenticeship program, initiated in 1991, deserves mention for a track record of nearly 30 years of service to students and to the employer community. With 4,000 youth apprentices annually and an organization comprised of 33 regional consortiums, the program is a proven success (Wisconsin Department of Labor, 2019). And it appears to be exemplary in the close working relationship it has forged among the state, employers, and the public schools.

Expanding the Spectrum

When the National Apprenticeship Act was approved in 1937, apprenticeships were found primarily in construction, manufacturing, and utilities industries—arenas still served well by RA programs. For individuals seeking

SIDEBAR
The Chicagoland Example

A 2019 story in the *Chicago Sun-Times* describes a new form of apprenticeship as an *alternative* to a four-year degree that leads to employment through a blend of classroom study and practical experience in fields such as insurance, finance, and consulting (Issa, 2019).

Harper College (IL), a community college participating in the Chicago-based initiative known as "Apprenticeship 2020," stands in "the forefront of a small but growing movement that is changing how some students enter white-collar jobs" (Johnson, 2019). Photos of the college's apprenticeship programs show students engaged in banking and finance, insurance, cybersecurity, and marketing in addition to those training to be machinists and industrial maintenance mechanics. The first of Harper's (2021) "white-collar" employer partners was Zurich North America. Similar opportunities are offered in graphic arts and supply chain management. A further accelerant in the Chicago area appears in an initiative of two corporations, Aon and Accenture, **the Chicago Apprentice Network**. With funding of $3.2 million by foundations including JPMorgan Chase, MacArthur, and Joyce, the network supports the creation of "infrastructure to build capacity and accelerate the growth of nontraditional apprenticeships" (Chicagoland Workforce Funder Alliance, 2019). A beneficiary of this initiative, **City Colleges of Chicago** (CCC), has received $1.25 million to expand its capacity "to support employer relationships, recruit students to apprenticeship opportunities, and implement academic curriculum for apprenticeship and work-based learning programs" (Chicagoland, 2019). The CCC now offer apprenticeships including culinary arts, retail management, banking and insurance, energy, and health care in cooperation with partners such as Walgreens, McDonald's, Pepsico, and the Rush University Medical Center (CCC, 2020).

opportunities in these arenas, apprenticeships still lead to qualifications that may well prove of greater immediate value than baccalaureate degrees.

The apprenticeship spectrum began to expand in the mid-20th century as RA programs emerged in sectors such as emergency medical care and public safety. That expansion continues. At present, according to the USDL (2018b),

> there are almost 24,000 Registered Apprenticeship programs providing education and training for approximately 400,000 apprentices in emerging and high-growth sectors such as energy conservation, health care, and

information technology, in addition to traditional industries such as manufacturing and construction.

Good news. But as we have noted, the number of those pursuing apprenticeship programs still reflects only a small percentage of the potential workforce. Perhaps the most promising approach to increasing that percentage may lie in initiatives that recall the recommendations of the Burning Glass/Harvard study. See the sidebar for a notable example.

Employers and Community Colleges

Not surprisingly, given their shared interests in apprenticeship programs, alliances between community colleges and employers have proliferated. In January 2019, the AACC announced a partnership with the USDL to "dramatically increase the number of apprenticeships entering the workforce." According to Walter Bumphus, president of the AACC (2019), the initiative "will result in thousands of students who are job-ready and a newly imagined network of apprenticeships that will serve industry and employers' needs for decades to come." Clearly, one incentive lies in the community college commitment to support local and regional economies. But the mission of the association is far broader: to "ensure access to lifelong learning to benefit individuals, communities, and society in general" and "to prepare learners to be effective in a global society" (AACC, n.d.).

Exerting Political Leadership

Even before the Burning Glass/Harvard study documented the likely advantages of an expansion of the "apprentice spectrum," the priority had been embraced by some national and state political leaders on both sides of the aisle.

On July 24, 2014, President Obama convened the "first-ever" White House summit on apprenticeships "to dramatically increase apprenticeship in America" (para. 2). The president's priority had an equity component: "With women and African Americans comprising only 6 percent and 10 percent of our apprentices respectively, we are clearly not tapping the full extent and diversity of the nation's talent" (Perez & Zients, 2014, para. 5).

The contrast between the limited focus of most U.S. apprenticeships (though that is changing) and the far broader focus found in nations such as Switzerland and Germany surfaces in an interview with Martin Dahinden, in 2016 the Swiss ambassador to the United States. In Switzerland, business and "government" (public education) collaborate. Apprenticeship costs are shared by public funds (one third) and the private sector (two thirds). Students can choose from 238 careers and professions. And because an apprentice in Switzerland may "end up as a CEO of a multinational company," apprenticeships are considered an alternate path for promising students, not a default for those unlikely to succeed in college.

Increased access to apprenticeships consistent with this model was one of the few issues on which Presidents Obama and Trump appear to have agreed. An executive order issued by the Trump White House on June 15, 2017, echoed President Obama's earlier summons: "It shall be the policy of the Federal Government to provide more affordable pathways to secure, high paying jobs by promoting apprenticeships" (Trump, 2017, para. 6). Though representing a different political sector, the Center on Education & Skills (now the Center on Education and Labor) at New America (2019) has expressed comparable enthusiasm: "Apprenticeships can meet the talent development needs of a wide range of industries while increasing access to good jobs for many more Americans" (para. 2).

SIDEBAR
"Bolstering" the Registered Apprenticeship

Less than a month into his administration, President Biden announced significant initiatives in support of Registered Apprenticeships. He endorsed the National Apprenticeship Act of 2021, a bill that would "create and expand registered apprenticeships, youth apprenticeships and pre-apprenticeship programs"—an estimated 1 million new opportunities. He asked the USDL to reinstate the National Advisory Committee on Apprenticeships and explained that the committee would "focus on making sure that Black and brown Americans, immigrants, and women can access the training and jobs of the future." In March some details became clearer through the release of the American Jobs Plan. While the proposal for an ambitious investment in infrastructure appeared to face an uncertain future in the Congress, broad support for the creation of "one to two million new registered apprenticeships slots" signaled a fresh emphasis on programs initiated by or offered in partnership with community colleges (White House, 2021b).

An "Alternate" Approach to Apprenticeships

An alternative to the registered apprenticeship developed just as the distractions and disruptions of 2020–2021 were becaming conspicuous. The impediments to the scaling of apprenticeships listed by Robert Lerman—insufficient funding, a "complex administrative structure," approval delays, inadequate auditing—were cited as some of the reasons for IRAPs proposed by the National Network of Business and Industry Associations. Although IRAPS were authorized by the USDL in March 2020, in November 2021 the USDL issued a proposal to rescind that authorization.

They would offer a different model. Quality assurance would be achieved not through compliance with the venerable national standards for the RA but through the evaluation of programs by third-party assessors in the context of industry needs. And programs would award industry-recognized credentials rather than the completion certificates awarded by RA programs. In a "final rule" authorizing the new approach, the secretary of labor in the Trump administration, Eugene Scalia, described IRAPs as offering "employers, community colleges, and others a flexible, innovative way to quickly expand apprenticeship in telecommunications, health care, cybersecurity, and other sectors where apprenticeships currently are not widely available" (USDL, 2020, para. 3).

The risk behind this alternate approach, voiced by Mary Alice McCarthy of the Center on Education & Skills at New America (CESNA), was that it might "open the door to low-quality programs," thereby destabilizing a system "that has been the closest thing to a guaranteed pathway into the middle class for over 80 years" (McCarthy, 2019, para. 5). Caroline Preston was

---

SIDEBAR
Apprenticeships and Other "Practicums"

The apprenticeship represents only one of several educational approaches that combine academic learning with practical experience—but it is the most likely to award a *credential.* Other such approaches include internships offered by academic institutions. While many undergraduate internships focus on service assignments or cultural experience, a 2012 survey of 50,000 employers by *The Chronicle of Higher Education* and public radio's *Marketplace* showed that the internship has more recently become *primarily* a step toward employment (The Chronicle of Higher Education and American Public Media, 2012). Others include the clerkship (through which a recent legal graduate, e.g., may work with an experienced judge), residencies in various professional specialties (medical appointments are the most familiar), university postdoctoral fellowships, especially in scientific disciplines, and employment that provides built-in opportunites for continued career education.

more blunt. Writing for *The Hechinger Report*, she expressed a concern "that this parallel push for industry-recognized apprenticeships could be a stealth means of watering down standards for apprenticeships, making it easier for businesses to avoid wage gains and other requirements of the apprenticeship model" (Preston, 2018, para. 10).

McCarthy's concern that the alternate system would offer inadequate protection for students and taxpayers would inform the later action proposing recission. Earlier, a February 17, 2021, executive order from the Biden White House had asserted that such programs "have fewer quality standards than registered apprenticeship programs . . . and they lack the standardized training rigor that ensures employers know they are hiring a worker with high-quality training" (White House, 2021a, para. 6).

Following the European Example: Three Initiatives
In 2010 a German automotive company, BMW, was facing a dilemma at its production facility in Spartanburg, SC, difficulty in recruiting "those multiskilled employees out there who have all the mechanical, electrical, robotics, and other skills we need" (Labi, 2012). So BMW decided to invest in a competitive "BMW Scholars Program" to be offered in partnership with three technical colleges in the area. The program enables successful applicants to gain experience at the plant working part-time while earning credits as full-time students at the colleges. Moreover, *BMW offers students chosen for the program tuition assistance toward obtaining their degrees* (Greenville Technical College, 2019).

In New Jersey, an "Earn While You Learn" partnership between Hudson County Community College (HCCC, Jersey City) and Eastern Millwork, Inc., a custom woodworking company, has led to a four-year "European style dual educational program" offered through the company's Holz Technik Academy. High school graduates selected for the academy receive full benefits and a starting salary of nearly $25,000. Four days each week, they follow a systematic curriculum combining instruction and on-the-job experience at Eastern Millwork. On Fridays, they take classes at HCCC. After four years of study and training, apprentices will have earned regular increments in compensation, an associate degree (from HCCC), and a four-year credential in engineering. They may then qualify for a salary of $70,000 (Eastern Millwork, 2019).

In Chattanooga, TN, the location of its principal U.S. production facility, Volkswagen convened a regional discussion of apprenticeships. Although VW shares an industry with BMW, the initiatives prompted by this discussion were not limited to automobile manufacture. For instance, Northeast State Community College (Blountville, TN) and the Regional Center for Advanced Manufacturing (RCAM) now offer an RA with a variety of employers in different industries. Quoted in the (Kingsport, TN) *Times-News,* Jeff Frazier, the RCAM dean, describes the process: "We're able to put a [USDL] registered apprenticeship structure together for them and deliver it as a turn-key package . . . to any size company whether it has one apprenticeship or 20. This allows them to take advantage of the same level of training available to Fortune 500 companies" (Wilson, 2020).

In Sum

An entire chapter on apprenticeships? We considered that question at the outset but concluded that in addition to offering a beachhead for innovation with a potential for impressive growth—in the number of apprenticeships, in the spectrum of professional opportunities, in participants, and, most notably, in prestige—the contemporary apprenticeship represents a singular synthesis among credentials. Apprenticeships can combine academic study and workplace mentoring, on-the-job compensation and practical experience, the completion of degrees, and the securing of employment. If there were a single motivating paradigm for the evolution of postsecondary education in the 21st century, it might be the apprenticeship.

Takeaways

Colleges and universities that seek the best for their students (and wish to remain competitive) should explore expanding their students' access to apprenticeships. There are specific initiatives well worth considering.

Administrators could

- determine whether there are prominent industries or corporations within the institution's service area that might benefit from additional apprenticeship programs and challenge disciplines within the institution to develop such programs in consultation with employers;
- survey students regarding their potential interest in apprenticeships and invite disciplines within the institution to respond; and
- create stronger linkages between community colleges and four-year institutions (in both directions) that could expand participation in apprenticeships.

Faculty members could

- determine whether there are models of apprenticeships, internships, and residencies within their disciplines that deserve consideration; and
- discuss how schedules, curricula, and student services within their disciplines or departments might be modified to facilitate student participation in apprenticeships and other practicum experiences.

Academic advisors could

- familiarize themselves with apprenticeship agreements and contracts so as to assist students in evaluating such opportunities;
- seek out apprenticeship opportunities that students might otherwise overlook; and
- contribute to the development of criteria for evaluating and assigning appropriate credit to learning achieved through apprenticeships.

PART THREE

Implications for Action

We have acknowledged both the objective and subjective values of credentials.

We have cited labor market information to document income gains promised by credentials. We have observed how a successful experience in the pursuit of a nondegree credential can lead to a job or to admission to a degree program. And we have questioned the distinction between credentials focused on eligibility for entry-level positions and those offering pathways to careers, advancement, and leadership. We have argued against regarding any assumption as "terminal."

We have also recognized important subjective values. As commencement exercises demonstrate, receiving a credential can mean far more than qualifying for employment or advanced study. Credentials are sources of pride for recipients and for their families and friends. Credentials differentiate them throughout their lives. They create opportunity, but they also "hang on the wall" as a testament to talent and persistence and as a bid for respect.

Therein lies a concern, however. As Michael Sandel has defined the issue, academic credentials while "congratulating the winners" can "denigrate the losers, even in their own eyes." The result? "Resentment borne of humiliation" creates deep and long-lasting divisions (Sandel, 2020, pp. 25–26). Drawing on Sandel's book for his *New York Times* column, Thomas L. Friedman perceives the paradox at the heart of Sandel's argument, that "a seemingly attractive ideal—the meritocratic promise that if you work hard and go to college, you will rise . . . sends a double message" (Friedman, 2020, p. A26).

On the one hand, earning a college degree can lead to both financial and social advancement. On the other hand, failing to do so can bar an individual from such advancement and fuel a sense of estrangement and humiliation. "Elites have so valorized a college degree . . . that they have difficulty understanding the hubris a meritocracy can generate, and the harsh judgment it imposes on those who have not gone to college" (Sandel, 2020, p. 26).

Eric Kelderman wrote the cover story for the November 13, 2020, issue of *The Chronicle of Higher Education* headlined, "The College Degree is Dividing America." Reflecting on the presidential election then just concluded, he warned that "the Trump era may foreshadow a deep and enduring schism between those who have a college credential and those who do not" (Kelderman, 2020, p. 20). The possible consequences for postsecondary education—further reductions in public funding, increased (and increasingly more critical) oversight, and a continued erosion of belief in higher education as a public good—could be long lasting.

Of course, the problem that Sandel, Friedman, and Kelderman describe is not by any means attributable solely, or perhaps even principally, to actions on the part of credential providers. "Credentialism," the use of credentials to create or protect castes in society, thrives most vigorously in a labor market that creates stark winners and losers. Worker protections formerly offered by strong labor union contracts and regular adjustments to a "living" minimum wage once limited the differentials in the marketplace. Now, such disparities, exacerbated by factors including a decline in union membership and influence, a stagnant minimum wage, the exporting of domestic employment, and the replacement of workers by technology have had the greatest negative impact on those without a college degree.

But if credential providers do not deserve all the blame, colleges, universities, and other providers do share a measure of responsibility. We have documented a lack of transparency about credentials, acknowledged the academy's resistance to change, objected to the stratification of credential categories, and taken issue with the principle that privileged groups *should* find their way to preferred paths while others should be content with lower tiers.

The good news is that there is much that credential providers can and should do to address the problem. In fact, we reserve the "Takeaways" at the conclusion of chapter 11 for practical strategies that both acknowledge and seek to address credentialism. Principal among them is a commitment to recognize and celebrate individuals who may choose not to earn postsecondary credentials but nevertheless have much to offer.

We argue also that one effective approach to achieving genuine equity must focus on credentials themselves—on the institutions and organizations that award them, on the faculty members whose teaching makes them possible, and, above all, on the students and potential students who benefit from them. But we will also argue that to focus on achieving greater equity so far as credentials are concerned without giving equal attention to their quality is worse than meaningless. Encouraging students to seek inferior credentials will not bridge the divide but deepen it.

In chapter 12, we will consider how administrators, faculty members, and academic advisors can and should take lead roles in improving both equity and quality. The takeaways following each chapter have so far been largely tactical, practical initiatives. But our emphasis in concluding this book will shift to overarching strategies, to the clarification and pursuit of commitments that can and should make a difference in the credentials environment.

II

QUALITY AND EQUITY IN THE CREDENTIALS MARKETPLACE

The synthesis of quality and equity, always a challenge to maintain, has become an even greater challenge. Increased political polarization, a heightened focus on racial justice, public health concerns associated with the pandemic, and existential concerns within many academic institutions are some of the reasons. Some academic leaders may conclude that circumstances require them to prioritize one or the other. But doing so would be a strategic error for institutions and a disservice to students and to society. There are practical steps that administrators, faculty members, and academic advisors can take that will enable them to serve students more effectively and equitably while making their institutions both more competitive and more sustainable.

Academic Leadership at a Critical Time

Prior to 2020, postsecondary educators, policymakers, and opinion leaders appeared to be nearing consensus on an answer to the question posed by the title of Goldie Blumenstyk's 2015 book: *American Higher Education in Crisis?* That consensus? Yes. Blumenstyk (2015) focuses on three issues: the extent to which postsecondary education serves (or fails to serve) students, increases in the costs of education and commensurate increases in student debt, and challenges for leadership within and beyond the academy.

Each issue proves multifaceted, not surprisingly, but there is a leitmotif of two themes that are audible throughout. The first sounds a growing concern about quality (fueled by employer dissatisfaction with new employees, increases in postsecondary education costs, breakdowns in accountability, institutional closures, etc.). The other theme evokes demonstrable inequities created by economic barriers, discriminatory testing, unequal access to technology, deep variances in the quality of secondary school systems, and the like.

Each of these concerns was exacerbated by the events of 2020–2021. Quality has suffered and inequities have become more conspicuous. At the same time, however, these unprecedented challenges for society have reaffirmed quality credentials as the essential commitment of postsecondary education, a critical asset for the economy, a clear benefit for individuals, and an effective engine for addressing (and one would hope) resolving inequities. As a result, improving quality and building equity with respect to credentials—seen not as separate issues but as one priority—has become the single most important challenge for postsecondary education and for society. Rising to that challenge will include the pursuit of many of the reforms we have proposed.

The Promise of Social Mobility—and the Reality

Individuals who obtain credentials with recognized value can gain access to successful careers and satisfying lives. And there are benefits for society as well. Credential earners on average are more likely to maintain good health, to exercise civic responsibility, and to have an appreciation for racial and ethnic diversity (Doyle, 2017; Gurin et al., 2002).

That's the promise. And that's the justification for public investment in postsecondary education as both an individual and a social good. But because the promise is not made available to all groups equally, not all qualified and motivated students are able to benefit from it. To the contrary, as we have seen, the complicated and often inscrutable credentials marketplace offers risks as well as opportunities, and both are disproportionately distributed.

Although quality and equity should go hand in hand, the inequities conspicuous in society—in income, in access to health care, in the availability of technology, in opportunities for advancement—tarnish the credentials marketplace as well. Learners from disadvantaged backgrounds, particularly students of color, are less likely to pursue credentials associated with the most positive outcomes. Some find their preparation inadequate for competitive programs. Others, despite being fully qualified, may find themselves steered toward credentials of lesser value. And they may be less likely to attain even these! National Student Clearinghouse data on students who start at four-year public institutions show significant differences in completion rates: 48% and 57% for Black and Hispanic students, respectively, which is much lower than the rate for White students, 72% (Shapiro et al., 2018).

Moreover, Black and Hispanic students who do attain credentials are likely to incur disproportionate levels of debt—in itself a disincentive to seek a credential. Those who complete a bachelor's degree acquire on average $7,400 more in debt (Scott-Clayton, 2018) than their White classmates. And that differential represents a continuing weight, one factor contributing to a substantial net worth differential between Black and White families (McIntosh et al., 2020).

SIDEBAR
Talk the Talk, Walk the Walk
Published in October 2020, *From Equity Talk to Equity Walk: Expanding Practitioner Knowledge for Racial Justice in Higher Education* (Wiley) identifies impediments to equity and suggests strategies for confronting them. Responding to questions about the book posed by Scott Jaschik (2020) of *Inside Higher Ed*, the authors (Tia Brown McNair, Estela Mara Bensimon, Lindsey Malcolm-Piquex) urge faculty, staff, students, and administrators to "take on the role of 'anthropologists' and identify how their familiar routines, practices, policies, documents, language, values, etc. reproduce racial inequality and privilege" (n.p.). Informed by data disaggregated by race, campus leaders should examine institutional practices and "identify specific actions needed to realize equity" (n.p.). Drawing on the experience of AAC&U and the Center for Urban Education, the book offers many examples of progress being made.

The expansion of postsecondary education, as shown in a sustained growth in college enrollments, has led to an increase in opportunities for all. But that increase has not benefited everyone equally. Advantaged in many ways—more effective K–12 preparation, better pre-college advising, greater reliance on advanced placement and other means of educational acceleration, and more reliable access to technology—privileged students are more likely to qualify for admission to the nation's most competitive and prestigious institutions. And while many less advantaged students may prosper at community colleges, regional universities, and other institutions offering good value for money, others will make poor choices that with better advice they would have been able to avoid. Institutions enabling first-generation college students to achieve a measure of social mobility take pride in that mission, and rightly so. But the extent to which the stratification of postsecondary education reflects and reinforces that of society is part of the problem.

Indeed, the societal costs of stratification are high, whether the divide be between prestigious and run-of-the-mill credentials or between some credential and no credential. Although postsecondary education offers our most reliable pathway to the alleviation of poverty and inequality, its hierarchical structure can contribute to their perpetuation. If there is any value to be found in the coruscating experiences of 2020–2021, it may lie in a renewed awareness of social injustice and the inequities that result. Whether that awareness will continue to sustain a thirst for reform—as it should!—remains an open question.

Commendable Efforts

Even as the problems Blumenstyk describes in her 2015 book were growing worse, there were commendable efforts under way to address them: books, task forces, conferences, legislation, whitepapers. A clear focus on improving and assuring quality appears, for instance, in the following:

- a 2016 collaborative work edited by Richard Arum, Josipa Roksa, and Amanda Cook, *Improving Quality in American Higher Education*
- HR 4579, the Quality Higher Education Act, introduced on October 8, 2019, which proposed enhancements in accreditation "to ensure that colleges are graduating students with meaningful degrees and preparing them for workplace success" (Wilson, F. S., 2019, para. 1)
- a 2019 publication by the Council on Higher Education Accreditation, *Conversations About Quality in Higher Education*
- an annual "International Conference on Quality in Higher Education," which attracts educators to share ideas focused on elements of quality and quality assurance

During the same period, a commensurate focus on improving equity and removing injustices was apparent as well. Consider, for instance, the following:

- Achieving the Dream (ATD, 2020), "the most comprehensive non-governmental reform movement for student success in higher education history" (para 3). Focused on community college students, the initiative brings together nearly 300 institutions, a corps of coaches and advisors, investors, and partners with the aim of enabling community college students to "realize greater economic opportunity."
- Books such as *Stand Up and Lead for Equity* and *America's Unmet Promise: The Imperative for Equity in Higher Education* (Witham et al.), both published in 2015 by AAC&U, illuminate this issue and offer strategies for addressing it.
- The state-by-state approach of The Education Trust has encouraged the development and pursuit of racial equity goals in more than

40 states. "In such a diverse nation—where more than half of public school students are students of color—this educational inequality is a threat to a healthy economy, which depends on well-trained workers, as well as to a healthy democracy, which depends on well-informed citizens" (Jones & Berger, 2019, para. 2).

Each of these initiatives has value. All express the understanding that educational quality depends in part on diversity within the learning environment and in part on a determined effort to identify and address injustice. And they share the recognition that inequities in postsecondary education contribute to and reinforce injustice in society—racial, social, economic, geographic. It is similarly obvious that compromises in quality inevitably undermine the effort to achieve genuine equity. Nevertheless, there remains an implicit assumption in many of these undertakings that progress must be sought through efforts that emphasize *either* quality *or* equity.

A Concerted Approach

We subscribe instead to a recognition voiced by a task force of 20 (college presidents, association heads, accreditors, analysts, etc.) convened in 2018 by Lumina Foundation. The group's given task was to develop recommendations that would reflect its name, the Quality Credentials Task Force. But at the first of four in-person meetings, the members of the QCTF achieved a breakthrough that would guide their work, namely, the recognition that *no distinction should be made between quality and equity.* The final report of the task force, *Unlocking the Nation's Potential: A Model to Advance Quality and Equity in Education Beyond High School,* asserts that "quality and equity are inextricably linked and that future reform approaches must integrate these priorities. Without improved quality, there can be no meaningful equity. Without improved equity, claims for quality ring hollow" (Lumina Foundation, 2019, p. 2).

That perception—that quality and equity represent one priority—articulates the first axiom of the two we advance in this chapter. The second is like unto it. The most direct and effective means by which an institution may pursue this single multifaceted priority is through a focus on credentials—those they offer and those they should be offering.

Our suggestions are for initiatives at two levels: (a) institutional and (b) statewide and national. Our greater emphasis lies with priorities that fall within the immediate jurisdiction of institutional leaders—administrators, faculty members, and academic advisors. But given the influence of such leaders on priorities at the state and national level, we regard these as also within their proper purview.

Institutional Priorities for Action

Throughout this book, we have proposed various "takeaways" and, where appropriate, have observed the implications in them for quality | equity. But an inverted approach could be useful as well, one that *begins* with the quality | equity imperative as a prompt for practical strategies. From the wide range of approaches that might be considered, we suggest those we believe to have the greatest potential. Though they would be feasible as a sequence, they are suggested here rather as components of a comprehensive commitment.

Determine Whether the Basic Elements Crucial to Student Success Are in Place

Colleges and universities must make sure that the credentials they offer will deliver for those who receive them. That requires careful design cognizant of employer needs, of how such credentials might work within a variety of learning pathways (recall the Lego analogy), and of the extent to which credential recipients will qualify for additional education. Coherence is no less important. Students should be able to appreciate the value of every element in the curriculum they are following, even of those elements that may at first appear tangential to the credentials they are seeking. But there is a larger value behind curricular design: Institutions should be able to demonstrate through the thoughtfulness and discipline of the curriculum the priority they place on their students. Some of the questions that might be asked are the following:

- Do the institution's recruitment and admissions practices and its provisions for needs-based financial support express a determination to address inequities?
- Does the institution demonstrate awareness of—and a determination to address—less visible impediments to student success? Does it offer or facilitate childcare? Does it provide assistance for students who may be experiencing hunger and homelessness? Does it attempt to accommodate those who are employed outside the institution?
- Does instruction exemplify effective pedagogy and cultural competence? Is effectiveness measured by and improved through assessment?
- Is instruction provided by a faculty whose diversity reflects that of the student body? If not, is there a clear commitment to move in that direction?

- Are "high-impact practices" of proven efficacy (first-year seminars, writing-intensive courses, learning communities, undergraduate research, internships, diversity/global learning, service learning, and capstone courses and projects) made widely available throughout the curriculum? (See Kuh, 2008.)
- Is the institution's commitment to student success apparent in the availability of comprehensive advising?
- Does the institution follow clear and effective policies for the recognition of prior learning and for the reclamation of "stranded" credits?

Bring the Quality | Equity Priority to Bear on Both a Credentials Inventory and a Credentials Needs Analysis

Institutions that seek to become more effective, more efficient, and more highly regarded are likely to find a systematic focus on credentials—those they offer and those they should be offering—both a principled and a rewarding strategy. Questions that should inform both the inventory and the needs analysis are as follows:

- When disaggregated by race, ethnicity, gender, and other distinguishing factors, does data on student participation and success within the institution's programs reveal reasons for concern and, thus, opportunities for improvement?
- Has the institution encouraged its students, faculty members, alumni, and supporters to consider how familiar conventions and practices may contribute to racial injustice and other inequities? Do all stakeholders have opportunities to share their candid perspectives on issues of quality | equity, particularly so far as credentials are concerned?
- Have the institution's leaders made clear their commitment to a quality | equity agenda? Have their actions mirrored their words?
- Have administrators and faculty members consulted with the institution's academic advisors—often a reliable source of advice on the many issues and opportunities discussed in this book?

Conduct the Credentials Inventory

No institution can provide all of the credentials that its constituents might find profitable, but most could do more than they are doing at present. A strategic approach begins with a thorough canvassing of credentials currently on offer. Every inventory should address a few essential questions:

SIDEBAR
Clearer Pathways

A useful approach to improving student success can be found through implementation of clear curricular pathways supported by effective advising. In addition to the advantages for students—improved curricular continuity, assured alignment with clear learning outcomes—there can be advantages for institutions in terms of greater curricular efficiency and increased student retention and success. Such pathways should be evident within programs, but as some of the examples we have provided suggest, they can also link programs. *Career pathways* help create systems of stackable credentials and useful supports that enable students to choose wisely from multiple entry and exit points to education and work. For instance, restructuring a baccalaureate program to include the completion of a certification can create a straightforward and very appealing pathway. *Guided pathways* can help at the institutional level through the reorganization of programs to support better informed and more deliberate student choice (Bailey et al., 2015). Proactive academic advising with respect to programs aggregated into a few broad areas or "meta-majors" could simplify decision-making and help students make progress. Although pathways are found more often in community colleges, administrators, faculty members, and academic advisors at all institutions should consider their advantages.

- What enrollment trends are evident during the past five and 10-year periods, both for each credential and for each category? (Categories include both hierarchical divisions, such as associate, bachelor's, master's, etc., and broad disciplinary divisions, such as the liberal arts, the social sciences, STEM disciplines, etc.)
- What factors other than enrollment trends should the inventory consider? Student success and alumni accomplishment? Cost effectiveness? Alignment with specific needs? Institutional mission and identity?
- Does the institution's portfolio of programs reflect labor market trends? A program with below average enrollments may nevertheless offer a credential essential to the regional economy or to a particular constituency within the student body.
- Is the current mix of credentials offered by the institution attuned to the abilities and interests of its *current* student body—including first-generation students, disadvantaged students, and students of color?

- In what ways have program enrollments suggested sustained shifts in demand? Are they likely to prove temporary or are they likely to continue?
- What challenges would follow from decisions to discontinue the offering of underperforming credentials so as to reallocate funds to the development and initiation of credentials with greater potential? How might such challenges be addressed?

Identify Unmet Credential Needs
While the inventory is in progress, the institution should consider three factors in its effort to identify credentials not on offer that should be: advancements in knowledge and pedagogy within its disciplines, its current and potential capacity to offer additional credentials, and the unmet needs of current students, potential students, and concerned employers. It should consider these factors in particular:

- Do the credentials reflect advances in knowledge and pedagogy? Or have legacy academic structures and programs been given deference that might be reconsidered? (Consultants may be useful in identifying opportunities.)
- Has the institution expanded its offerings of NDCs in response to emerging demands? If not, is there a persuasive rationale for *not* considering such offerings? If so, has it developed pathways that capitalize on the flexibility of the Lego pieces it offers?
- How well aligned are the credentials on offer with the expertise of the faculty? (Recent hires may make possible opportunities that formerly would have been problematic. Conversely, recent retirements may suggest the need for reevaluation of the curriculum.) Expanded opportunities for faculty development and possible reorientation should support such transitions.
- If the credentials inventory cannot identify potential sources of savings to fund the pursuit of additional opportunities, are there other sources that might be tapped—projected revenues, the securing of an endowment or grant, or corporate partnerships or sponsorships?
- Has every discipline consulted with employers who hire (or might hire) those awarded its credentials? And reviewed labor market information? Are there opportunities to become more responsive to employer and labor market needs?
- Should reforms be deferred until enrollment, financial, and other issues are resolved? Or does "the new normal" point to the urgency of such reforms?

Implement Credentials That Will Declare the Institution's Commitment to Quality | Equity

Strategic reallocation of resources from underperforming programs to ones more closely aligned with the diversity of students and their aspirations could enhance the delivery of credentials, both degrees and NDCs, that expand both opportunity and the commitment to quality.

- One model of a concerted approach to quality | equity appears in the task force report we have cited, *Unlocking the Nation's Potential.* A practical guide rather than a rhetorical statement, the report urges credential redesign (to improve coherence, alignment with needs, and the likelihood of completion), an explicit focus on outcomes (to bolster motivation and to clarify resulting competencies), and a renewed commitment to well-informed and comprehensive student advising.
- A complementary model can be found in a project at Rutgers University focused specifically on NDCs. Its "conceptual framework to guide measurement" proposes a system "to measure quality and ensure these credentials do not offer false promises, particularly to individuals from marginalized groups who may be particularly drawn to non-degree credentials" (Van Noy et al., 2019, para. 1).
- Although these and similar efforts offer administrators, faculty members, and academic advisors useful prompts for leadership, their personal commitment will be critical as they respond to such prompts. The initiatives that succeed will be those that develop collaboratively through energetic discussion of institutional missions, resources, values, and, above all, student needs.

State and National Priorities for Action

Institutional and professional accreditors, academic sector associations, and state and federal agencies all can provide important leadership in the pursuit of quality | equity. But if such organizations stand at one remove from institutional administrators, faculty members, and academic advisors, they should both express and influence the priorities of their constituents. Accrediting commissions include representatives of member institutions. Academic sector associations such as AAC&U and the Council of Independent Colleges, while created to offer leadership, also consider and choose in part from priorities their members identify. State and federal agencies benefit from the continuity offered by civil servants, but policies and priorities are determined largely by individuals either elected or appointed by elected officials. So the actions recommended should be regarded not as the purview of distant bureaucracies but as objectives deserving our advocacy. We have met the reform leaders, as Pogo might have said, and they is us. Or should be. Steps to create an environment for meaningful reform may include the following:

Merge Quality Assurance With "Equity Assurance"
Given their engagement with programs and institutions, both professional and institutional accreditors can exert a positive influence:

- Accreditors can follow the lead of a few accreditation innovators by asking that their members report *disaggregated* data for quality indicators such as credential completion rates, licensure pass rates, employment placements, access to additional credentials, and so on, so as to identify both institutional accomplishments and challenges with respect to racial groups in particular and underrepresented groups in general. Accreditors can recommend good practices for addressing challenges, negotiate benchmarks for improvement, and monitor the results.
- Many accreditors convene their members at least annually for discussion of shared interests and best practices. A renewed and more conspicuous commitment to quality | equity would be timely.
- Specialized accreditors drawing on the experience of professionals within their disciplines should define and recommend good practices for addressing issues of underrepresentation, especially so far as students of color are concerned.
- National accreditors that emphasize career preparation could demonstrate leadership by giving attention to evidence of underrepresentation within particular career tracks, by providing a forum for consideration of strategies to address identified issues, and by facilitating a consensus on benchmarks to which successful institutions and programs should aspire.

Exercise Governmental Authority to Support Leadership in the Pursuit of Quality | Equity
State and federal agencies have important regulatory functions to perform, but they also serve important ancillary roles as information clearinghouses, as conveners, and as mobilizers. Such roles are especially important with regard to quality | equity in the credentials marketplace. Examples of initiatives in this regard may include the following:

- A state higher education or workforce agency could (a) mandate dis-aggregation of quality indicators such as program-level employment outcomes, licensure pass rates, program-level debt repayment, and average income to document differences among racial and ethnic groups; (b) invite practitioners, advocates, and students to reflect on possible root causes for differences that appear and to propose solutions; and (c) offer leadership in the pursuit of such solutions.

- Criteria used in performance-based funding, an effective stimulus to institutional improvement in many states, might include documentation of satisfactory progress toward greater quality | equity.

A Modest Proposal

Success in the pursuit of quality | equity in credentials will depend above all on the commitment and leadership of those we have consistently addressed throughout this book: administrators, faculty members, and academic advisors. But such success would be more likely if there were a concerted national effort to promote the importance of such leadership and to provide support for it.

Many of the priorities of such an effort are implicit in the recommendations for action we have proposed. But there are two priorities in particular that lie beyond the purview of individual institutions—or even that of their sector associations—and that should invite an overarching perspective for any reform effort.

The first would clarify and celebrate the value of *all* postsecondary credentials through explicit recognition of the distinct value of *each* credential. As we have observed, in Switzerland, an apprenticeship may offer a more direct path to the corner office than an MBA. In the United States, a certificate or certification may prove more advantageous than a baccalaureate degree—and combining the NDC with the degree may prove more advantageous than either alone. That is a reality that might be far more widely acknowledged.

The second would address directly the two prejudices that Sandel and Friedman identify, first, that some degrees are innately better than others, second, that possessing a degree is innately better than not possessing one.

We must focus on college readiness, on improving access to and support within postsecondary education, and on improving strategies for completion. We must weave safety nets enabling those who fall through the cracks to rebound and catch the rungs once more. We must enable those who will benefit from a college education to obtain a good one.

Above all, we must engage in the self-scrutiny that Sandel's book prescribes. That should include examining the differences in status we assign to credentials. Giving appropriate value to the opportunities that NDCs offer—and to those who earn them—would be helpful. Perhaps graduation ceremonies should recognize those who have earned certificates, certifications, and badges as well as those who have earned degrees.

But beyond offering such recognition, we should also acknowledge learning and experience that may not be recognized by the award of academic credentials. First, we can implement institutional hiring practices and standards that recognize credentials may not always provide the most reliable indicator of potential for employment. Second, even if we must acknowledge that the world does for the most part rely on credentials in apportioning opportunity, we might also consider awarding new credentials that could document and affirm otherwise unauthenticated competencies. Many organizations already categorize their employees through internal ranks and titles that recognize accomplishment and incentivize advancement. But "degrees of difference," by whatever name, could enable the formerly noncredentialed to achieve greater recognition.

Similarly, there must also be a priority on ways to affirm those employed by the college or university (carpenters, plumbers, law officers, chefs) who demonstrate significant (but perhaps not academic) competences. Although competitive compensation and benefits remain the *sine qua non* for correcting credentialism, less tangible forms of recognition might also play a part. For instance, colleges and universities that separate recognitions of faculty from those honoring staff members might consider combining them! Faculty clubs, where they exist, might extend a membership invitation to all employees. Imagine inviting opportunities for academic administrators, faculty members, food service employees, buildings and grounds workers, campus security officers, and many others to mingle informally and become acquainted!

In Sum

A priority on creating more effective strategies to achieve greater quality and equity in institutions, in programs, and in credentials could engage accreditors, associations (e.g., AAC&U, AACC), foundations (e.g., Gates, Ford, Lumina), sector organizations (CIC, AASCU, APLU, etc.), federal and state agencies, and the employer community. But leadership, most likely in the form of a nongovernmental task force drawing on all of these sources, could offer guidance in the pursuit of a strong, simply stated consensus on the elements of quality in postsecondary education, an identification of the most compelling quality | equity issues that require attention at the national level, a mobilization of appropriate players to provide guidance, and a clarification of metrics for assessing the results of reform.

Why now? The answer should be obvious. We have had ample reason to recognize the continuing educational and social costs of a credentials environment that exacerbates inequities. Insurrection, contempt for expertise, and the radical prioritization of individual rights over societal needs—all have their roots in grievances related to credentialism.

The "takeaways" that ordinarily would appear at this point have been embedded throughout because the chapter as a whole focuses explicitly on what administrators, faculty members, and academic advisors can and should "take away" from the discussion in order to serve students more effectively and to strengthen their institutions. There is an overriding assumption implicit throughout that the priority on quality | equity can be pursued most effectively through attention to credentials and how they are delivered, classroom by classroom, program by program, institution by institution. Such attention, if it is to prove effective, will come from leadership that embodies above all a principled and well-informed commitment to the success of *all* students.

ACADEMIC LEADERSHIP
AT A CRITICAL TIME

A volatile period in American history has had a marked influence on postsecondary education—creating a "new normal," as the catch phrase has it. What has not changed? The essential elements of an effective response to the opportunities and risks presented by the credentials environment remain the same. But the need for effective leadership has become both more important and more urgent. Hence the three priorities of our title: Understand the problems. Identify the opportunities. Create the solutions.

Laudable Initiatives

There is no lack of initiatives bearing on the credentials environment. No fewer than 36 such efforts are documented in a March 2019 survey, the "Learn-and-Work Ecosystem Guide." The survey identifies agencies and associations that are addressing different audiences through different strategies but that appear to agree on six broad goals:

- building greater transparency throughout the credentials environment
- accelerating progress in this environment through coordination and cooperation of participating agents
- creating and implementing improved technology, developing more useful data, and defining clearer standards to facilitate the alignment of discrete systems
- advancing employer and workforce "signaling" for credential transparency
- improving navigation tools and quality assurance in the credentials database
- improving and expanding communications related to credential transparency (Zanville, 2020)

Taken together, these objectives offer a multifaceted yet coherent effort to understand and elucidate the credentials "ecosystem" as a means toward making opportunities more accessible and risks more transparent. But the objective concerning the need for more and better data appears especially critical. In particular, if the credentials environment is to be understood more fully and monitored more effectively for quality assurance, noncredit courses and programs must also be documented in IPEDS and other relevant databases. As they are increasingly important to students, so, too, have they become increasingly important for institutions and for the agencies that assess their effectiveness.

The true measure of all such objectives will appear in action plans to accomplish them, sector by sector, institution by institution, leader by leader. That is where the volatility of the past few years has made matters more complicated. Change processes within institutions have had to adapt to a "new reality" in which faculty members, administrators, and students are choosing more often to meet online rather than on campus. Within regions, many of the institutional reforms regarded as "substantive" by accrediting commissions qualified for a fast track to approval—temporarily. Nationally, changes in student aid and accreditation implemented in July 2020 may now startle those who have been paying attention to more immediate challenges. The hope is that we can continue to use what we learned during a crisis in order to make good use of opportunities and options that have emerged.

We will defer to Levine and Van Pelt for prophecy. (See the sidebar, p. 201.) As brokers warn, "past performance is no guarantee of future results." Hence this "capstone" chapter focuses on *practical* steps that administrators, faculty members, and academic advisors can take in the near term with respect to credentials so as to strengthen their institutions and serve their students more effectively. The recommendations (which align approximately with the preceding chapters) appear as propositions. Some may be easily implemented. In fact, some are already in the works at some institutions. Others may raise hackles. And, depending on the emergence of further unprecedented developments, some may turn out to be unrealistic, unfeasible, or simply untimely.

But that is OK! Leo Damrosch's masterful account of stimulating discussions in 19th-century England, *The Club* (Yale, 2019), shows world-class arguers such as Samuel Johnson and Edmund Burke deliberately provoking their colleagues so as to stimulate a productive exchange of views. While neither of us would have qualified for membership, we rather admire the members for their collegial and constructive (if occasionally heated) arguments. So if our propositions make you want to email a colleague, to schedule a meeting, to snap a pencil in half, or simply to inform yourself more fully about pros and cons, cheers! You're in the club!

SIDEBAR
Two Sages Predict the Future

A book should ordinarily avoid offering predictions. Prophets who get it wrong risk losing credibility altogether. But a book may acknowledge predictions by authoritative voices when they correspond closely to the issues on which it focuses. In the September 3, 2021, issue of the *Chronicle of Higher Education,* two prominent authorities on postsecondary education, Arthur Levine and Scott Van Pelt, share their views as to five ways in which higher education may be "upended" in the coming decades (pp. 21–25). Because every one of their "ways" takes up issues our book considers, we summarize them in brief:

(a) "Consumers" rather than institutions will become dominant. That is, students, rather than colleges or other institutions, will increasingly determine the priorities of higher education.

(b) Students captivated by the internet and contemporary media will demand that education become no less innovative and appealing.

(c) "A host of new institutions, organizations, and programs have cropped up . . . and constitute a harbinger of things to come." For more details, see chapters 2 and 3.

(d) The priorities of a "knowledge economy . . . rooted in outcomes" will prevail over an increasingly obsolete focus on "time, process, and teaching." As we have observed, making programs stronger begins with clarifying their objectives.

(e) Nondegree credentials, sharp in focus and efficient in delivery, will challenge the dominance of traditional degrees that combine breadth and depth.

Such an abbreviated summary cannot do justice to a prophecy based on long experience and made stronger by wise caveats. But the Latin cliché prompts us to take wise prognosticators seriously: *Praemonitus, praemunitus.* Or, in our paraphrase, if you **understand the problems** (are *forewarned*), you are prepared to **identify the opportunities** and **create the solutions** (are *forearmed*). The article is available at https://www.chronicle.com/article/5-ways-higher-ed-will-be-upended-in-the-decades-to-come?cid2=gen_login_refresh&cid=gen_sign_in

What Can Be Known, What Cannot Be Known, and What Should Be Done Anyway

As we have shown, within the past few years the credentials environment has become more complicated, not simpler. Riskier, not safer. And—barring steady progress—more likely to lead to further stratification of postsecondary education, to deeper inequities, and to greater frustration for students and employers.

Why? First, constraints on the proliferation of credentials, never robust to begin with, have further eroded. For instance, although the leveling of a familiar partition between "regional" and "national" institutional accreditation may prove to be positive, the immediate consequence is likely to be greater confusion. Second, while increased reliance on online learning in 2020–2021 led to some technological and pedagogical improvements, the abrupt shift away from in-person learning created some memorably poor experiences for many. The fallout may have a long half-life. Finally, while the necessity for a temporary enforced absence from campus may have awakened in students and faculty members alike a deep appreciation for learning as part of a community, the opposite trend, that formerly traditional students will henceforth opt for distributed learning, seems possible as well. Even as traditional "campus life" and institutional culture continue to rebound, questions concerning priorities, especially during a period of financial challenges, will continue to demand attention. Another recreation center "lazy river," anyone?

The issue is not the appropriateness of particular adjustments undertaken prior to, despite, or because of events in 2020–2021. Some were overdue. But those that have occurred and are continuing to occur appear unlikely to make the credentialing environment more transparent, easier to negotiate, or more reliable. Hence administrators, faculty members, and academic advisors face a heightened challenge to interpret the most relevant changes for the benefit of their colleagues and to undertake efforts that will inform, guide, and protect their students. Some suggested priorities in this regard will conclude our book.

Priorities for Leaders

Leadership priority 1: Recognizing that the changing environment of postsecondary education in the 2020s will continue to necessitate continued innovation and responsiveness, determine which trends so far as credentials are concerned create opportunities appropriate to the institution and its students and seek a realistic and data-driven approach to realize those opportunities. *See especially chapters 4–10.*

Leadership priority 2: While attending to immediate priorities that must be addressed to ensure the continued viability of your institution and the value for its students of the credentials it awards, give some attention also to priorities that bear on the transparency, usefulness, and competitiveness of the credentials that are offered—and of those that should be. See especially *chapters 1–3.*

Leadership priority 3: Seek a clearer understanding of how well the credentials awarded by the institution are "working" for the students who earn them. With an awareness of social and economic inequities in postsecondary education, disaggregate institutional tracking of student success so as to identify and address concerns *credential by credential, demographic by demographic.* Be attentive to ways in which the "transactional" dimensions of credentials may be changing as hiring practices evolve and as the nation seeks a closer alignment between the needs of the economy and the qualifications of the workforce. But be wary of unstated and unexamined assumptions concerning prestige and entitlement. *See chapters 1 and 11 in particular.*

Leadership priority 4: Acknowledge that the distribution of credentials awarded by category may continue to shift in favor of those that can be completed in less time and at less expense. Because of inadequate data on noncredit credentials, it is particularly important that administrators, faculty members, and academic advisors become familiar with trends within their disciplines—and with the opportunities they offer. By exploring ways of linking short-term noncredit credentials to for-credit programs, institutions can take a cost-effective approach to expanding opportunities for students. But degree programs, which have by and large retained their "branding" advantage, also should become a platform for innovation. They can be strengthened by defining explicit learning outcomes for each, implementing pedagogy meant to encourage the accomplishment of those outcomes, assessing the resulting effectiveness, and using what is learned to improve continuously. *See especially chapters 4–9.*

Leadership priority 5: Community college administrators, faculty members, and academic advisors should consider how the associate degree might more effectively link to (and perhaps incorporate) nondegree credentials (NDCs). And administrators, faculty members, and academic advisors at four-year institutions should spruce up their welcome ramps for associate degree recipients and their community college credits. In fact, community college graduates may represent the single largest potential pool for new enrollments at small liberal arts colleges and regional universities. *See Chapter 4 in particular.*

Leadership priority 6: Although there has been increasing interest in the advantages of short-term credentials, both credit and noncredit, savvy baccalaureate institutions should take advantage of the bachelor's degree "brand" as the iconic postsecondary credential—the most frequently awarded, the most widely recognized, and the most often used as a platform for advanced professional study. But if the advantages of the bachelor's degree should not be underestimated, neither should they be overestimated. Degrees that fail to document explicit learning outcomes may place graduates at a disadvantage relative to their peers presenting focused NDCs. Administrators, faculty members, and academic advisors have an obligation to set aside comfortable platitudes about a liberal arts education in favor of explicit educational objectives, including "liberalizing" ones. Assessment of effectiveness should in turn support strategic reinvestment in programs closely aligned with student needs and labor market demands. *See chapter 5 in particular.*

Leadership priority 7: In confusion lie opportunities for competitive innovation. The master's degree, the most protean of credentials, may be the most versatile Lego piece in the set. However, for the credential to offer students and the economy distinctive value, its particular merit as both a terminal or transitional qualification must be made clear through the publication of explicit, rigorous, and easily assessed learning outcomes that set it apart from all other credentials. *See chapter 6.*

Leadership priority 8: Institutions that offer the doctorate, whether it be the traditional research degree, the PhD, the EdD, or doctoral credentials offering access to the practice of a profession belong to a selective and influential club. Unfortunately, despite an urgent need for coordination and cooperation, the members of this club too often go their own way. Administrators, faculty members, and academic advisors at doctoral institutions face a dual challenge, that of protecting the distinctive value of a long-esteemed credential (e.g., the PhD) while responding to an increased demand within practitioner disciplines (mostly in health care) for doctoral education. *See chapter 7.*

Leadership priority 9: Embrace the dual nature of NDCs. Most conspicuously, they can offer students at all educational levels opportunities to develop highly focused expertise closely aligned with opportunities for employment. Increasingly, however, they are being combined with other NDCs and with degree programs to create "covalent bonds" that are strong compounds. Savvy administrators, faculty members, and academic advisors in all institutional categories should embrace this trend and expand the range of "connectable" options. *See chapters 8 and 9 in particular.*

Leadership priority 10: Many apprenticeships combine academic preparation appropriate to an associate degree with hands-on instruction offered by master mentors. These merit particular attention because of (a) the increasing influence of the apprenticeship as a model of effective education and (b) the extent to which apprenticeships linking institutions (particularly community colleges) and employers can offer a particularly advantageous bridge between postsecondary education and the world of work. Administrators, faculty members, and academic advisors should consider not only the potential for their institutions in new "white-collar" apprenticeship programs, but also how the "spirit of apprenticeship" might be extended to reinvigorate disciplines and programs in general. *See chapter 10.*

Leadership priority 11: The synthesis of quality and equity, which has always been a challenge, has become a particular priority now, one expressed through a commitment to reliable guidance, to trustworthy providers, and to credentials with demonstrable returns. By making inequities more conspicuous, the experience of 2020–2021 may have clarified the importance of addressing and ameliorating them, but administrators, faculty members, and academic advisors must continue working to fulfill that commitment. By so doing, they will serve their students more effectively while making their institutions more competitive. See *chapter 11.*

Leadership priority 12: As this review has attempted to suggest, the future of higher education belongs to institutions led by administrators, faculty members, and academic advisors who understand credentials and their contexts, who take seriously their shared responsibility for guiding students through an inchoate complex of opportunities, and who embrace the need for thoughtful, consultative, and evidence-based innovation—the kinds of innovation we have advocated throughout this book.

A Final Word—Four, Actually

Through the priorities suggested and, indeed, the many listed in the more detailed "Takeaways" that conclude chapters 1–10, there are four principles that any administrator, faculty member, and academic advisor should keep in mind. They are obvious. They are worth repeating.

Information

Never has the need for clear and complete data been greater. Since 2010 the "Strong Foundations" initiative of the State Higher Education Executive Officers Association (SHEEO) has led to marked improvement in state postsecondary data systems. And through its "Communities of Practice" project SHEEO encourages states to make more effective use of its data to identify and address issues. A recent (SHEEO, 2021) report summarizes progress being made through both initiatives.

This is good news for institutions as well, in that state-level data in many states now offers reliable contexts for an institution's analysis of its own effectiveness. Given such contexts, questions—

- How does the institution define its "signature" credentials? Which are they?
- Which credentials most clearly represent the values and reputation of the institution?
- Which credentials most clearly represent a competitive advantage for the institution? For its students?
- Which of the credentials offered by the institution are most directly associated with student success—before and following graduation?
- Which credentials are defined most fully in terms of clearly stated learning outcomes? Which should be more clearly defined?
- Which credentials reflect consultation with employers and continuing attention to workforce data?
- Are there credentials not currently offered that would address documented student interests or regional needs?

—can be addressed both in absolute and relative terms. How effective is the institution relative to its own strategic priorities? And how does its effectiveness compare with that of its competitors?

The answers will of course depend on the quality of the data available—in national databases, in improved state databases, in urban and regional databases, and through the institution's own research. But—to make the point tactfully—data will not be useful unless it is used. Far too often, an institution's credentials reflect unexamined assumptions, traditional preroga-tives, and a preference for the status quo. The institutions that thrive in this era will be those willing to ask and address hard questions. In this book we have identified several exemplars. Others are emerging.

Entrepreneurship

Our concern throughout has been to emphasize not that postsecondary institutions should necessarily be "run like businesses," but that if they are to thrive, they must exemplify values essential to any effective organiza-tion. We have described many of these values, including that of a reliance on information, which we have just emphasized, but underneath them all lies the entrepreneurial question that Dennis Jones, a former president of NCHEMS, used to ask regularly: "Is everything you are doing now more important than what you *might* be doing?"

As we suggest, effective organizations rely on data in reviewing the credentials they offer and in asking hard questions about them. Their quality and equity measured in terms of student success must be the primary con-sideration, but questions of entrepreneurship should be considered as well. Which credential offerings are performing well relative to marketplace needs? Which should be promoted more aggressively? Which should be improved if the organization is to remain competitive? And which have seen better days? By considering such questions regularly and by responding boldly to the answers that emerge, administrators, faculty members, and academic advisors honor the academic enterprise and serve their students and their other constituencies more effectively.

Consultation

We have emphasized the necessity for the continued engagement of our three primary audiences—administrators, faculty members, and academic advisors—not only with the issues we have outlined, *but with each other.* Each of these has experience and expertise to contribute, and each has a responsibil-ity to work with and support the efforts of the others. Administrators should consult more regularly with faculty members not only out of respect for their traditional prerogative concerning curricular matters, but also because fac-ulty knowledge of academic fields is essential to wise decisions concerning credentials. In turn, faculty members joining the discussion must be willing to assume an institutional perspective focused on "our students" rather than "my courses." Notwithstanding their dedication to a discipline, they must be willing to "think like administrators" so as to participate in institutional leadership. And academic advisors work at the heart of the matter from an encompassing vision of postsecondary credentials and the opportunities available to students. Too often relegated to routine tasks (course scheduling, graduation checks) and limited by burdensome advisee loads, they may not often have the opportunity to offer their perspectives. But enabling, empowering, and consulting with academic advisors should be a critical priority for every institution. And everyone responsible for leadership should have Institutional Research among the "favorite" contacts on their phones.

Quality and Equity

The three principles presented so far are likely to prove of little value without a fourth: a commitment to the continued pursuit of improved quality and strengthened equity in the design, evaluation, and offering of credentials. If either quality or equity is compromised, the institution will fail its students and fail society. You can't have one without the other. Period.

REFERENCES

AACSB. (2018). *2013 eligibility procedures and accreditation standards for business accreditation.* https://www.aacsb.edu/-/media/aacsb/docs/accreditation/business/standards-and-tables/2018-business-standards.ashx?la=en&hash=B9AF18F3FA0DF19B352B605CBCE17959E32445D9

Achieving the Dream. (2020). *About us.* https://www.achievingthedream.org/about-us-0

Adelman, C. (2009). *The Bologna Process for U.S. eyes: Re-learning higher education in the age of convergence.* Institute for Higher Education Policy. https://files.eric.ed.gov/fulltext/ED504904.pdf

Akron. (2009). *The Akron Advantage.* The University of Akron [Video]. https://www.youtube.com/watch?v=kuPv9LwATMI

Alfeld, C., Charner, I., Johnson, L., & Watts, E. (2013). *Work-based learning opportunities for high school students.* University of Louisville, National Research Center for Career and Technical Education.

Althauser, R. (1989). Internal labor markets. *Annual Review of Sociology, 15,* 143–161.

American Association of Colleges of Nursing. (2019). *Fact sheet: The impact of education on nursing practice.* https://www.aacnnursing.org/Portals/42/News/Factsheets/Education-Impact-Fact-Sheet.pdf

American Association of Community Colleges. (n.d.). *Mission statement.* https://www.aacc.nche.edu/about-us/mission-statement/

American Association of Community Colleges. (2019, January 24). *AACC, DOL partner to expand apprenticeships.* Community College Daily. http://www.ccdaily.com/2019/01/aacc-dol-partnership-aims-expand-apprenticeships/

American Association of Community Colleges. (2020). *Fast facts.* https://www.aacc.nche.edu/wp-content/uploads/2020/03/AACC_Fast_Facts_2020_Final.pdf

American Historical Association. (2021). *Tuning the history discipline in the United States.* https://www.historians.org/teaching-and-learning/tuning-the-history-discipline

American Nurses Association. (2011). *IOM future of nursing report.* https://www.nursingworld.org/practice-policy/iom-future-of-nursing-report/

American Speech-Language-Hearing Association. (2020). *Audiology: Frequently asked questions.* https://www.asha.org/aud/faq_aud/#4

Angrist, J. D., & Chen, S. H. (2011). Schooling and the Vietnam-era GI Bill: Evidence from the draft lottery. *American Economic Journal: Applied Economics, 3*(2), 96–118.

Applbaum, A. I. (2017). The idea of legitimate authority in the practice of medicine. *AMA Journal of Ethics, 19*(2), 207–213.

Apprenticeship.gov. (n.d). *Industry recognized apprenticeship program.* U.S. Department of Labor. https://www.apprenticeship.gov/industry-recognized-apprenticeship-program

Areekkuzhiyil, S. (2017). Emergence of new disciplines. *Edutracks, 17*(4), 20–22. ERIC. https://files.eric.ed.gov/fulltext/ED578910.pdf

Association of American Colleges & Universities. (2019). *Essential learning outcomes.* https://www.aacu.org/leap/essential-learning-outcomes

Association of American Medical Colleges. (2020). *Why pursue an MD-PhD?* https://students-residents.aamc.org/choosing-medical-career/article/why-pursue-md-phd/

Association of Specialized and Professional Accreditors. (2008). *Statement on professional doctorates.* https://www.aspa-usa.org/wp-content/uploads/2015/02/ASPA-Statement-Professional-Doctorates-2008.pdf

Backes, B., Holzer, H. J., & Velez, E. D. (2015). Is it worth it? Postsecondary education and labor market outcomes for the disadvantaged. *IZA Journal of Labor Policy 4*, 1. https://doi.org/10.1186/s40173-014-0027-0

Bailey, T. (2017). *Guided pathways at community colleges: From theory to practice.* American Association of College & Universities.

Bailey, T., Jaggers, S., & Jenkins D. (2015). *Redesigning America's community colleges: A clearer path to student success.* Harvard University Press.

Bartlett, K. (2004). *The signaling power of occupational certification in the automobile service and information technology industries.* National Dissemination Center for Career and Technical Education. https://files.eric.ed.gov/fulltext/ED483201.pdf

Bauman, D., & Blumenstyk, G. (2018). A sector in flux: How for-profit higher ed has shifted. *The Chronicle of Higher Education, 64*(28). https://www.chronicle.com/article/a-sector-in-flux-how-for-profit-higher-ed-has-shifted/

Becker, G. S. (1993). *Human capital: A theoretical and empirical analysis, with special reference to education.* The University of Chicago Press.

Bell, N. (2010). *Data sources: The effect of changes to IPEDS categories on graduate education data.* Council of Graduate Schools. https://cgsnet.org/ckfinder/userfiles/files/DataSources_2010_10.pdf

Berkeley Extension. (2020). *Certificate program in marketing.* https://extension.berkeley.edu/public/category/courseCategoryCertificateProfile.do?method=load&certificateId=17111

Berrett, D. B. (2012, May 13). Artists debate whether the discipline needs a doctorate. *The Chronicle of Higher Education.* https://www.chronicle.com/article/Artists-Debate-Whether-the/131833/?sid=at&utm_medium=en&utm_source=at

Best Cosmetology Schools. (n.d.). *Cosmetology license requirements.* https://bestcosmetologyschool.com/cosmetology-license-requirements/

Bills, D. B. (1988a). Credentials and capacities: Employers' perceptions of the acquisition of skills. *The Sociological Quarterly, 29*, 439–449.

Bills, D. B. (1988b). Educational credentials and promotions: Does schooling do more than get you in the door? *Sociology of Education, 61*, 52–60.

Bills, D. B. (2003). Credentials, signals, and screens: Explaining the relationship between schooling and job assignment. *Review of Educational Research, 73*(4), 441–469.

Bills, D. B. (2004). *The sociology of education and work*. Wiley.

Blumenstyk, G. (2015). *American higher education in crisis?* Oxford University Press.

Blumenstyk, G. (2019a, August 7). What a tech company's big shift portends for the future of the master's degree. *The Chronicle of Higher Education*. https://www.chronicle.com/newsletter/the-edge/2019-08-07?cid=wcontentlist

Blumenstyk, G. (2019b, December 4). Why isn't it a no-brainer to embed "certifications" into bachelor's degrees? *The Chronicle of Higher Education*. https://www.chronicle.com/article/Why-Isn-t-It-a-No-Brainer-to/247648

Blumenstyk, G. (2020, January 15). The gloves are off: What a deal between a mega-university and a community-college system says about the fight for students. *The Chronicle of Higher Education*. https://www.chronicle.com/article/The-Gloves-Are-Off-What-a/247854?utm_source=at&utm_medium=en&cid=at&source=ams&sourceId=4415

Boggs, G. (2012). The evolution of the community college in America: Democracy's colleges. *Community College Journal, 82*(4), 36–39. https://eric.ed.gov/?id=EJ970327

Boston University. (2019). *Financial planning certificate program*. https://financialplanningonline.bu.edu/?creative=248175795508&keyword=certified%20financial%20planner&matchtype=e&network=g&device=c&gclid=Cj0KCQjwrrXtBRCKARIsAMbU6bH28sqXETWO6ReiH-qaaMUXWGeW-yO92dXKIryFLFIKFiBjPteNdFIYaAojoEALw_wcB

Bourdieu, P. (1984). *Distinction: A social critique of the judgment of taste*. Harvard University Press.

Bowen, K., & Thomas, A. (2014). Badges: A common currency for learning. *Change: The Magazine of Higher Learning, 46*(1), 21–25. https://doi.org/10.1080/00091383.2014.867206

Bowles, S., & Gintis, H. (2002). Schooling in capitalist America revisited. *Sociology of Education, 75*, 1–18.

Brint, S., & Karabel, J. (1989). *The diverted dream: Community colleges and the promise of educational opportunity in America, 1900–1985*. Oxford University Press.

Brooks, D. (2020, November 26). The rotting of the Republican mind. *The New York Times*. https://www.nytimes.com/2020/11/26/opinion/republican-disinformation.html

Brooks, P. (2011). Our universities: How bad? How good? *The New York Review, 58*(5), 10–13. https://www.nybooks.com/articles/2011/03/24/our-universities-how-bad-how-good/

Brown, D. K. (1995). *Degrees of control: A sociology of educational expansion and occupational credentialism*. Teachers College Press.

Brown, D. K. (2001). The social sources of educational credentialism: Status cultures, labor markets, and organizations. *Sociology of Education, 74*, 19–34.

Brown, J., & Kurzweil, M. (2017). *The complex universe of alternative postsecondary credentials and pathways.* The Academy of Arts and Science. www.amacad.org/sites/default/files/publication/downloads/CFUE_Alternative-Pathways.pdf

Brown University. (2020). *Graduate school: Fifth-year master's degree.* https://www.brown.edu/academics/gradschool/fifth-year

Bruch, E., & Feinberg, F. (2017). Decision-making processes in social contexts. *Annual Review of Sociology, 43*(1), 207–227. htttps://doi.org/10.1146/annurev-soc-060116-053622

Bureau of Statistics of Labor. (1907). *Thirty-seventh annual report.* Wright & Potter. https://books.google.com/books?id=4xYoAAAAYAAJ&pg=PA3&lpg=PA3&dq=%22from+the+introduction+of+the+first+labor+saving+machine%22&source=bl&ots=QXv_kTyEga&sig=4fQjH2C7_FxuoiWIRYaRIl7VaF0&hl=en&sa=X&ved=0ahUKEwi78cCO_b7YAhVkqlQKHegkA34Q6AEIJTAA#v=onepage&q=%22from%20the%20introduction%20of%20the%20first%20labor%20saving%20machine%22&f=false

Burke, L. (2021, May 16). A case against Lambda School. *Inside Higher Ed.* https://www.insidehighered.com/news/2021/05/18/three-students-allege-false-advertising-lambda-school

Burning Glass Technologies. (2020). *Bad bets: The high cost of failing programs.* https://www.burning-glass.com/research-project/bad-bets-high-cost-failing-programs/

Bushway, D. J., Dodge, L., & Long, C. S. (2018). *A leader's guide to competency-based education: From inception to implementation.* Stylus.

Busteed, B. (2020, September 1). The fastest, most scalable path to work-readiness for college students. *The Evolllution.* https://evolllution.com/programming/credentials/the-fastest-most-scalable-path-to-work-readiness-for-college-students/

Bustillo, D., & Laitenen, A. (2021, April 20). Letting employers off the hook. *Inside Higher Ed.* https://www.insidehighered.com/views/2021/04/20/offering-pell-grants-short-term-training-could-have-adverse-consequences-opinion?utm_source=Inside+Higher+Ed&utm_campaign=1ee3d9d16e-DNU_2021_COPY_02&utm_medium=email&utm_term=0_1fcbc04421-1ee3d9d16e-197550369&mc_cid=1ee3d9d16e&mc_eid=68cfb0a26d

California Polytechnic State University. (2019). *Blended programs.* https://academicprograms.calpoly.edu/content/academicpolicies/policies-undergrad/blended4plus1

Cantor, J. A. (1993). *Apprenticeship and community colleges.* University Press of America.

Cappelli, P. (1997). *Change at work.* Oxford University Press.

Cappelli, P. (2012). *Why good people can't get jobs: The skills gap and what companies can do about it.* Wharton School Press.

CareerWise Colorado. (2019). *A shift in thinking: Not your grandfather's apprenticeship.* https://www.careerwisecolorado.org/en/a-shift-in-thinking/

Carey, K. (2021, August 5). The great master's-degree swindle. *The Chronicle of Higher Education.* https://www.chronicle.com/article/the-great-masters-degree-swindle?cid=gen_sign_in

Carlson, S. (2017). Everyone agrees on value of apprenticeships. The question is how to pay for them. *The Chronicle of Higher Education, 64*(16). https://www.chronicle.com/article/Everyone-Agrees-on-Value-of/241961

Carnegie Classification of Institutions of Higher Education. (2017). *About the Carnegie Classification.* http://carnegieclassifications.iu.edu/

Carnevale, A. P., Garcia, T. I., Ridley, N., & Quinn, M. Q. (2020). The overlooked value of certificates and associate's [sic] degrees: What students need to know before they go to college. *Georgetown University Center on Education and the Workforce.* https://1gyhoq479ufd3yna29x7ubjn-wpengine.netdna-ssl.com/wp-content/uploads/CEW-SubBA.pdf

Carnevale, A. P., Rose, S. J., & Hanson, A. R. (2012, June). *Certificates: Gateway to gainful employment and college degrees.* Georgetown University Center on Education and the Workforce. https://www.luminafoundation.org/wp-content/uploads/2017/08/certificates.pdf

Casilli, C., & Hickey, D. (2016). Transcending conventional credentialing and assessment paradigms with information-rich digital badges. *The Information Society, 32*(2), 117–129.

Cassuto, L., & Weisbuch, R. (2020, December 9). The PhD isn't working right now. *The Chronicle of Higher Education.* https://www.chronicle.com/article/the-ph-d-isnt-working-right-now?utm_source=Iterable&utm_medium=email&utm_campaign=campaign_1801897_nl_Academe-Today_date_20201210&cid=at&source=ams&sourceId=4415

Catalano, F., & Doucet, K. J. (2013, August). *Digital "badges" emerge as part of credentialing's future.* Professional Examination Service.

Certified Financial Planning Board of Standards. (2019). *Become a CFP® professional.* https://www.cfp.net/get-certified/certification-process

Certified Financial Planning Board of Standards. (2020). *Find an education program.* https://www.cfp.net/get-certified/certification-process/education-requirement/certification-coursework-requirement/find-an-education-program

CHE Staff. (2019, September 20). How 3 "super innovators" made their mark. *The Chronicle of Higher Education,* A4.

Chen, G. (2020, November 5). *New bachelor's degrees offered at community colleges.* Community College Review. https://www.communitycollegereview.com/blog/new-bachelors-degrees-offered-at-community-colleges

Cheney, S., & Sponsler, B. (2020, September 5). *Credential pollution: Workers need better information to navigate a hazy labor market.* Working Nation. https://workingnation.com/credential-pollution-workers-need-better-information-to-navigate-a-hazy-labor-market/

Chicagoland Workforce Funder Alliance. (2019). *Apprenticeship 2020.* https://chicagoworkforcefunders.org/apprenticeship-2020/

The Chronicle of Higher Education and American Public Media. (2012). *The role of higher education in career development: Employer perceptions.* https://chronicle-assets.s3.amazonaws.com/5/items/biz/pdf/Employers%20Survey.pdf

Chronicle Staff. (2019, Feburary 24). Which colleges are best and worst in enrolling and graduating women in computer science and engineering. *The Chronicle of*

Higher Education, 65(24). https://www.chronicle.com/article/which-colleges-are-best-and-worst-at-enrolling-and-graduating-women-in-computer-science-and-engineering/

City Colleges of Chicago. (2020). *Apprenticeship at City Colleges of Chicago.* http://apprenticeship.ccc.edu/

Coffey, C., Sentz, R., & Saleh, Y. (2019). *Degrees at work: Examining the serendipitous outcomes of diverse degrees.* Emsi. https://www.economicmodeling.com/wp-content/uploads/2019/07/Degrees-at-Work_Full-Report.pdf

Cohen, A., & Brawer, F. (2003). *The American community college* (4th ed.). Jossey-Bass.

College Art Association. (2015, January 12). *Statement on terminal degree programs in the visual arts and design.* https://www.collegeart.org/standards-and-guidelines/guidelines/terminal-degree-programs

Collins, R. (2019). *The Credential Society: An historical sociology of education and stratification.* Columbia University Press.

Community College of Philadelphia. (2020). *Cisco CCNA certification training.* https://www.ccp.edu/academic-offerings/professional-development/non-credit-courses/cisco-ccna-certification-training

Competency-Based Education Network (C-BEN). (2020). *About C-BEN.* https://www.cbenetwork.org/about/

Complete College America. (2010, December). *Certificates count: An analysis of sub-baccalaureate certificates.* https://files.eric.ed.gov/fulltext/ED536837.pdf

Council of Graduate Schools. (2017). *Articulating learning outcomes in doctoral education.* https://cgsnet.org/publication-pdf/4923/ArticulatingLearningOutcomesinDoctoralEducationWeb.pdf

Council on Higher Education Accreditation. (2021). *Almanac quarterly updates.* chea.org/chea-almanac-online

Craig, R. (2020, September 4). Colleges should go back to school on remote learning. *Inside Higher Ed.* https://www.insidehighered.com/views/2020/09/04/have-colleges-seized-or-missed-opportunity-improve-remote-learning-opinion?utm_source=Inside+Higher+Ed&utm_campaign=2ed575b9f5-DNU_2020_COPY_02&utm_medium=email&utm_term=0_1fcbc04421-2ed575b9f5-197671373&mc_cid=2ed575b9f5&mc_eid=ad94bacc49

Credential Engine. (2018, April 5). *Counting U.S. secondary and postsecondary credentials – April 2018 Report.* https://credentialengine.org/2018/04/05/counting-u-s-secondary-and-postsecondary-credentials-april-2018-report/

Credential Engine. (2019, September 24). *Counting U.S. secondary and postsecondary credentials – September 2019 Report.* https://credentialengine.org/2019/09/24/counting-u-s-postsecondary-and-secondary-credentials/

Credential Engine. (2021, February). *Counting U.S. postsecondary and secondary credentials.* http://credentialengine.org/wp-content/uploads/2021/02/Counting-Credentials-2021.pdf

Crosby, O. (2002/2003). Two years to a career or a jump start to a bachelor's degree. *Occupational Outlook Quarterly, 46*(4), 2–13.

Cutter, C. (2021, May 5). Some CEOs suggest dropping degree requirements in hiring. *Wall Street Journal.* https://www.wsj.com/articles/some-ceos-suggest-dropping-degree-requirements-in-hiring-11620233566?st=4qm68bcp3akitfl&reflink=desktopwebshare_permalink

Deil-Amen, R., & Rosenbaum, J. (2004). Charter building and labor market contacts in two-year colleges. *Sociology of Education, 77*(3), 245–265.

Delgado Community College. (2019, August 23). *Delgado Community College offers new certified health coach program.* http://www.dcc.edu/news/health-coach.aspx

DeSilver, D. (2019, August 29). *10 facts about American workers.* Pew Research Center. https://www.pewresearch.org/fact-tank/2019/08/29/facts-about-american-workers/

Desrochers, D., & Hurlburt, S. (2014). *Trends in college spending: 2001–2011.* Delta Cost Project, American Institutes for Research.

Distance Education Accrediting Commission. (2020). *(SEA)RESULTS distance education effectiveness assessment.* https://www.deac.org/Resources/Distance-Education-Effectiveness-Assessment.aspx

Dougherty, K., Lahr, H., & Smith Morest, V. (2017). *Reforming the American community college: Promising prospects and their challenges* (Working paper no. 98). Community College Research Center, Teacher's College, Columbia University.

Doyle, W. (2017). Does postsecondary education result in civic benefits? *The Journal of Higher Education, 88*(6), 863–893.

Drake University. (2020, September 1). *John Dee Bright College at Drake University to offer two-year degrees.* https://news.drake.edu/2020/09/01/new-john-dee-bright-college-at-drake-university-to-offer-two-year-degrees/

Dyjur, P., & Lindstrom, G. (2017). Perceptions and uses of digital badges for professional learning development in higher education. *TechTrends, 61,* 386–392.

Eastern Millwork. (2019). *Apprentice program with Eastern Millwork.* http://www.easternmillworks.com/apprentice-program/

EC/EACEA/Eurydice. (2018). *The European Higher Education Area in 2018: Bologna Process implementation report.* European Commission, Education and Culture Executive Agency, & Eurydice. Publications Office of the European Union.

Education Commission of the States. (2018, June). *50-state comparison: Transfer and articulation.* http://ecs.force.com/mbdata/MBquest3RTA?Rep=TR1803

edX. (2020). *MicroMasters programs.* https://www.edx.org/micromasters

Embry-Riddle Aeronautical University. (2020). *General education.* https://catalog.erau.edu/daytona-beach/general-education/

Ewert, S., & Kominski, R. (2014, January). *Measuring alternative educational credentials: 2012.* U.S. Census Bureau. https://www.census.gov/prod/2014pubs/p70-138.pdf

Fain, P. (2020, August 27). Alternative credentials on the rise. *Inside Higher Ed.* https://www.insidehighered.com/news/2020/08/27/interest-spikes-short-term-online-credentials-will-it-be-sustained

Ferenstein, G. (2018). *How history explains America's struggle to revive apprenticeships.* Brookings. https://www.brookings.edu/blog/brown-center-chalkboard/2018/05/23/how-history-explains-americas-struggle-to-revive-apprentic-eships/

Finkelstein, J., Knight, E., & Manning, S. (2013). *The potential and value of using digital badges for adult learners.* American Institutes for Research.

Finley, A. (2021). *How college contributes to workforce success.* AAC&U. https://www.aacu.org/sites/default/files/files/research/AACUEmployerReport2021.pdf

Flores-Lagunes, A., & Light, A. (2007). *Interpreting sheepskin effects in the returns to education.* Princeton University Press.

Franciscan University. (n.d.). *MA in Catholic studies.* https://spt.franciscan.edu/programs/ma-in-catholic-studies/

Friedman, T. (2020, September 9). Who can win America's politics of humiliation? *The New York Times,* A26.

Freidson, E. (2001). *Professionalism, the third logic: On the practice of knowledge.* The University of Chicago Press.

Fry, R. (2014, May 14). *Young adults, student debt and economic well-being.* Pew Research Center Social and Demographic Trends Project. https://www.pewresearch.org/social-trends/2014/05/14/young-adults-student-debt-and-economic-well-being/

Fuller, J., & Sigelman, M. (2017). *Room to grow: Identifying new frontiers for apprenticeships.* Burning Glass Technologies. https://www.burning-glass.com/research-project/apprenticeships/

Fulton, M. (2015). *Community colleges expanded role into awarding bachelor's degrees.* Education Commission of the States. https://files.eric.ed.gov/fulltext/ED556034

Gallagher, S. (2016). *The future of university credentials: New developments at the intersection of higher education and hiring.* Harvard Education Press.

Gallagher, S., & Zanville, H. (2021, March 25). *More employers are awarding credentials. Is a parallel higher education system emerging?* EdSurge. https://www.edsurge.com/news/2021-03-25-more-employers-are-awarding-credentials-is-a-parallel-higher-education-system-emerging

Gaston, P. (2014). *Higher education accreditation: How it's changing, why it must.* Stylus.

Gedye, G. (2020). Masters of none. *Washington Monthly.* https://washington-monthly.com/magazine/january-february-march-2020/the-education-masters-degree-scam/

Georgia Tech. (2020). *Master of Science in cybersecurity.* https://www.iisp.gatech.edu/masters-degree

Georgia Tech Professional Education. (2016, April 13). *What's special about professional master's degrees.* https://pe.gatech.edu/blog/what%E2%80%99s-special-about-professional-master%E2%80%99s-degrees

Gibson, D., Ostashewski, N., Flintoff, K., Grant, S., & Knight, E. (2015). Digital badges in education. *Education and Information Technologies, 20*(2), 403–410. https://link.springer.com/content/pdf/10.1007/s10639-013-9291-7.pdf

Gomillion, D. L. (2017). The role of industry certifications in an AACSB-accredited institution. *Information Systems Education Journal, 15*(1), 68–79. https://files.eric.ed.gov/fulltext/EJ1135360.pdf

Google. (2020). *Google career certificates.* https://grow.google/certificates/

Gordon, A. V. (2018, February 13). "MicroMasters" surge as MOOCs go from education to qualification. *Forbes.* https://www.forbes.com/sites/adamgordon/2018/02/13/voice-of-employers-rings-out-as-moocs-go-from-education-to-qualification/?sh=e9bfdff564b6

Grant, S. (2016). Building collective belief in badges: Designing trust network. In D. Ifenthaler, N. Bellin-Mularski, & D. Mah (Eds.), *Foundation of digital badges and micro-credentials* (pp. 97–114). Springer. https://doi.org/10.1007/978-3-319-15425-1

Greenville Technical College. (2019). *BMW scholars program.* https://www.gvltec.edu/academics_learning/exp_learning/bmw-scholars.html

Gurin, P., Dey, E., Hurtado, S., & Gurin, G. (2002, September). Diversity and higher education: Theory and impact on educational outcomes. *Harvard Educational Review, 72*(3), 330–367. https://doi.org/10.17763/haer.72.3.01151786u134n051

Harmon, A. M. (Trans.). (1913). *Lucian* (Vol. 1). Macmillan.

Harper Apprenticeship. (2021, August 19). *Harper apprenticeship programs.* https://library.educause.edu/-/media/files/library/2015/6/elib1503-pdf.pdf

Hickey, D., Willis, J., & Quick, J. (2015). *Where badges work better. EDUCAUSE Learning Initiatives.* https://library.educause.edu/resources/2015/6/where-badges-work-better

Holyoke Community College. (n.d.). *Latinx studies.* https://www.hcc.edu/latinx-studies

Horn, L. (1996). *Nontraditional undergraduates: Trends in enrollment from 1986 to 1992 and persistence and attainment among 1989–90 beginning postsecondary students.* National Center for Education Statistics. https://nces.ed.gov/pubs/97578.pdf

Iasevoli, B. (2015, March 2). *How an oversupply of PhDs could threaten American science.* The Hechinger Report. https://hechingerreport.org/oversupply-phds-threaten-american-science/

IMS Global Learning Consortium. (2021). *Open badges.* https://www.imsglobal.org/activity/digital-badges

Indiana State University. (2019). *Indiana State online: LPN/LVN to BSN.* https://www.indstate.edu/academics/online/undergraduate/lpntobs

Interstate Passport. (2020). *The innovation of Interstate Passport.* http://interstatepassport.wiche.edu/about/overview/

Issa, N. (2019, January 19). New apprenticeship 2020 program lets Chicago students skip 4-year degree. *Chicago Sun-Times.* https://chicago.suntimes.com/2019/1/29/18340683/new-apprenticeship-2020-program-lets-chicago-students-skip-4-year-degree

Ivy Tech Community College. (2020). *Network infrastructure program.* https://www.ivytech.edu/network-infrastructure/index.html

Jacoby, T. (2021). *The indispensable institution: Taking the measure of community college workforce education.* Opportunity America. https://opportunityamericaonline.org/wp-content/uploads/2021/10/FINAL-survey-report.pdf

James Madison University. (2020). *Independent scholars major overview.* https://www
.jmu.edu/academics/undergraduate/majors/independent-scholars.shtml

Jaschik, S. (2020, October 6). From equity talk to equity walk. *Inside Higher Ed.*
https://www.insidehighered.com/news/2020/10/06/authors-discuss-new-book-
equity-higher-education

Jenkins, D., & Fink, J. (2015). *What we know about transfer.* Community
College Research Center, Teacher's College, Columbia University. https://ccrc
.tc.columbia.edu/media/k2/attachments/what-we-know-about-transfer.pdf

Jepsen, C., Troske, K., & Coomes, P. (2014). The labor-market returns to community college degrees, diplomas, and certificates. *Journal of Labor Economics, 32*(1),
95–121. https://doi.org/10.1086/671809

John Carroll University. (2020). *Bachelor of Science in interdisciplinary physics.*
https://jcu.edu/academics/physics/programs-of-study/bachelor-of-science-in-
interdisciplinary-physics

Johnson, S. (2019, June 21). There's a new pipeline to white-collar jobs. It starts with
apprenticeships. *The Chronicle of Higher Education.* https://www.chronicle.com/
article/There-s-a-New-Pipeline-to/246543

Joint Commission on Allied Health Personnel in Ophthalmology. (2019). *Get
certified today.* https://www.jcahpo.org/certification-recertification/

Jones, D. A. (2011). Apprenticeships back to the future. *Issues in Science and
Technology, 27*(4). https://issues.org/auer_jones/

Jones, T., & Berger, K. (2019, January 9). *Aiming for equity.* The Education Trust.
https://edtrust.org/resource/aiming-for-equity/

Jyotishi, S. (2021, March 10). *This employer-aligned & stackable college bootcamp
delivers* [Blog post]. New America. https://www.newamerica.org/education-
policy/edcentral/employer-aligned-stackable-college-bootcamp-delivers/

Kahneman, D. (2011). *Thinking fast and slow.* Farrar, Strauss and Giroux.

Kamin, D. (2020, November 18). Struggling colleges are unloading dorms. *The New
York Times,* B6.

Kelderman, E. (2020, November 13). The great divide. *The Chronicle of Higher
Education,* p. 20.

Kelling, T. (2020, April 29). *How coronavirus tested a graduate program launch.*
University Business. https://universitybusiness.com/launching-a-masters-of-
business-creation-program-during-a-crisis/?eml=20200512&oly_enc_id=
8686E2238256D3S

Kim, J. (2019, December 1). Netflix, low-cost online master's programs and
"that will never work." *Inside Higher Ed.* https://www.insidehighered.com/blogs/
technology-and-learning/netflix-low-cost-online-masters-programs-and-will-
never-work%E2%80%99

Kleiner, M. M. (2011). *Occupational licensing: Protecting the public interest or pro-
tectionism?* (Policy paper 2011-009). W.E. Upjohn Institute. https://research.
upjohn.org/cgi/viewcontent.cgi?article=1008&context=up_policypapers

Kleiner, M. M., & Vorotnikov, E. (2017). Analyzing occupational licensing among
the states. *Journal of Regulatory Economics, 52*(2), 132–158. https://doi.org/
10.1007/s11149-017-9333-y

Knight, E., & Casilli, C. (2012). Mozilla open badgers. In D. G. Oblinger (Ed.), *Game changers: Education and information technology* (pp. 279–284). EDUCAUSE. https://www.educause.edu/ir/library/pdf/pub7203.pdf

Korn, M., & Fuller, A. (2021, July 8). "Financially hobbled for life": The elite master's degrees that don't pay off. *Wall Street Journal.* https://www.wsj.com/articles/financially-hobbled-for-life-the-elite-masters-degrees-that-dont-pay-off-11625752773

Kreighbaum, A. (2019, July 8). Brewing battle over Pell grants. *Inside Higher Ed.* https://www.insidehighered.com/news/2019/07/08/debate-over-proposed-expansion-pell-grants-short-term-job-training

Kuh, G. (2008). *High-impact educational practices: What they are, who has access to them, and why they matter.* American Association of Colleges and Universities.

Labi, A. (2012, November 26). Apprenticeships make a comeback in the United States. *The Chronicle of Higher Education.* https://www.chronicle.com/article/Apprenticeships-Make-a/135914?cid=rclink

Lao, M. (2001). Discrediting accreditation? Antitrust and legal education. *Washington University Law Review, 79*(4), 1035–1102. https://openscholarship.wustl.edu/law_lawreview/vol79/iss4/2/

Lavinson, R. (2021, May 27). Paving an efficient transfer pathway to a bachelor's degree. *Inside Higher Ed.* https://www.insidehighered.com/blogs/tackling-transfer/paving-efficient-transfer-pathway-bachelor%E2%80%99s-degree?utm_source=Inside+Higher+Ed&utm_campaign=ad609a066b-DNU_2021_COPY_02&utm_medium=email&utm_term=0_1fcbc04421-ad609a066b-197550369&mc_cid=ad609a066b&mc_eid=68cfb0a26d

Lederman, D. (2019, October 30). Professors' slow, steady acceptance of online learning: A survey. *Inside Higher Ed.* https://www.insidehighered.com/news/survey/faculty-support-online-learning-builds-slowly-steadily-not-enthusiastically?utm_source=Inside+Higher+Ed&utm_campaign=2945ba851e-DNU_2019_COPY_01&utm_medium=email&utm_term=0_1fcbc04421-2945ba851e-197550369&mc_cid=2945ba851e&mc_eid=68cfb0a26d

Lee, D. (2013). *Quarterly report on household debt and credit.* Federal Reserve Bank of New York. https://www.newyorkfed.org/medialibrary/media/newsevents/mediaadvisory/2013/lee022813.pdf

Lerman, R. L. (2018, October 17). *The virtue of apprenticeship.* The American Interest. https://www.the-american-interest.com/2018/10/17/the-virtue-of-apprenticeship/

Levine, A. (2005, March). *Educating school leaders.* The Education Schools Project. http://edschools.org/pdf/Final313.pdf

Levine, A., & Van Pelt, S. (2021, September 3). 5 ways higher ed will be upended in the decades to come. *The Chronicle of Higher Education.* https://www.chronicle.com/article/5-ways-higher-ed-will-be-upended-in-the-decades-to-come

Levy, F., & Murnane, R. (2004). *The new division of labor: How computers are creating the next job market.* Princeton University Press.

Loprest, P. J., & Sick, N. (2018, November 1). *Career prospects for certified nursing assistants.* Urban Institute. https://www.urban.org/research/publication/career-prospects-certified-nursing-assistants/view/full_report

Lumina Foundation. (2014). *Degree qualifications profile*. www.luminafoundation.org/files/resources/dqp.pdf

Lumina Foundation. (2019). *Unlocking the nation's potential: A model to advance quality and equity in education beyond high school.* https://www.luminafoundation.org/wp-content/uploads/2019/08/unlocking-the-nations-potential.pdf

MacCullough, D. (2009). *Christianity: The first three thousand years.* Viking.

Mah, D. K. (2016). Learning analytics and digital badges: Potential impact on student retention in higher education. *Technology, Knowledge and Learning, 21*(3), 285–305. https://doi.org/10.1007/s10758-016-9286-8

Marcus, J. (2020, November 20). *More people with bachelor's degrees go back to school to learn skilled trades.* Hechinger Report. https://hechingerreport.org/more-people-with-bachelors-degrees-go-back-to-school-to-learn-skilled-trades/

Markow, W., Restuccia, D., & Taska, B. (2017). *The narrow ladder: The value of industry certifications in the job market.* Burning Glass Technologies.

Maryland State Department of Labor. (2019). *Apprenticeship Maryland.* http://www.marylandpublicschools.org/programs/Pages/CTE/ApprenticeshipMD.aspx

MCC. (2021). *Degrees of distinction close to home.* Macomb Community College. https://www.macomb.edu/future-students/choose-program/university-center/index.html

McCarthy, M. A. (2019, January 22). Deregulating apprenticeship. *Inside Higher Ed.* https://www.insidehighered.com/views/2019/01/22/essay-risks-trump-administrations-plans-deregulate-apprenticeship-opinion

McIntosh, K., Moss, E., Nunn, R., & Shambaugh, J. (2020, February 27). *Examining the Black-White wealth gap.* Brookings. https://www.brookings.edu/blog/up-front/2020/02/27/examining-the-black-white-wealth-gap/

Meyer, J. (1977). The effects of education as an institution. *American Journal of Sociology, 83*(1), 55–77.

Meyer, J., Ramirez, F., Frank, D., & Schoffer, E. (2007). Higher education as an institution. In Gumport, P. (Ed.), *Sociology of higher education: Contributions and their contexts* (pp. 187–221). Johns Hopkins University Press.

Minnesota State. (2020). *Ready to plan your education?* https://careerwise.minnstate.edu/education/degrees.html

Mintz, S. (2019, February 4). Educating versus training and credentialing. *Inside Higher Ed.* https://www.insidehighered.com/blogs/higher-ed-gamma/educating-versus-training-and-credentialing

Missouri State University. (2020). *Transferring an associate degree or the 42-hour block.* https://www.missouristate.edu/transfer/transferring-associate-degree.htm

Montana State University-Northern. (2019). *Automotive technology.* http://www.msun.edu/academics/cots/program-autotech.aspx

Mortrude, J. (2014). *Shared vision, strong systems: The alliance for quality career pathways.* Center for Law and Social Policy. https://www.clasp.org/publications/report/brief/shared-vision-strong-systems-alliance-quality-career-pathways-framework

Myskow, W., & Hansen, P. (2020, May 12). *Virtual commencement receives mixed reactions from students.* The State Press. https://www.statepress.com/article/2020/05/spcommunity-asu-students-upset-with-virtual-graduation

National Academies. (2011). *The future of nursing: Leading change, advancing health.* https://pubmed.ncbi.nlm.nih.gov/24983041/

National Association of Colleges and Employers. (2018, December 12). *Employers want to see these attributes on students' resumes.* https://www.naceweb.org/talent-acquisition/candidate-selection/employers-want-to-see-these-attributes-on-students-resumes/

National Association of Colleges and Employers. (2019, February 6). *The difference a master's degree can have on starting salary.* https://www.naceweb.org/job-market/compensation/the-difference-a-masters-degree-can-have-on-starting-salary/

National Association of Colleges and Employers. (2020). *What is career readiness?* https://www.naceweb.org/career-readiness/competencies/career-readiness-defined/

National Center for Education Statistics. (2015). *Web tables: Demographic and enrollment characteristics of nontraditional undergraduates: 2011–12.* https://nces.ed.gov/pubsearch/pubsinfo.asp?pubid=2015025

National Center for Education Statistics. (2018, May). *Trends in student loan debt for graduate school completers.* https://nces.ed.gov/programs/coe/indicator_tub.asp

National Center for Education Statistics. (2019a). *Table 318.40: Degrees/certificates conferred by postsecondary institutions, by control of institution and level of degree/certificate: 1970–71 through 2017–18.* https://nces.ed.gov/programs/digest/d19/tables/dt19_318.40.asp

National Center for Education Statistics. (2019b). *Parent and student expectations of highest education level.* https://nces.ed.gov/pubsearch/pubsinfo.asp?pubid=2019015

National Center for Education Statistics. (2019c). *Table 104.10: Rates of high school completion and bachelor's degree attainment among persons age 25 and over, by race/ethnicity and sex: Selected years, 1910 through 2018.* https://nces.ed.gov/programs/digest/d18/tables/dt18_104.10.asp

National Center for Education Statistics. (2019d). *Table 306.10: Total fall enrollment in degree-granting postsecondary institutions, by level of enrollment, sex, attendance status, and race/ethnicity or nonresident alien status of student: Selected years, 1976 through 2018.* https://nces.ed.gov/programs/digest/d19/tables/dt19_306.10.asp

National Center for Education Statistics. (2020). *Graduation rates.* https://nces.ed.gov/fastfacts/display.asp?id=40

National Conference of State Legislatures. (2020). *The national occupational licensing database.* https://www.ncsl.org/research/labor-and-employment/occupational-licensing-statute-database.aspx

National Council for Workforce Education. (2020). *2016 NCWE exemplary program awards.* https://www.ncwe.org/page/2016_exemp_awards

National Governors Association. (2019, February 1). *States' role in advancing high-quality youth apprenticeship.* Medium. https://medium.com/@NatlGovsAssoc/states-role-in-advancing-high-quality-youth-apprenticeship-87efb0fafccb

National Science Foundation. (2020a). *Table A-1. Types of research doctoral degrees recognized by the survey of earned doctorates: 2007 and 2008.* https://wayback.archive-it.org/5902/20150819055037/http://www.nsf.gov/statistics/nsf10309/pdf/taba1.pdf

National Science Foundation. (2020b). *Survey of earned doctorates.* https://www.nsf .gov/statistics/srvydoctorates/#tabs-2

National Student Clearinghouse Research Center. (2019, May 30). *Current term enrollment–Spring 2019.* https://nscresearchcenter.org/currenttermenrollmentestimate-spring2019/

National Student Clearinghouse Research Center. (2020, September 29). *Tracking transfer.* https://nscresearchcenter.org/tracking-transfer/?hilite=%27transfer%27

New America. (2019, February). *Building strong and inclusive economies through apprenticeship.* https://www.newamerica.org/education-policy/reports/state-policy-agenda-2019/

Nittier, K. (2019, September 26). *You don't get what you pay for: Paying teachers more for master's degrees.* National Council on Teacher Quality. https://www.nctq.org/blog/You-dont-get-what-you-pay-for:-paying-teachers-more-for-masters-degrees

Northeastern University. (2017, July 19). *The benefits of a master's in today's job market.* https://www.northeastern.edu/graduate/blog/masters-degree-benefits/

Northeastern University. (2019, April 11). *Is earning a graduate certificate worth it?* https://www.northeastern.edu/graduate/blog/graduate-certificate-value/

Oberlin College and Conservatory. (2020). *Individual major.* https://www.oberlin .edu/registrar/policies-procedures-forms/IM

O'Connor, S. (2019, September 12). *EdD vs. PhD in education: what's the difference?* Northeastern University Graduate Programs. https://www.northeastern.edu/graduate/blog/edd-vs-phd-in-education/

Ohio Department of Higher Education. (2020). *Certificate programs.* https://www .ohiohighered.org/students/find-a-career/certificate-programs

The Ohio State University. (2020). *DPT/PhD dual degree.* https://hrs.osu.edu/academics/graduate-programs/clinical-doctorate-in-physical-therapy/dptphd-dual-degree

Opportunity America. (2021). *Who are noncredit students?* https://opportunityamer-icaonline.org/ccsurvey/

Oregon State University-Cascades. (2020, January 27). *OSU-Cascades to launch bachelor's degree in outdoor products.* https://osucascades.edu/news/osu-cascades-launch-bachelors-degree-outdoor-products

Oreopoulos, P., & Petronijevic, U. (2013). *Making college worth it: A review of research on the returns to higher education* (Working paper no. 19053). National Bureau of Economic Research. https://doi.org/10.3386/w19053

Oxford English Dictionary. (1989). *Associate.* Oxford University Press.

Pager, T. (2019, March 5). She delivered babies for one community. Then came the police. *The New York Times,* A21.

Partnership to Advance Youth Apprenticeship. (2020). *About the Partnership to Advance Youth Apprenticeship.* https://s3.amazonaws.com/newamericadotorg/documents/PAYA_11x17_v6b-pages3.pdf

Penn Online. (2021). *Bachelor's degree.* https://lpsonline.sas.upenn.edu/academics/bachelors-degree

Pennsylvania Commission for Community Colleges. (2020, January 8). *Pennsylvania community college leaders sign seamless transfer agreement with Southern New*

Hampshire University. https://pacommunitycolleges.org/pennsylvania-community-college-leaders-sign-seamless-transfer-agreement-with-southern-new-hampshire-university/

Perez, T., & Zients, J. (2014, July 14). *The first-ever White House summit on American apprenticeship.* The White House, President Barack Obama. https://obamawhitehouse.archives.gov/blog/2014/07/14/first-ever-white-house-summit-american-apprenticeship-helping-american-workers-punch

Pew Research Center. (2014, February 11). *The rising cost of not going to college.* http://www.pewsocialtrends.org/2014/02/11/the-rising-cost-of-not-going-to-college/

Prebil, M., & McCarthy, A. (2018). *Building better degrees using industry certifications: Lessons from the field.* New America. https://www.newamerica.org/education-policy/reports/building-better-degrees-using-industry-certifications/

Preston, C. (2018, April 15). *Are apprenticeships the new on-ramp to good jobs?* The Hechinger Report. https://hechingerreport.org/are-apprenticeships-the-new-on-ramp-to-middle-class-jobs/

Quilantan, B. (2018, May 25). Should colleges let ailing majors die or revamp them? *The Chronicle of Higher Education, 64*(34), A8–A10. https://www.chronicle.com/article/should-colleges-let-ailing-majors-die-or-revamp-them/

Quillian, L., Pager, D., Hexel, O., & Midtboen, A. (2017). Meta-analysis of field experiments shows no change in racial discrimination in hiring over time. *Proceedings of the National Academy of Sciences, 114*(41), 10870–10875. https://www.pnas.org/content/early/2017/09/11/1706255114

Raelin, J. A. (2008). *Work-based learning: Bridging knowledge and action in the workplace.* Wiley.

Rafel, E., Briones, J., & Montenegro, E. (2020, September 23). *Getting involved in credential transparency: A roadmap for states.* Credential Engine. https://credentialengine.org/2020/09/23/getting-involved-in-credential-transparency-a-roadmap-for-states/

The Real Yellow Pages. (2019). *Colleges in Atlanta, GA.* https://www.yellowpages.com/search?search_terms=colleges&geo_location_terms=Atlanta%2C+GA

Richardson, R. (1995). *Emerson: The mind on fire.* University of California Press.

Rocky Mountain College. (n.d.) *Doctor of Medical Sciences.* https://www.rocky.edu/dmsc

Rogers, K. L. (2020, December 2). 10 steps to reform graduate education in the humanities. *The Chronicle of Higher Education.* https://www.chronicle.com/article/10-steps-to-reform-graduate-education-in-the-humanities?utm_source=Iterable&utm_medium=email&utm_campaign=campaign_1823216_nl_Academe-Today_date_20201216&cid=at&source=ams&sourceId=4415&cid2=gen_login_refresh

Rose, M. (2011, June 3). Making sparks fly. *The American Scholar.* https://theamericanscholar.org/making-sparks-fly/

Rosenfeld, R. (1992). Job mobility and career processes. *Annual Review of Sociology, 18*, 39–61.

Rubin, M. (2020, February 4). What happens after the MBA bubble bursts? *Inside Higher Ed.* https://www.insidehighered.com/views/2020/02/04/business-schools-must-reconsider-what-future-workforce-really-needs-opinion

Rughiniș, R., & Matei, S. (2013). Digital badges: Signposts and claims of achievement. In C. Stephanidis (Ed.), *Communications in computer and information science* (Vol. 374, pp. 84–88). Springer.

Rutgers Business School. (2020). *Mini-MBA: Business essentials.* https://www.business.rutgers.edu/executive-education/business-essentials

Ryan, C. L., & Bauman, K. (2016). *Educational attainment in the United States: 2015 population characteristics population reports.* U.S. Census Bureau. ERIC. https://files.eric.ed.gov/fulltext/ED572028.pdf

Salisbury University. (2019). *Emphasizing hands on learning.* https://www.salisbury.edu/explore-academics/research/undergraduate-and-graduate-student-research.aspx

Sandel, M. (2020). *The tyranny of merit: What's become of the common good?* Farrar, Strauss & Giroux.

San Diego Workforce Partnership. (2015). *San Diego County middle-skill jobs: Gaps and opportunities* [Special report]. https://workforce.org/wp-content/uploads/2018/06/middle-skill_jobs_gaps_and_opportunities_2015.pdf

Saxenian, A. (1994). *Regional advantage: Culture and competition in Silicon Valley and Route 128.* Harvard University Press.

Schneider, C. (2019). Report provided by the author.

Schneider, C. G., Gaston, P. L., Adelman, C., & Ewell, P. T. (2015). *The degree qualifications profile 2.0: Defining US degrees through demonstration and documentation of college learning.* American Association of Colleges and Universities. https://www.aacu.org/publications-research/periodicals/degree-qualifications-profile-20-defining-us-degrees-through#:~:text=The%20student%2C%20not%20the%20institution%2C%20is%20the%20primary%20reference%20point.&text=The%20DQP%20is%20presented%20as,particular%20areas%20of%20specialized%20knowledge

Schneider, M., & Sigelman, M. (2018). *Saving the Associate of Arts degree: How an A.A. degree can become a better path to labor market success.* American Enterprise Institute and Burning Glass Technologies. burning-glass.com/wp-content/uploads/RPT_Saving_the_Associates_of_Arts_Degree.pdf

Scott-Clayton, J. (2011). *The shapeless river: Does a lack of structure inhibit students' progress at community colleges?* [Working paper no. 25]. Community College Research Center, Teacher's College, Columbia University. https://ccrc.tc.columbia.edu/publications/lack-of-structure-students-progress.html

Scott-Clayton, J. (2018). The looming student loan default crisis is worse than we thought. *Evidence Speaks Reports, 2*(34). Economic Studies at Brookings. https://www.brookings.edu/wp-content/uploads/2018/01/scott-clayton-report.pdf

Selingo, J. (2016). *There is life after college: What parents and students should know about navigating school to prepare for the jobs of tomorrow.* HarperCollins.

Selingo, J. (2017, November 5). Six myths about choosing your college major. *The New York Times*, A8. https://www.nytimes.com/2017/11/03/education/edlife/choosing-a-college-major.html

Selingo, J. (2018, May 25). It's time to end college majors as we know them. *The Chronicle of Higher Education, 64*(34), A10. https://www.chronicle.com/article/its-time-to-end-college-majors-as-we-know-them/

Shapiro, D., Dundar, A., & Huie, F. (2018). *Completing college: A national view of student completion rates—fall 2012 cohort.* National Student Clearinghouse Research Center. https://nscresearchcenter.org/wp-content/uploads/SignatureReport16.pdf

Shields, R., & Chugh, R. (2017). Digital badges – rewards for learning? *Education and Information Technologies, 22*(4), 1817–1824. https://doi.org/10.1007/s10639-016-9521-x

Snyder, T. (Ed.). (1993). *120 Years of American Education: A Statistical Portrait.* U.S. Department of Education, Office of Educational Research and Improvement, National Center for Education Statistics. https://nces.ed.gov/pubs93/93442.pdf

SoftwareGuild. (2020). *Boot up your software development career.* https://www.thesoftwareguild.com/digital-coding-badges/

Southwest Tennessee Community College. (2020, September 13). *Southwest Tennessee Community College launches $1M U.S. Department of Labor IT apprenticeship program* [Press release]. https://www.pr.com/press-release/821101

St. Amour, M. (2020, June 9). The future of apprenticeships. *Inside Higher Ed.* https://www.insidehighered.com/news/2020/06/09/are-virtual-apprenticeships-future-after-pandemic?utm_source=Inside+Higher+Ed&utm_campaign=c9b8131562-DNU_2019_COPY_02&utm_medium=email&utm_term=0_1fcbc04421-c9b8131562-197550369&mc_cid=c9b8131562&mc_eid=68cfb0a26d

St. Louis Community College. (2020). *Education for life.* https://stlcc.edu/about/

State Higher Education Executive Officers Association. (2021). *State postsecondary data.* https://postsecondarydata.sheeo.org/

Staver, M. D., & Staver, A. L. (2003). Lifting the veil: An exposé on the American Bar Association's arbitrary and capricious accreditation process. *The Wayne Law Review, 49*(1), 3–91.

Strada Education Network. (2020, August 26). *The new education consumer—what's driving Americans' interest in short-term and virtual skills training options.* https://www.stradaeducation.org/publicviewpoint/

Trainor, S. (2015, October 20). How community colleges changed the whole idea of education in America. *Time.* https://time.com/4078143/community-college-history/

Treisman, R. (2020, December 13). *Op-ed urging Jill Biden to drop the "Dr." sparks outrage online.* National Public Radio. https://www.npr.org/2020/12/13/946068319/op-ed-urging-jill-biden-to-drop-the-dr-sparks-outrage-online

Trump, D. (2017, June 15). *Presidential executive order expanding apprenticeships in America.* The White House. https://trumpwhitehouse.archives.gov/presidential-actions/3245/

Twenge, J. M., & Cooper, A. B. (2020). The expanding class divide in happiness in the United States, 1972–2016. *Emotion.* https://doi.org/10.1037/emo0000774

University of Central Florida, College of Business. (2020). *Admission standards and academic policies.* https://business.ucf.edu/centers-institutes/office-of-professional-development/cba-policies/#admission

University of Hawai'i Maui College. (2020). *Home page.* http://maui.hawaii.edu/

University of Illinois Urbana-Champaign. (2019). *Computer Science and Liberal Arts and Sciences disciplines.* https://las.illinois.edu/admissions/faqcsx

University of Maryland, Baltimore County. (2021). *Credly.* https://www.credly.com/organizations/umbc/badges?id=umbc&page=1&sort=-state_updated_at

U.S. Chamber of Commerce. (2020). *LER information and resources.* https://www.uschamberfoundation.org/t3-innovation-network/ilr-pilot-program

U.S. Department of Education. (2018). *Degree and nondegree credentials held by labor force participants.* https://nces.ed.gov/pubs2018/2018057.pdf

U.S. Department of Labor. (n.d.). *Certification finder.* Career One Stop. https://www.careeronestop.org/Toolkit/Training/find-certifications.aspx

U.S. Department of Labor. (2016). *Data and statistics.* https://www.dol.gov/agencies/eta/apprenticeship/about/statistics/2016

U.S. Department of Labor. (2018a). *Apprenticeship.* https://www.dol.gov/apprenticeship/

U.S. Department of Labor. (2018b, April 3). *Apprenticeship history and Fitzgerald Act.* https://www.dol.gov/agencies/eta/apprenticeship/policy/national-apprenticeship-act

U.S. Department of Labor. (2020, March 10). *USDL issues industry-recognized apprenticeship program final rule.* https://www.dol.gov/newsroom/releases/eta/eta20200310

U.S. News & World Report. (2020). *U. S. News best colleges.* https://www.usnews.com/best-colleges#more-rankings

Van Noy, M. (2011). *Credentials in context: The meaning and use of associate degrees in the employment of IT technicians* [Unpublished doctoral dissertation]. Columbia University. https://smlr.rutgers.edu/faculty-research-engagement/education-employment-research-center-eerc/eerc-projects/re

Van Noy, M., Jacobs, J., Korey, S., Bailey, T., & Hughes, K. L. (2008). *The landscape of noncredit workforce education: State policies and community college practices.* Community College Research Center, Teachers College, Colombia University.

Van Noy, M., James, H., & Bedley, C. (2016). *Reconceptualizing learning: A brief on informal learning.* Rutgers, the State University of New Jersey. https://smlr.rutgers.edu/faculty-research-engagement/education-employment-research-center-eerc/eerc-projects/re

Van Noy, M., McKay, H., & Michael, S. (2019). *Non-degree credential quality: A conceptual framework to guide measurement.* Education and Employment Research Center, Rutgers University School of Management and Labor Relations. https://

smlr.rutgers.edu/faculty-research-engagement/education-employment-research-center-eerc/eerc-projects/non-degree

Vasquez, M. (2019). The nightmarish end of the Dream Center's higher-ed empire. *The Chronicle of Higher Education, 65*(27). https://www.chronicle.com/article/the-nightmarish-end-of-the-dream-centers-higher-ed-empire/

Walden University. (2019). *Earn your degree faster with an accelerated master's program.* https://www.waldenu.edu/online-masters-programs/resource/earn-your-degree-faster-with-an-accelerated-masters-program#deOFs55DUHipHuQ3.99

Weinburg, A. (2020). Google just changed the higher education game. *Business Insider.* https://www.businessinsider.com/google-careers-certificate-program-changed-game-universities-should-pay-attention-2020-9

Weinstein, P. (2018). *Which colleges offer three-year bachelor's and why aren't they working?* Progressive Policy Institute. https://www.progressivepolicy.org/wp-content/uploads/2018/05/PPI_ThreeYearDegrees2018.pdf

Western Illinois University. (2020, February 10). *Cannabis production minor to launch at WIU in fall 2020.* http://www.wiu.edu/news/newsrelease.php?release_id=16995

White House. (2021a, February 17). *Fact sheet: Biden administration to take steps to bolster registered apprenticeships.* https://www.whitehouse.gov/briefing-room/statements-releases/2021/02/17/fact-sheet-biden-administration-to-take-steps-to-bolster-registered-apprenticeships/

White House. (2021b, March 31). *Fact sheet: The American Jobs Plan.* https://www.whitehouse.gov/briefing-room/statements-releases/2021/03/31/fact-sheet-the-american-jobs-plan/

Williams, J. J. (2019). The new humanities. *The Chronicle of Higher Education, 66*(15). https://www.chronicle.com/interactives/20191113-TheNewHumanities?cid=wsinglestory_hp_1a&cid=db&source=ams&sourceId=4415

Wilson, F. S. (2019). *Congresswoman Wilson introduces the Quality Higher Education Act.* https://wilson.house.gov/media-center/press-releases/congresswoman-wilson-introduces-the-quality-higher-education-act

Wilson, M., Karon, J., & Alamuddin, R. (2020, June 11). *Transfer pathways to independent colleges.* Ithaka S-R. https://sr.ithaka.org/publications/transfer-pathways-to-independent-colleges/

Wilson, T. (2020, July 6). Northeast State/RCAM apprenticeship strategy. *TimesNews.* http://www.timesnews.net/frontpage/2018/03/18/Northeast-State-RCAM-Apprenticeship-strategy

Wisconsin Department of Labor. (2019). *Youth Apprenticeship Program information.*

Witham, K., Malcom-Piqueux, L., Dowd, A., & Bensimon, E. (2015). *America's unmet promise: The imperative for equity in higher education.* Association of American Colleges and Universities.

WorkCred. (2020). *Embedding certifications into bachelor's degrees.* https://workcred.org/Our-Work/Aligning-and-Embedding-Industry-Certifications-with-Bachelor-Degrees.aspx

Xu, D., & Ran, F. X. (2019). Noncredit education in community college: Students, course enrollments, and academic outcomes. *Community College Review, 48*(1), 77–101.

Xu, D., & Trimble, M. (2016). What about certificates? Evidence on the labor market returns to nondegree community college awards in two states. *Educational Evaluation and Policy Analysis, 38*(2), 272–292.

Yale University. (2021, February 1). *Report of the humanities doctoral education advisory working group.* https://image.message.yale.edu/lib/fe311570756405787c1278/m/1/0bfeafd2-c069-43b3-b529-bd6a7460fb89.pdf

Zanville, H. (2020, March 16). *An updated map to help us navigate the learn-and-work highway.* The Evolllution. https://evolllution.com/programming/credentials/an-updated-map-to-help-us-navigate-the-learn-and-work-highway/

ABOUT THE AUTHORS

Paul L. Gaston, trustees professor emeritus at Kent State University (Ohio), has served four universities as a faculty member, dean, and provost. Having offered 14 years of university service as a provost (Northern Kentucky and Kent State), he has focused more recently on teaching, writing, and consulting.

His recent books include *General Education Transformed: How We Can, Why We Must* (AAC&U, 2015); *Higher Education Accreditation: How It's Changing, Why It Must* (Stylus, 2014); *General Education and Liberal Learning* (AAC&U, 2010); *The Challenge of Bologna: What U.S. Higher Education Has to Learn from Europe and Why It Matters That We Learn It* (Stylus, 2010); and *Revising General Education*, with Jerry Gaff (AAC&U, 2009). His most recent book prior to this one, *Ohio's Craft Beers* (Kent State University Press, 2017), explores alternate approaches to "higher" education.

His more than 50 published articles on literature and higher education include studies of the British hymn tradition, Anthony Powell, George Herbert, the role of the provost in university fundraising, the Bologna Process, minor league baseball, accreditation reform, *Il Gattopardo*, interart analogies, and the cultures of futures markets. He is one of the four original authors of the influential *Degree Qualifications Profile* (Lumina Foundation, 2011, 2014).

He received his degrees from Southeastern Louisiana University (BA) and from the University of Virginia (MA, PhD), where he was a Woodrow Wilson fellow. He is now distinguished fellow at the Association of American Colleges and Universities and a consultant to Lumina Foundation.

He lives in Northeast Ohio with his wife, Eileen, (a volunteer proofreader for this book) and two cats. His son, Tyler (1980–2004), continues to offer the inspiration of his values and spirit. His daughter, Beth, works in financial services in Chicago. For recreation, he enjoys hiking, cycling, reading, and supporting Chelsea (soccer) and the St. Louis Cardinals. His Twitter name is CardsFaninOhio.

Michelle Van Noy is an associate research professor in the Labor Studies and Employment Relations Department and the director of the Education and Employment Research Center at the School of Management and Labor Relations at Rutgers, the State University of New Jersey. She is also on the faculty of the Higher Education PhD program at Rutgers. Previously, she has conducted research at the Heldrich Center for Workforce Development at Rutgers; the Community College Research Center at Teachers College, Columbia University; and Mathematica Policy Research.

She has 25 years of research experience on the connection between education and work. Her research has included studies of technician education, community college noncredit education, student decision-making about majors and careers, quality in nondegree credentials, higher education labor market alignment, and effective practices in workforce education.

She recently published an edited volume for New Directions for Community Colleges, *Lessons Learned From TAACCCT*, documenting findings from the Department of Labor's $2 billion investment in community colleges through the TAACCCT grant program. She has published articles in the *Community College Review* and *Economics of Education Review*. She publishes widely for practitioner audiences with over 50 papers and reports on workforce- and education-related topics.

She holds a PhD in sociology and education from Columbia University, Graduate School of Arts and Sciences, an MS in public policy from the Bloustein School of Planning and Public Policy, Rutgers, and a BA in psychology and Spanish from Douglass College, Rutgers.

She lives in central New Jersey with her two sons, Evan and Andre, and her cat, Momo. She enjoys running, reading, cooking, and watching her sons play in local youth soccer.

academic advisors, 42, 61–62, 156,
180
academic credentials, 20–21, 25, 41
academic leadership, within
licensing, 156
accommodations, for students, 51
accreditation, xiii–xiv, 37–38, 153,
195
Accrediting Council on Education
in Journalism and Mass
Communication (ACEJMC), 37
Achieving the Dream, 188
action lines, reforms of, 64
active learning, changes within, 35
administrators, xvi, 61, 62, 156,
179
advising, student, 4, 13, 42, 48, 59
advisors, academic, 42, 61–62, 156,
180
Alamo Colleges District (TX), 71
Alfred P. Sloan foundation, 115
alma mater, majors *versus*, 38
American Association of Colleges of
Nursing (AACN), 155
American Bar Association (ABA),
12–13, 33
American Historical Association
(AHA), 93
American Public University, 100
American Speech-Language-Hearing
Association (ASHA), 124
American Welding Society
certification, 152
analysis paralysis, 47

anthropologies of credentials, 187
applied associate degree, 75–76, 80
applied baccalaureate programs, 26
applied doctorate degree, 125
applied programs, benefits of, 41
Apprenti, 167–168
Apprenticeship 2020 (Harper
College), 174
Apprenticeship Maryland, 173
apprenticeship programs
alternate approach to, 176–178
barriers to, 170
benefits of, 41, 167, 170
characteristics of, 168–169
community colleges and, 172,
175
competencies within, 36
employers and, 175
expansion of, 174–175
for high school students,
172–173
innovation within, 167–168
leadership priorities within, 205
for licensing, 154
limitations of, 168
open-ended, 173
overview of, 164–167
political leadership and, 175–179
registered, 165–167
revitalization of, 171–179
scaling, 169–171
solutions for, 170, 171
underinvestment of, 170
unregistered, 166

Degrees That Matter

Moving Higher Education to a Learning Systems Paradigm

Natasha A. Jankowski and David W. Marshall

Sponsored by the National Institute for Learning Outcomes Assessment

Concerned by ongoing debates about higher education that talk past one another, the authors of this book show how to move beyond these and other obstacles to improve the student learning experience and further successful college outcomes. Offering an alternative to the culture of compliance in assessment and accreditation, they propose a different approach that they call the learning system paradigm. Building on the shift in focus from teaching to learning, the new paradigm encourages faculty and staff to systematically seek out information on how well students are learning and how well various areas of the institution are supporting the student experience and to use that information to create more coherent and explicit learning experiences for students.

The authors begin by surveying the crowded terrain of reform in higher education and proceed from there to explore the emergence of this alternative paradigm that brings all these efforts together in a coherent way. The learning system paradigm presented in chapter 2 includes four key elements—consensus, alignment, student-centeredness, and communication. Chapter 3 focuses upon developing an encompassing notion of alignment that enables faculty, staff, and administrators to reshape institutional practice in ways that promote synergistic, integrative learning. Chapters 4 and 5 turn to practice, exploring the application of the paradigm to the work of curriculum mapping and assignment design. Chapter 6 focuses upon barriers to the work and presents ways to start and options for moving around barriers, and the final chapter explores ongoing implications of the new paradigm, offering strategies for communicating the impact of alignment on student learning.

The Transfer Experience

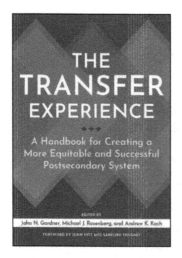

A Handbook for Creating a More Equitable and Successful Postsecondary System

Edited by John N. Gardner, Michael J. Rosenberg, and Andrew K. Koch

Foreword by John Hitt and Sanford Shugart

Copublished with the Gardner Institute

"The achievement and graduation of transfer students in higher education is one of the most important issues confronting colleges and universities. Given that nearly half the undergraduate enrollees are in community colleges, we have to work together across the community college and 4-year sector to find structures, *programs*, and policies to strengthen their success. The authors provide nuanced perspectives on how transfer student success must be addressed."—*Scott E. Evenbeck, Founding President, Stella and Charles Guttman Community College, City University of New York*

"Helping students achieve their educational goals is a win for everyone, and brings the 'American Dream' closer to reality. A key, underutilized strategy in reaching this goal is an effective, holistic transfer system that begins when a student enters an institution of higher education and continues through completion. *The Transfer Experience: A Handbook for Creating a More Equitable and Successful Postsecondary System* is authored by 'transfer warriors' who understand and are passionate about transfer. The book is a comprehensive educational masterpiece that challenges and inspires higher education leaders and policy makers to skillfully and purposefully foster transfer student success, thereby enhancing the quality of life for students." —*Paula K. Compton, Associate Vice Chancellor, Articulation and Transfer, Ohio Department of Higher Education*

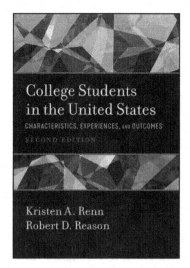

College Students in the United States, Second Edition

Characteristics, Experiences, and Outcomes

Kristen A. Renn and
Robert D. Reason

In this book, the authors bring together in one place essential information about college students in the United States in the 21st century. Synthesizing existing research and theory, they present an introduction to studying student characteristics, college choice and enrollment patterns, institutional types and environments, student learning, persistence, and outcomes of college.

Substantially revised and updated, this new edition addresses contemporary and anticipated student demographics and enrollment patterns, a wide variety of campus environments (such as residential, commuter, online, hybrid), and a range of outcomes including learning, development, and achievement.

The book is organized around Alexander Astin's inputs-environment-outputs (I-E-O) framework. Student demographics, college preparation, and enrollment patterns are the "inputs." Transition to college and campus environments are the substance of the "environment." The "outputs" are student development, learning, and retention/persistence/completion.

The authors build on this foundation by providing relevant contemporary information and analysis of students, environments, and outcomes. They also provide strategies for readers to project forward in anticipation of higher education trends in a world where understanding "college students in the United States" is an ongoing project. By consolidating foundational and new research and theory on college students, their experiences, and college outcomes in the United States, the book provides knowledge to inform policies, programs, curriculum, and practice.

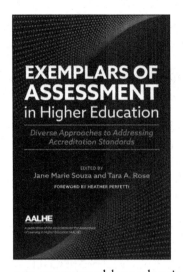

Exemplars of Assessment in Higher Education

Diverse Approaches to Addressing Accreditation Standards

Edited by Jane Marie Souza and Tara A. Rose

Foreword by Heather Perfetti

Copublished with AALHE

"*Exemplars of Assessment in Higher Education* celebrates institutional and program success as measured by authentic assessment and student learning, providing a welcome respite from a national higher education environment that so often equates higher education's success solely with student loan metrics and graduation rates. It illustrates cooperation, partnership, and shared purpose among accreditors and the institutions and programs that they accredit. Faculty, administrators, and accreditors will find ideas and inspiration from others who have gone before on the assessment journey."—***Laura Rasar King***, *Executive Director, Council on Education for Public Health*

Colleges and universities struggle to understand precisely what is being asked for by accreditors, and this book answers that question by sharing examples of success reported by schools specifically recommended by accreditors. This compendium gathers examples of assessment practice in 24 higher education institutions: 23 in the United States and one in Australia. All institutions represented in this book were suggested by their accreditor as having an effective assessment approach in one or more of the following assessment focused areas: assessment in the disciplines, cocurricular, course/program/institutional assessment, equity and inclusion, general education, online learning, program review, scholarship of teaching and learning, student learning, or technology. These examples recommended by accrediting agencies makes this a unique contribution to the assessment literature.

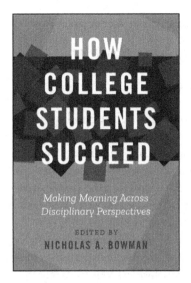

How College Students Succeed

Making Meaning Across Disciplinary Perspectives

Edited by Nicholas A. Bowman

"Essential. Timely. Requisite reading. This interdisciplinary compendium not only provides a theoretical framework to advance our knowledge of college student success, but also serves as an indispensable guide for higher education institutions to anticipate the post-pandemic needs of our students and eliminate the institutional barriers that inhibit their success. *How College Students Succeed* will help inform practice for years to come." —*Doneka R. Scott, Vice Chancellor and Dean for the Division of Academic and Student Affairs, North Carolina State University*

Receiving a college education has perhaps never been more important than it is today. While its personal, societal, and overall economic benefits are well documented, too many college students fail to complete their postsecondary education. As colleges and universities are investing substantial resources into efforts to counter these attrition rates and increase retention, they are mostly unaware of the robust literature on student success that is often bounded in disciplinary silos.

The purpose of this book is to bring together in a single volume the extensive knowledge on college student success. It includes seven chapters from authors who each synthesize the literature from their own field of study, or perspective. Each describes the theories, models, and concepts they use; summarizes the key findings from their research; and provides implications for practice, policy, and/or research.

The disciplinary chapters offer perspectives from higher education, public policy, behavioral economics, social psychology, STEM, sociology, and critical and poststructural theory.

HIGHER EDUCATION ACCREDITATION

HOW IT'S CHANGING, WHY IT MUST

PAUL L. GASTON

Higher Education Accreditation

How It's Changing, Why It Must

Paul L. Gaston

"Accreditation is the lighting rod of higher education, but few understand the nuanced complex changes in the field. Political leaders want to assure that students can transition from two- to four-year institutions without losing credits. University leaders want accreditation to cost less and be less intrusive. Students want it to make colleges more affordable. Few authors could write a book on accreditation that diverse stakeholders would demand in their library, but Paul Gaston has crafted a balanced, thoughtful explanation of accreditation. With higher education changing faster than it has at any period in its history, Gaston's book is a must-read to understand the sea change impacting higher education and how accreditation can impact our future."—***Robert G. Frank**, President, The University of New Mexico*

The Challenge of Bologna

What United States Higher Education Has to Learn From Europe, and Why It Matters That We Learn It

Paul L. Gaston

Foreword by Carol Geary Schneider

"*The Challenge of Bologna* is an informed, comprehensive and rich analysis of the efforts of Europe to lead a major transformation of higher education during the last decade. Even more important, Dr. Gaston offers a robust, intriguing, and insightful comparison of Bologna and U.S. efforts in higher education during the same time period. He is astute in his grasp of both the similarities of higher education tradition that bind the United States and Europe and the differences in government and culture that result in our approaching major challenges in quite different ways."
—*Judith S. Eaton, President, Council for Higher Education Accreditation*

Also available from Stylus

Pursuing Quality, Access, and Affordability

A Field Guide to Improving Higher Education

Stephen C. Ehrmann

Foreword by Jillian Kinzie

"In *Pursuing Quality, Access, and Affordability*, Steve Ehrmann advances a compelling narrative on how higher education can be improved. Basing his analysis on six extensive institutional case studies, he outlines how it is possible for institutions to create what he terms '3fold gains' in educational quality, equitable access, and stakeholder affordability. These gains are achieved through Integrative learning-based constellations of mutually supportive educational strategies, organizational foundations, and interactions with the wider world. The book offers a cogent rationale for how such coordinated efforts can enhance quality, access, and affordability on an institutional scale. As higher education prepares for a post-COVID educational landscape much changed by current challenges, now is the time for forward-thinking institutions to imagine this future. And the author's careful study, based on actual experiences of institutions that have achieved success in these areas at the core of higher education's mission and purpose, provides an excellent blueprint for success."—*David Eisler, President, Ferris State University*

22883 Quicksilver Drive
Sterling, VA 20166-2019   Subscribe to our email alerts: www.Styluspub.com